S0-AVX-372

LEARNING GERMAN

A Journey through Language and Culture

James Pfrehm, PhD

THE GREAT COURSES®

Published by

THE GREAT COURSES

Corporate Headquarters

PHONE: 1.800.832.2412
FAX: 703.378.3819
WEB: www.thegreatcourses.com

4840 Westfields Boulevard, Suite 500
Chantilly, Virginia, 20151-2299

Copyright © The Teaching Company, 2019

Printed in the United States of America

This book is in copyright. All rights reserved. Without limiting the rights under copyright reserved above, no part of this publication may be reproduced, stored in or introduced into a retrieval system, or transmitted, in any form, or by any means (electronic, mechanical, photocopying, recording, or otherwise), without the prior written permission of The Teaching Company.

James Pfrehm, PhD

Associate Professor of German and Linguistics
Ithaca College

James Pfrehm is an Associate Professor of German and Linguistics at Ithaca College. He received a master's degree in German Literature from the University of Washington and a doctorate in Germanic Linguistics from the University of Wisconsin–Madison.

Dr. Pfrehm's teaching and research are intentionally interdisciplinary and include the German language; the literature and culture of German-speaking countries; and several subfields of linguistics, primarily sociolinguistics, dialectology, linguistic anthropology, and technolingualism. He has taught at universities in Heidelberg and Münster, has written and presented his research at numerous academic conferences, and has led several workshops at universities across the United States on teaching foreign languages with technology.

Dr. Pfrehm has received recognition from the Student Governance Council at Ithaca College for his outstanding teaching and commitment to his students, and he has earned various institutional grants to take students abroad for short-term study experiences.

Dr. Pfrehm is the author of *Technolingualism: The Mind and the Machine* and *Austrian Standard German: Biography of a National Variety of German*. He is also the author or coauthor of two foreign language textbooks: *Kunterbunt und kurz geschrieben: An Interactive German Reader* and *Textures: Pour approfondir la communication orale et écrite*.

Dr. Pfrehm is also a published playwright and has had multiple plays produced by theaters in the United States and Canada. ∎

TABLE OF CONTENTS

INTRODUCTION

LESSON GUIDES

SUPPLEMENTARY MATERIALS

LEARNING GERMAN
A Journey through Language and Culture

Hallo und herzlich willkommen! If you're reading this right now, it's safe to assume that you've begun your journey through the German language with the video lessons and you're serious enough in your endeavor to learn German that you're ready and willing to solidify your new knowledge by working through the activities in this workbook. *Das ist großartig!*

Meine Damen und Herren: Each lesson in this workbook has been designed to review, reinforce, and drill the content that is covered in the corresponding video lesson, and each lesson is organized as follows:

- a summary of grammar
- grammar tables
- a list of important vocabulary, organized by word class, gender, or theme
- texts from the video lessons
- grammar exercises
- vocabulary exercises
- translations: German into English and English into German
- workbook answers

The summaries, tables, lists, exercises, and texts in this workbook are meant to provide you with the opportunity to thoroughly review and put into practice the material presented in the video lessons. After you've finished with the exercises in this workbook, you are strongly encouraged to seek out additional venues for practice. Perhaps the best way to go about this is to type the phrase "German grammar exercises" into your preferred web browser and then explore the options that appear. Four outstanding online sources are the following:

The Goethe-Institut: https://www.goethe.de/en/index.html

Deutsch-Lernen.com: https://www.deutsch-lernen.com/learn-german-online/beginners/exercises_summary.htm

German.net: https://german.net/exercises/

Lingolia's German site: https://deutsch.lingolia.com/en/

Ich wünsche Ihnen viel Spaß, und viel Erfolg in Ihrer Reise durch die deutsche Sprache!

WILLKOMMEN!

SUMMARY

Welcome to your tour through the German language!

Your journey will include a comprehensive grounding in German's sounds, words, and grammar in a way that echoes the unpredictable and exciting path of learning a language in a natural setting.

> German <u>, as in the phrase *Guten Tag!*, is deeper and has a purer tone than English <oo>, as in "boot."

> German <ü>, as in the phrase *Grüß Gott!*, is not a sound in English; it's formed by pronouncing the German <u> sound with your lips rounded but with your tongue in the place for the English vowel <ee>.

> German <w>, as in the phrase *Auf Wiedersehen*, is pronounced like the English <v>.

> German <ch>, as in the phrases *Gute Nacht* and *Ich spreche ein bisschen Deutsch*, is pronounced either as a throaty fricative, as in *Nacht*, or a palatal fricative, as in *ich*.

Speakers of English are intrinsically suited to learn German because German and English are historically closely related; the languages share many cognates.

Worldwide, approximately 100 million people speak German as a first language, and more than 15 million speak it as a second language.

German is listed as an official language in nine countries and as an official minority language in another 13 countries.

VOCABULARY

Nouns (singular und plural)

der Biergarten ¨-	beer garden
der Kühlschrank ¨-e	refrigerator (literally "cool cabinet")
der Handschuh -e	mitten (literally "hand shoe")
der Türsteher -	bouncer (literally "door stander")
der Wiederbelebungsversuch -e	resuscitation attempt (literally "again bringing to life attempt")
das Bier -e	beer
das Brot -e	bread
das Sauerkraut	sauerkraut
die Aussprache -n	pronunciation
die Bäckerei -en	bakery

Adjectives and Adverbs

großartig	great
schön	nice, beautiful
wunderbar	wonderful

Phrases

Alles klar?	Got it? Is that clear?
Also dann	So then
Auf Wiedersehen!	Goodbye!
Das ist richtig!	That's right/correct!
Grüß Gott!	Hello! (southern German and Austrian)
Guten Abend!	Hello / Good evening!
Guten Morgen!	Hello / Good morning!
Gute Nacht!	Goodbye! / Good night!
Guten Tag!	Hello! / Good day!
Hallo!	Hello! (informal)
Herzlich Willkommen!	Welcome!
Ich spreche ein bisschen Deutsch.	I speak a little German.
Keine Panik!	Don't worry! (literally "No panic!")
Ich lebe in …	I live in …
Los geht's!	Let's go!
Meine Damen und Herren	Ladies and gentlemen
Mein Name ist …	My name is …

A. Willkommen

Meine Damen und Herren: Hallo und herzlich willkommen! Mein Name ist James Pfrehm. Ich bin Professor für Deutsch am Ithaca College. Ich lebe in New York. Es ist wunderbar, dass Sie da sind.

B. On Kulm Peak

MIA: Entschuldigung. Können Sie bitte ein Foto von uns machen?
Excuse me. Can you please take a picture of us?

ME: Gerne. Drei, zwei, eins.
Gladly. Three, two, one.

MIA: Vielen Dank.
Thank you very much.

ME: Bitte sehr.
You're welcome.

RALF: Diese Aussicht ist schön, oder?
This view is gorgeous, don't you think?

ME: Ja, sehr schön.
Yes, really gorgeous.

RALF: Woher sind Sie, wenn ich fragen darf?
Where are you from, if I may ask?

ME: Ich komme aus den USA.
I come from the United States.

RALF: Sie sprechen aber gut Deutsch!
You speak German very well!

ME: Danke. Ich lerne Deutsch gern. Und woher sind Sie?
Thanks. I like learning German. And where are you from?

MIA: Wir sind aus Deutschland. Wir wohnen in Augsburg.
We are from Germany. We live in Augsburg.

ME: Ach so. Wo ist Augsburg?
I see. Where is Augsburg?

VOCABULARY EXERCISES

A. Fill in the appropriate phrase for the given situation.

1. You run into a friend in the grocery store: _____!

2. You turn off the bedside lamp with your significant other: _____!

3. Your friend gets a flat tire but you know how to change it: _____!

4. You meet a new colleague who is from Munich: _____!

5. A family member asks if you're learning German: _____!

6. Your supervisor is leaving work for the day: _____!

7. You and a friend are about to head out on a hike: _____!

8. You run into your supervisor in the elevator in the morning: _____!

B. Fill in the appropriate vocabulary word from the list. Don't forget to conjugate verbs.

1. _____ New York.

2. _____ James Pfrehm.

3. Sie lernen Deutsch! Das ist _____!

4. Der _____ ist für den Winter.

5. Ich lerne _____ für Deutsch.

6. Ich trinke _____.

7. _____ in Berlin!

8. _____ ist in der Bäckerei.

A. Translate from German into English.

1. Meine Damen und Herren!

   _____

2. Eine Reise durch die deutsche Sprache.

   _____

3. Herzlich Willkommen!

   _____

4. Ich lebe in New York.

   _____

5. Es ist wunderbar, dass Sie da sind.

   _____

B. Translate from English into German.

1. My name is ...

   _____

2. That is great!

   _____

3. Thank you very much!

   _____

4. I come from the United States.

   _____

5. You're welcome.

   _____

Answers on page 242

DEFINITE ARTICLES, GENDER, AND NOUNS

SUMMARY

All German nouns have one of three genders: masculine, feminine, or neuter.

For the most part, you have to memorize a noun's gender.

German nouns can be preceded by a definite article, which expresses its gender: *der* for masculine, *die* for feminine, and *das* for neuter nouns. These definite articles correspond to "the" in English.

If a noun refers to a person or an animal in the real world with a physical/biological gender, the noun will have the corresponding grammatical gender: *der Mann, die Frau, der Tiger, die Tigerin, der Pilot, die Pilotin.*

Some German nouns have endings that indicate their grammatical gender: nouns ending in *-e, -heit, -keit, -schaft,* and *-ung* are almost always feminine (e.g., *die Katze, die Freiheit, die Freundschaft, die Endung*); nouns ending in *-er* and *-or* are almost always masculine (e.g., *der Computer, der Professor*); and nouns ending in *-um, -ment,* and *-chen* are almost always neuter (e.g., *das Museum, das Monument, das Brötchen*).

The German alphabet has 27 letters plus three vowels with umlauts:

German Letter	German Name	Approximate Pronunciation in English
A	Ah	box
Ä	Ah-Umlaut	said
B	Beh	boy
C	Tseh	cake
D	Deh	day
E	Eh	day
F	Eff	fair
G	Geh	good
H	Hah	happy
I	Ee	me
J	Yott	yes
K	Kah	kite
L	Ell	like
M	Emm	me
N	Enn	no
O	Oh	boat
Ö	Oh-Umlaut	---
P	Peh	pa
Q	Kuh	kvitt
R	Err	---
S	Ess	see
T	Teh	tea
U	Uh	boot
Ü	Uh-Umlaut	---
V	Fau	fair
W	Weh	vase
X	Iks	ax
Y	Üpsilon	---
ß	Eszett	bass
Z	Tzett	sets

GRAMMAR

Definite Articles

Singular			Plural
masculine	feminine	neuter	
der	**die**	**das**	**die**

VOCABULARY

Nouns

der Arm -e	arm
der Computer -	computer
der Hund -e	dog
der Mann	man / male spouse
die Frau -en	woman / female spouse
die Hand ¨-e	hand
die Hauptstadt ¨-e	capital city
die Milch	milk
das Bier -e	beer
das Haus ¨-er	house
das Land ¨-er	country

Places

Österreich	Austria
Deutschland	Germany
Luxemburg	Luxembourg
die Schweiz	Switzerland
die Stadt Luxemburg	Luxembourg City
Wien	Vienna
Zürich	Zurich

Adjectives and Adverbs

ausgezeichnet	excellent
feminin	feminine (gender of noun)
männlich	masculine / manly
maskulin	masculine (gender of noun)
neutral	neuter (gender of noun)
sächlich	neuter
sehr	very
weiblich	feminine / womanly

Phrases

Achtung!	Pay attention! / Careful!
also dann	all right then
auf Deutsch	in German
Bis gleich!	See you soon!
Das heißt ...	That is ...

Danke schön!	Thank you!
Einverstanden?	Okay? / Agreed?
Hören Sie zu!	Listen!
Ich bin interessiert!	I am interested!
Jawohl!	Yes indeed! / Certainly!
Los geht's!	Let's go! / Here we go!
Sind Sie bereit?	Are you ready?
Wiederholen Sie, bitte.	Please repeat.

Directions

im Osten von	in the east of
östlich von	to the east of
im Norden von	in the north of
nördlich von	to the north of
im Süden von	in the south of
südlich von	to the south of
im Westen von	in the west of
westlich von	to the west of

TEXTS

A. How Professor Pfrehm Got Started on His Journey through German

Ach, wer ist dieser junge Mann? Das bin ich! Ich bin sechszehn Jahre alt und ich lerne Deutsch in der Schule.

Da bin ich wieder. Es ist Sommer und ich bin in Deutschland.

Ach! Der arme, junge James ... Er hat keinen Tanzpartner.

Hallo. Mein Name ist Katharina.

Hallo. Mein Name ist James. Ich komme aus Oregon.

B. Letter to Katharina

Liebe Katharina,

Wie geht es dir? Es geht mir sehr gut. Das Wetter hier ist nicht so gut. Es regnet viel. Wie ist das Wetter in Neu Ulm? Hoffentlich komme ich im Sommer wieder nach Deutschland. Kannst du nach Oregon kommen? Ich bin sehr froh. Ich vermisse dich.

Dein,
James

GRAMMAR EXERCISES

A. Give the gender of the following nouns.

1. _____ Trainer

2. _____ Individuum

3. _____ Woche

4. _____ Landschaft

5. _____ Hoffnung

6. _____ Lippe

7. _____ Instrument

8. _____ Faulheit

9. _____ Traktor

10. _____ Seife

B. Fill in the blanks with *der*, *die*, or *das*.

Simone, a personal fitness trainer, returns home after a long day of work only to discover that her pet ferret has knocked over her lamp and her aquarium.

(1) _____ Fitnesstrainerin Simone kommt nach Hause. „Wo ist (2) _____ Lampe?" denkt sie. (3) _____ Dunkelheit macht sie nervös. Dann findet sie Wasser und Glas auf dem Boden. „Ach nein", schreit sie, (4) „_____ Aquarium ist kaputt!" Es ist klar, wer (5) _____ Täter ist: (6) _____ Frettchen. „Wo ist (7) _____ Tierchen?" denkt sie. (8) _____ Suche beginnt.

VOCABULARY EXERCISES

A. Complete the short exchanges between speakers A and B with an appropriate phrase.

1. A: Wo liegt Deutschland?
   B: _____ Italien

2. A: Sind Sie bereit?
   B: _____! Los geht's

3. A: _____! Krokodil im Wasser!

   B: Danke schön!

4. A: Auf Wiedersehen!
   B: _____!

5. A: Wo liegt die Schweiz?
   B: _____ Österreich.

6. A: _____: „Ich lerne Deutsch.“
   B: „Ich lerne Deutsch.“

B. Fill in the missing word. Don't forget the definite article, where appropriate.

1. Das Nomen „der Kaffee“ ist _____.

2. _____ gut!

3. _____ heißt Liechtenstein und es ist südlich von Deutschland.

4. _____ von Österreich ist Wien.

5. Das Nomen „das Sofa“ ist _____.

6. Was ist „dog“ _____?

7. _____ ist frisch von der Kuh.

8. _____ ist ein neuer MacBook Pro.

9. _____ ist frisch von der Brauerei.

10. Mein Deutsch ist _____!

TRANSLATIONS

A. Translate from German into English.

1. Es ist Sommer und ich bin in Deutschland.

   _____

2. Ich bin sechszehn Jahre alt.

   _____

3. Das Wetter hier ist nicht so gut.

   _____

4. Ich bin sehr froh.

   _____

5. Hoffentlich komme ich im Sommer wieder nach Deutschland.

   _____

B. Translate from English into German.

1. That/This is excellent!

   _____

2. Germany lies to the north of Italy.

   _____

3. Switzerland lies to the west of Austria.

   _____

4. Listen and repeat!

   _____

5. Are you ready?

   _____

Answers on page 242

PERSONAL PRONOUNS AND THE VERB *SEIN*

SUMMARY

Personal pronouns are words that stand in for and refer to noun phrases.

Personal pronouns in German express

- three personal perspectives: first person, second person, and third person;
- two grammatical numbers: singular and plural;
- two social perspectives: formal and informal; and
- three grammatical genders: masculine, feminine, and neuter.

Gendered personal pronouns in German can refer to both people (e.g., *der Mann = er*) and objects (e.g., *der Computer = er*).

The verb *sein* means "to be" and has an irregular conjugation.

Most plural forms of German nouns must be memorized. However, certain noun suffixes take regular plural forms:

- nouns ending in an *-e* take an *-en* plural suffix;
- nouns with a suffix of *-heit*, *-keit*, *-schaft*, and *-ung* take an *-en* plural suffix; and
- nouns with the diminutive suffix *-chen* have no plural suffix.

GRAMMAR

Definite Articles

ich [I]	**wir** [we]
du [you/informal]	**ihr** [you guys/informal]
Sie [you/formal]	**Sie** [you/formal]
er [he]	
sie [she]	**sie** [they]
es [it]	

sein [to Be]

ich bin [I am]	**wir sind** [we are]
du bist [you are/informal]	**ihr seid** [you guys are]
Sie sind [you are/formal]	**Sie sind**[you are]
er ist [he is]	
sie ist [she is]	**sie sind** [they are]
es ist [it is]	

Singular	Plural	Plural Suffix
das Kind	die Kinder	**-er**
die Tochter	die Töchter	**none, but umlauted vowel**
die Schwester	die Schwestern	**-n**
der Sohn	die Söhne	**-e, and umlauted vowel**
das Messer (knife)	die Messer	**none**
der Pilot	die Piloten	**-en**
die Pilotin	die Pilotinnen	**-nen**
der Freund	die Freunde	**-e**
das Baby	die Babys	**-s**
der Wald (forest)	die Wälder	**-er, and umlauted vowel**
das Material	die Materialien	**-ien**

Nouns

der Bruder -¨	brother
der Cousin -s / der Vetter, -n	the male cousin
der Enkel -	grandson
der Großvater -¨	grandfather
der Junge -n	boy
der Mann ¨-er	man / husband
der Neffe -n	nephew
der Onkel -	uncle
der Opa -s	grandpa
der Schwiegersohn ¨-e	son-in-law
der Sohn ¨-e	son
der Tisch -e	table
der Vater ¨-e	father
der Zungenbrecher -	tongue twister
die Endung -en	ending
die Enkelin -nen	granddaughter
die Frau -en	woman / wife
die Freiheit -en	freedom
die Freundschaft -en	friendship
die Großmutter -¨	grandmother
die Kusine -n	female cousin
die Möglichkeit -en	possibility
die Mutter -¨	mother
die Nichte -n	niece
die Oma -s	grandma
die Schwester -n	sister
die Schwiegertochter -¨	daughter-in-law
die Tante -n	aunt
die Tochter -¨	daughter
das Baby -s	baby
das Brötchen -	roll
das Kind -er	child
das Mädchen -	girl
die Eltern	parents
die Großeltern	grandparents

Verbs	
sein	to be

Adjectives and Adverbs	
brav	good (behavior)

Phrases	
Hören Sie zu.	Listen.
Sehen Sie?	Do you see?

TEXTS

A. Mias Familie

Das ist meine Familie. Ich bin Mia. Ich bin die Mutter. Das ist mein Mann, Ralf Gruber. Er ist der Vater. Wir sind die Eltern von Rahel und Hans. Sie sind die Kinder. Rahel ist die Tochter, und Hans ist der Sohn. Die Personen hier sind Paul und Sabina. Sie sind die Eltern von Ralf, und die Großeltern von Rahel und Hans. Sabina ist die Oma und Paul ist der Opa. Die Familie Gruber ist klein, aber wir sind glücklich.

B. Die Familie Gruber

HANS

Der Junge ist Hans. Hans ist der Bruder von Rahel, und der Sohn von Mia und Ralf. Er ist auch der Enkel von Sabina und Paul.

RAHEL

Das Mädchen ist Rahel. Sie ist die Schwester von Hans, und die Tochter von Mia und Ralf. Sie ist auch die Enkelin von Sabina und Paul.

MIA

Die Frau ist Mia. Sie ist die Frau von Ralf, und die Mutter von Hans und Rahel. Sie ist auch die Schwiegertochter von Sabina und Paul.

RALF

Der Mann ist Ralf. Er ist der Mann von Mia, und der Vater von Hans und Rahel. Er ist auch der Sohn von Sabina und Paul.

SABINA und PAUL

Der Mann und die Frau sind Sabina und Paul. Sie sind die Eltern von Paul, und die Großeltern von Hans und Rahel. Sabina ist die Oma, und Hans ist der Opa.

V. Die deutsche Familienpolitik / German Government Family Policies

Since the 1950s, Germany has made it one of its political priorities to foster the viability and well-being of its families. The result of this institutional prioritization is that today Germany offers countless family programs that are either fully or partially funded by the federal government.

The average size of the German family is 3.5. In other words, most German families are made up of a married couple with one or two children. By comparison, American families generally have two or more children.

Also, around 55 percent of Germans aged 20 and over are married.

Furthermore, statistics show that the average German male is 35 when he has his first child, while the average German female is 30. For comparison, an American man typically becomes a first-time father at 30, while an American woman typically has her first child at 28.

While statistics have shown that birthrates in Germany have been falling over the past few decades, the German government has nevertheless continued to take measures to promote *die deutsche Familie*.

For instance, following the birth of a child, both the mother and father are allowed to take a paid break from work. In addition, the government pays a parental allowance amounting to 65 percent of net income for a total of 14 months.

In fact, every time a German family has a new child, each parent is eligible to receive *Elterngeld* ("parental money") for up to 12 months. Just how much *Elterngeld* depends on each family's financial need and tax bracket, but monthly allowances can be anywhere from 360 dollars to more than 2,100 dollars.

The German government also gives *die Eltern* cash for each child. This is called *das Kindergeld* program. The *Kindergeld* benefit pays 233 dollars per month for each of the first two children, 240 dollars for the third child, and then 270 dollars for the fourth child. And the German government continues to send parents this money until the child's 26th birthday!

GRAMMAR EXERCISES

A. Fill in the correct personal pronoun.

1. Das ist die deutsche Bundeskanzlerin. _____ heißt Angela Merkel.

2. „Hallo! _____ sind die Familie Gruber."

3. Das sind Mia und Ralf. _____ sind die Eltern von Hans und Rahel.

4. Hier ist der Computer. _____ ist neu.

5. Hier ist das Buch. _____ ist sehr gut.

B. Fill in the blanks for the short story „*Zwei Dackel und ein Ehepaar*" ("Two Dachshunds and One Married Couple") with the appropriate conjugated form of *sein*.

Zwei Dackel und ein Ehepaar

Manfred und Nina **1.**_____ verheiratet (*married*). Nina

2._____ Tierliebhaberin (*animal lover*) und sie liebt Hunde. Aber Manfred

3._____ allergisch gegen Hunde. An einem warmen Frühlingstag **4.**_____

die Eltern von Nina zu Besuch (*visiting*). Sie sagen, „Wir **5.**_____ besorgt

(*concerned*) über euch. Ihr **6.**_____ zu einsam (*lonely*)." Der Vater von

Nina geht zum Auto und bringt zwei Hunde ins Haus. Die Mutter von Nina sagt,

„Sie **7.**_____ Dackel. Ein Hund und eine Hündin." Nina sagt, „Danke

schön!" Sie nimmt den Dackel in die Hand und sagt, „Du **8.**_____ jetzt

Frida, und du **9.**_____ jetzt Diego!" Die Familie **10.**_____ jetzt

glücklich (*happy*). Manfred denkt, „Na ja, die Hündchen **11.**_____ hübsch

(*cute*), aber ich **12.**_____ allergisch!"

C. Give the correct plural for each noun.

1. die Tochter → die _____

2. die Landschaft → die _____

3. das Messer → die _____

4. das Gebäude   → die _____

5. das Baby   → die _____

6. das Kind   → die _____

7. der Junge   → die _____

8. die Wand   → die _____

9. das Mädchen   → die _____

10. die Meinung   → die _____

VOCABULARY EXERCISES

A. Determine which word is being described. (Note: Some may have more than one
answer, depending on the family member's perspective.)

1. der Junge von (*of*) dem Vater _____

2. das Mädchen von der Mutter _____

3. die Mutter und der Vater von dem Kind _____

4. eine Übung (*exercise*) für die Aussprache _____

5. der Sohn von dem Bruder _____

6. das kleine Kind _____

7. die Mutter von der Mutter _____

8. der Bruder von der Mutter _____

9. der Vater von der Mutter __._____

10. Die Kinder heißen Helmut und Sophie. Helmut ist _____

    und Frieda ist _____.

A. Translate from German into English.

1. Ich bin die Schwiegertochter.

   _____.

2. Wir sind die Großeltern von Westin.

   _____.

3. Er ist der Neffe von Mia.

   _____.

4. Das Mädchen ist die Enkelin von Sabina.

   _____.

5. Sie sind die Kinder von Ralf und Mia.

   _____.

B. Translate from English into German.

1. This is my family.

   _____.

2. You (formal) are the uncle of Mia.

   _____.

3. You guys (informal) are the parents of Westin.

   _____.

4. The tongue twister is excellent.

   _____.

5. They are very good (i.e., in behavior).

   _____.

Answers on page 243

REGULAR VERBS IN THE PRESENT TENSE

SUMMARY

Speakers use the phrases *Wie geht's Ihnen?* (formal) and *Wie geht's?* (informal) to inquire about another speaker's well-being.

All German verbs have an *-n* or *-en* suffix in their infinitive: *heißen* ("to be called"), *arbeiten* ("to work"), *segeln* ("to sail"), *tun* ("to do"), etc.

German verbs are conjugated with a subject noun or subject pronoun, according to perspective (first, second, or third person), number (singular or plural), and social address (formal or informal).

German verbs always require the subject to be stated along with the conjugated verb: **ich** *gehe*, **du** *arbeitest*, **wir** *segeln*, etc.

All present tense regular verbs are conjugated in the following way: 1) take off the *-en* or *-n* suffix from the infinitive; 2) add the conjugational ending.

Present tense regular verb conjugational endings are *ich → -e, du → -est, Sie → -en, er/sie/ es → -t, wir → -en, ihr → -t, Sie → -en, sie → -en.*

If a verb has a *-t* or *-d* at the end of its stem, after the *-en* suffix has been dropped from its infinitive, you add an extra *-e-* in the *du, er/sie/es*, and *ihr* conjugations: *du findest, er/sie/es arbeitet, ihr redet.*

If a verb has an *-s, -ß,* or *-z* at the end of its stem, after the *-en* suffix has been dropped from its infinitive, you leave out the *-s-* in the *du* conjugation: *du reist, du heißt, du sitzt.*

The German indefinite pronoun *man* conjugates as a singular third-person personal pronoun and translates as "one," "you," "a person."

GRAMMAR

Present Tense Conjugational Endings

	Sing. Pronouns	Conj. Ending	Plur. Pronouns	Conj. Ending
1st Per.	ich	-e	wir	-en
2nd Per. Inform.	du	-st	ihr	-t
2nd Per. Form.	Sie	-en	Sie	-en
3rd Per.	er/sie/es	-t	sie	-en

Present Tense Conjugation of Regular Verbs

wohnen

ich wohne	wir wohnen
du wohnst	ihr wohnt
Sie wohnen	Sie wohnen
er/sie/es wohnt	sie wohnen

Present Tense Conjugation of Verbs with Stem Ending in -t or -d

finden

ich finde	wir finden
du findest	ihr findet
Sie finden	Sie finden
er/sie/es findet	sie finden

Present Tense Conjugation of Verbs with Stem Ending in -s, -ß, or -z

sitzen

ich sitze	wir sitzen
du sitzt	ihr sitzt
Sie sitzen	Sie sitzen
er/sie/es sitzt	sie sitzen

VOCABULARY

Nouns

der Mann, ̈-er	man / husband
der Wortschatz, ̈-e	vocabulary
die Arbeit, -en	work
die Dusche, -n	shower (in bathroom)
das Gras, ̈-er	grass
das Land, ̈-er	country
das Museum/Museen	museum

Places and Peoples

Dänemark, der Däne / die Dänin	Denmark, Dane
Deutschland, der Deutsche / die Deutsche	Germany, German
England, Engländer, Engländerin	England, Englishman, Englishwoman
Europa, der Europäer / die Europäerin	Europe, European
Frankreich, der Franzose, die Französin	France, Frenchman, Frenchwoman
Irland, der Ire, die Irin	Ireland, Irishman, Irishwoman
Italien, der Italiener / die Italienerin	Italy, Italian
Japan, der Japaner / die Japanerin	Japan, Japanese
Österreich, der Österreicher / die Österreicherin	Austria, Austrian
die Schweiz, der Schweizer / die Schweizerin	Switzerland, Swiss
Spanien, der Spanier / die Spanierin	Spain, Spaniard
die Leute	people

Verbs

arbeiten	to work
finden	to find
gehen	to go
heißen	to be called
kaufen	to buy
kommen	to come
mähen	to mow

rauchen	to smoke
reisen	to travel
singen	to sing
sitzen	to sit
wohnen	to live

Adjectives and Adverbs

ausgezeichnet	excellent
gut	good / well
sehr gut	very good / very well
schlecht	bad / unwell

Phrases

Bleiben Sie dran!	Stay tuned!
Das weiß man nie.	You never know.
Die Reise geht weiter!	The journey continues!
Es geht.	Not too bad. (in response to "How are you?")
Ich habe Glück!	I'm lucky!
mit dem Zug	by train
Nicht so gut.	Not so well. (in response to "How are you?")
nördlich von	north of
östlich von	east of
So la la.	So-so. (in response to "How are you?")
Wie geht's?	How's it going? (informal)
Wie geht es dir?	How are you? (informal, to one person)
Wie geht es euch?	How are you? (informal, to more than one person)
Wie geht es Ihnen?	How are you? (formal, to one or more than one person)
Wie sagt man _____ auf Deutsch?	How do you say _____ in German?
Wo findet man _____	Where does one find _____
Wo kauft man _____	Where does one buy _____
Servus!	Hello! (informal, southern Germany and Austria)
südlich von	south of
Toll!	Great! / Super! (informal)
westlich von	west of
zu Fuß	by foot

A. Mias internationale Familie

Hallo! Ich bin Mia und meine Familie ist sehr international. Ich komme aus Deutschland. Das heißt, ich bin Deutsche. Meine Eltern wohnen in Deutschland, aber sie kommen aus Österreich. Mein Vater ist Österreicher und meine Mutter ist Österreicherin. Mein Onkel ist auch Österreicher, aber er wohnt in Japan. Meine Tante kommt aus Japan. Sie ist Japanerin. Wir sind eine internationale Familie!

B. Ein Gespräch beim Oktoberfest

MIA: Guten Tag!

FRAU: Guten Tag. Kommen Sie oft zum Oktoberfest?

MIA: Ja. Ich komme jedes Jahr. Mein Mann arbeitet in München.

FRAU: Wohnen Sie in München?

MIA: Nein. Wir wohnen in Augsburg.

FRAU: Ach so!

MIA: Mein Mann kommt mit dem Zug in die Arbeit.

FRAU: Wie lange sitzt er im Zug?

MIA: Fünfzig Minuten hin, und fünfzig Minuten zurück.

FRAU: Und Sie? Wie kommen Sie in die Arbeit?

MIA: Ich habe Glück. Ich gehe zu Fuß.

C. Die Länder in Europa

Das ist Europa. Ein Mann aus Europa ist der Europäer, und eine Frau aus Europa ist die Europäerin. Und hier sind die Länder und die Leute Europas.

Das Land heißt Irland. Ein Mann aus Irland ist der Ire, und eine Frau ist die Irin.

Östlich von Irland liegt England. Ein Mann aus England ist der Engländer, und eine Frau ist die Engländerin.

Östlich von England liegt Dänemark. Ein Mann aus Dänemark ist der Däne, und eine Frau ist die Dänin.

Südlich von Dänemark liegt Deutschland. Ein Mann aus Deutschland ist der Deutsche, und eine Frau ist die Deutsche.

Weiter südlich von Deutschland finden wir Österreich. Ein Mann aus Österreich ist der Österreicher, und eine Frau ist die Österreicherin.

Westlich von Österreich ist die Schweiz. Ein Mann aus der Schweiz ist der Schweizer, und eine Frau aus der Schweiz ist die Schweizerin.

Südlich von der Schweiz liegt Italien. Ein Mann aus Italien heißt der Italiener, und eine Frau nennt man die Italienerin.

Nordwestlich von Italien finden wir Frankreich. Ein Mann aus Frankreich heißt der Franzose, und eine Frau aus Frankreich heißt die Französin.

Westlich von Frankreich finden wir Spanien. Ein Mann aus Spanien ist der Spanier, und eine Frau aus Spanien heißt die Spanierin.

V. Der Multikulturismus in Deutschland / Multiculturalism in Germany

In many respects, Germany was a multicultural place long before its official unification as a nation-state in the nineteenth century. Starting as far back as the early Middle Ages, hundreds of thousands of Ashkenazi Jews have lived, worked, and created culture and art throughout Germany. In particular, the cities of Köln, Mainz, Worms, Speyer, and Regensburg hosted strong Jewish populations for centuries.

In fact, most people today don't realize that throughout time, many different ethnicities have migrated to the area now called Germany and put down roots. Among others, there have been French Huguenots, Slavic peoples, Ottoman Turks, Hungarians, and the Sinti and Roma (perhaps better known as Gypsies, though this term is now often considered derogatory).

Like the Ashkenazi, all of these peoples also made lasting sociocultural contributions to the German-speaking areas of Europe. Where do you think all those famous Austrian coffeehouses got their beans? The Turks. Guess who helped the Prussians recover and rebuild in the seventeenth century after the Thirty Years' War devastated their economy and infrastructure? The Huguenots!

Unfortunately, Germany's historically rich multicultural character experienced a radical change in the twentieth century. Prior to the National Socialist regime, for instance, it's estimated that more than half a million Jews lived in Germany. Today's resident Jewish population hovers at around one-fifth of pre-World War II numbers. And the ethnic groups mentioned previously also suffered terrible demographic losses.

Yet despite Germany's troubled history with ethnic tolerance and diversity, over the last six decades the government has worked tirelessly to show that the Germany of today is indeed a welcoming place for all peoples and cultures.

In fact, more than 20 percent of Germany's current population was not born in the country. That's one in every five people living in Germany! This is an important and widely unacknowledged fact—namely, that Germany is actually the second most popular migration destination in the world after the United States.

In 2015, annual migration to Germany hit an all-time high: More than 1.1 million people moved there—for family, work, or asylum, or simply because they aspired to make a better life for themselves or their loved ones.

In 2005, the German government passed its *Zuwanderungsgesetz* (*die Zuwanderung*, "migration to"; *das Gesetz*, "law"), a federal law promoting immigration to Germany. This *Zuwanderungsgesetz* is a major reason for the recent upward trend in migration to Germany. It is a deliberate, real-world demonstration that modern-day Germany regards newcomers as a benefit to its economy and culture.

However, in modern times, the first waves of foreigners to move to Germany actually started in the 1950s. Germany needed people to help rebuild its infrastructure and repopulate its workforce following the devastation from World War II, so the government invited foreign laborers from in and around Europe to help. And the German government gave them work permits, decent wages, and, much of the time, even housing.

These invited workers were called *Gastarbeiter* (*der Gast*, "guest"; *der Arbeiter*, "workers"). Turkey was one of the heaviest-recruited countries for *Gastarbeiter*. As a result, people with Turkish heritage make up Germany's largest minority group today. And here's a bit of interesting trivia: Nobody knows for certain how many Turks live in Germany. Germany's census doesn't let residents declare their ethnicity. So all we have are estimates, which range widely, from two to seven million!

But those are just numbers. It's the people and their culture that really matter. So guess where you can also find the best kebabs outside of Turkey? In Germany! And guess who won Best Foreign Language Film of 2017 at the 75th Golden Globe Awards for his drama *Aus dem Nichts* (*In the Fade*)? Fatih Akin, a German born in Hamburg to Turkish immigrants. And some of the most successful German-language hip-hop artists are *Deutsch-Türken*: Savaş Yurderi, who goes by the moniker Kool Savas, has put out more than a dozen albums since 1995.

Granted, nothing as complicated as societal multiculturalism is, or even can be, perfect. And of course, Germany's program of social and cultural progressiveness does have its fair share of critics and wrinkles. But the government's commitment to *Multikulturalismus* remains strong, and all indications are that Germany's policies will continue to make it one of the most welcoming nations in the world for foreigners.

GRAMMAR EXERCISES

A. Complete the verb conjugations.

1. Die Frau arbeit_____ bei Siemens.

2. Wir komm_____ oft zum Oktoberfest.

3. Du red_____ schnell.

4. Man find_____ gute Diskotheken in Heidelberg.

5. Ihr arbeit_____ in Luxemburg.

6. Ich sprech_____ Deutsch.

7. Mein Sohn wart_____ auf den Bus.

8. Wann reis_____ du in die Schweiz?

9. Der Mann wohn_____ in Österreich.

10. Die Kinder spiel_____ gern Fußball.

B. Fill in the appropriate conjugations for the verbs in the dialogue „*Ein Gespräch beim Oktoberfest.*"

MIA: Guten Tag! Ich heiß_____ (1) Mia.

FRAU: Guten Tag. Komm_____ (2) Sie oft zum Oktoberfest?

MIA: Ja. Ich komm_____ (3) jedes Jahr. Mein Mann arbeit_____ (4) in München.

FRAU: Wohn_____ (5) Sie in München?

MIA: Nein. Wir wohn_____ (6) in Augsburg.

FRAU: Wo lieg_____ (7) Augsburg?

MIA: Sechszig Kilometer westlich von hier. Mein Mann komm_____ (8) mit dem Zug ins Büro.

FRAU: Meine Güte! Wie lange sitz_____ (9) er im Zug?

MIA: Fünfzig Minuten hin, und fünfzig Minuten zurück.

Ich sag_____ (10) oft, „Ralf, du sitz_____ (11) hundert Minuten

 jeden Tag im Zug. Find_____ (12) du das nicht viel?"

FRAU: Ich denk_____ (13) auch, das ist viel. Mein Mann geh_____ (14)

zu Fuß ins Büro.

MIA: Schön!

VOCABULARY EXERCISES

A. Fill in the appropriate vocabulary word from the list. Don't forget to conjugate verbs.

1. Zwei Dänen _____ das Gras.

2. Frau Stein: „Guten Morgen. _____?" Herr Hammel: „Danke, gut!"

3. Ich _____ im Sommer nach Deutschland.

4. Spanien liegt _____ England.

5. Eine Frau aus Frankreich ist eine _____.

6. Du _____ bei BMW.

7. Mein Auto ist kaputt. Ich gehe _____ in die Arbeit.

8. _____ die Dusche?

9. Ralf: „Wie geht's dir, Mia?" Mia: „_____. Ich bin krank."

10. Prof. Pfrehm: „Wir reisen nach Österreich." Sie: „Das ist _____!"

TRANSLATIONS

A. Translate from German into English.

1. Die Dänen mähen das Gras.

   _____.

2. Du reist oft nach Europa.

   _____.

3. Die Frau kommt aus Spanien.

   _____.

4. Der Franzose singt gut.

   _____.

5. Die Irin wohnt in Frankreich.

   _____.

B. Translate from English into German.

   _____.

1. You (formal) work in Munich.

   _____.

2. His name is Ralf. (literally "He is called Ralf.")

   _____.

3. We are going by foot.

   _____.

4. You guys (informal) live in Spain.

   _____.

5. He smokes.

   _____.

Answers on page 243

INDEFINITE ARTICLES AND NUMBERS TO 100

SUMMARY

Indefinite articles in German work very similar to the indefinite articles "a" and "an" in English in that they always occur before the noun or nouns they're modifying (e.g., **ein** *Hammer*).

Indefinite articles express nonspecificity or contextual distance (e.g., *Wo ist* **der** *Hammer?* as opposed to *Wo ist* **ein** *Hammer?*).

German indefinite articles reflect their noun's gender (masculine, feminine, or neuter): *ein* is used for masculine and neuter nouns (*ein Hammer, ein Kind*), and *eine* is used for feminine nouns (*eine Katze*).

Just like English, there is no indefinite article before a plural noun (e.g., *a cats, *eine Katzen*).

Counting in German from 0 to 20 is very similar to English: *null, eins, zwei, drei, vier, fünf, sechs, sieben, acht, neun, zehn, elf, zwölf, dreizehn, vierzehn, fünfzehn, sechzehn, siebzehn, achtzehn, neunzehn, zwanzig.*

For the numbers 21 to 99 in German, you say the second integer first, followed by the base-10 quantity: e.g., "one-and-twenty," *einundzwanzig*; "two-and-twenty," *zweiundzwanzig*; and so on.

The base-10 sets for counting in German are as follows: *zwanzig, dreißig, vierzig, fünfzig, sechzig, siebzig, achtzig, neunzig.*

After the number *neunundneunzig* comes the number *einhundert* or *hundert*.

GRAMMAR

Indefinite Articles

Singular		
Masc.	Fem.	Neut.
ein	eine	ein

VOCABULARY

Nouns

-r Bahnhof ¨-e	train station
-r Berliner	custard-filled donut
-r Bierflaschensammler	beer bottle collector
-r Diesel -	a mixture of beer and cola
-r Kellner -	waiter (m.)
-r Radler -	shandy (beer with citrus)
-r Weißwein -e	white wine
-r Rotwein -e	red wine
-r Sekt -e	sparkling wine or champagne
-r Schnaps ¨-e	any clear alcohol (distilled from grain)
-r Obstbrand ¨-e / der Obstler -	fruit-flavored schnapps
-e Backware -n	baked good
-e Cola	cola / soft drink
-e Flasche -n	bottle
-e Getränkekarte -n	drink menu
-e Kellnerin -nen	waitress
-e Kneipe -n	bar / tavern
-e Matheaufgabe	math exercise
-e Rechnung	bill
-e Weinschorle -n	wine spritzer
-e Zahl -en	number
-s Bier vom Fass	draft beer
ein kleines Bier	a small beer
ein großes Bier	a large beer
-s Flaschenbier -e	bottled beer
-s Mineralwasser mit Sprudel	water with carbonation

-s Pils -e	pilsner beer
-s Wasser	water
ein stilles Wasser	uncarbonated water
ein helles Weizenbier	a light wheat beer
ein dunkles Weizenbier	a dark wheat beer

Verbs

bestellen	to order
glauben	to believe/think
kosten	to cost
zählen	to count

Adjectives and Adverbs

auch	Also / too
günstig	reasonable / convenient
teuer	expensive

Phrases

Achtung!	(Pay) Attention!
Entschuldigung!	Pardon/Excuse me!
Ich hätte gern ... / Ich möchte ...	I would like ...
Mensch!	My gosh!
Noch einmal!	Once more! / Again!
Probieren wir es!	Let's try it!
Sonst noch was?	Anything else?
Übung macht den Meister!	Practice makes perfect!
Was darf es sein?	What can I get you? / Can I get your order?
Was ist das?	What is that?
Wie viel?	How much?

TEXTS

A. Conversation in the Bar between Ralf and Me

RALF: Hier ist eine Getränkekarte.

ME: Danke. Hmm ... Eine Flasche Mineralwasser kostet nur fünfundneunzig (€ ,95) Cent.

RALF: Ja, das ist günstig.

ME: Eine Cola ist ein Euro neunzig (€ 1,90). Und ein großes Weizenbier kostet nur eins siebzig (€ 1,70).

RALF: Ja, das Bier ist auch günstig, aber der Wein ist teuer.

ME: Ja. Ein Weißwein kostet acht Euro fünfunddreißig (€ 8,35).

RALF: Und ein Rotwein kostet neun Euro neunundsiebzig (€ 9,79).

ME: Ein Glas oder eine Flasche?

RALF: Ich glaube, ein Glas.

ME: Mensch! Das ist teuer! Ich bestelle ein Weizenbier.

RALF: Und ich bestelle ein Pils.

ME: Und eine Flasche Mineralwasser.

RALF: Ein stilles Mineralwasser, oder ein Mineralwasser mit Sprudel?

ME: Ein stilles Mineralwasser.

RALF: Gut. Die Kellnerin kommt.

B. Conversation in the Bar between Ralf, Me, and Waitress

RALF: Die Kellnerin kommt.

KELLNERIN: Was darf es sein?

ME: Ich möchte ein stilles Mineralwasser und ein Weizenbier, bitte.

KELLNERIN: Vom Faß oder Flaschenbier?

ME: Vom Faß.

KELLNERIN: Und Sie?

RALF: Ich hätte gern ein Pilsener Bier vom Faß.

KELLNERIN: Sonst noch was?

RALF: Nein, danke.

KELLNERIN: Bitte schön. Kommt sofort.

GRAMMAR EXERCISES

A. Fill in the correct indirect article.

1. Das ist _____ Weinschorle.

2. Was kostet _____ Radler?

3. Wie viel kostet _____ Brezel?

4. Ich kaufe _____ frisches Brötchen.

5. Hier ist _____ Getränkekarte.

6. Wie viel kostet _____ Glas Weizenbier?

7. _____ Weißwein kostet sechs Euro.

8. Wir bestellen _____ Flasche Rotwein.

9. _____ stilles Wasser kostet ein Euro dreißig.

10. Ist das _____ Hund oder _____ Katze?

VOCABULARY EXERCISES

A. Determine which word is being described in each of the following.

1. Diese Person arbeitet im Restaurant. _____

2. eins, zwei, drei, vier, etc. _____

3. Etwas kostet viel Geld. _____

4. „Ich hätte gern ein Weizenbier." _____

5. Ein Kellner oder eine Kellnerin sagt das als Erstes. _____

6. Hier kann man Bier oder Wein trinken. _____

7. 238, 56, 9, etc. _____

8. „Ich _____, das ist günstig." _____

9. Ein Kellner oder eine Kellnerin sagt das als Letztes. _____

10. Ein Brötchen, ein Berliner, eine Brezel, etc. _____

B. Complete the math problems.

1. Wie viel ist fünf plus zehn minus drei?

   _____

2. Was macht zwanzig plus dreißig minus fünfundzwanzig?

   _____

3. Wie viel ist elf minus null plus neunundzwanzig?

   _____

4. Wie viel ist achtzig minus fünfzig plus dreizehn plus vierzig?

   _____

5. Was macht hundert minus siebzig minus sechs plus sechszehn?

   _____

6. Wie viel ist neunundneunzig minus sechzig plus dreiunddreißig?

   _____

TRANSLATIONS

A. Translate from German into English.

1. Wir haben Durst.

   _____.

2. Das Bier ist auch günstig.

   _____.

3. Mensch! Das ist teuer!

   _____.

4. Ich bestelle eine Flasche Mineralwasser mit Sprudel.

   _____.

5. Die Kellnerin kommt.

   _____.

B. Translate from English into German.

1. I would like an uncarbonated mineral water.

   _____.

2. My gosh! A glass of white wine is expensive.

   _____.

3. I think a dark wheat beer is reasonable.

   _____.

4. Let's try it!

   _____!

5. Practice makes perfect!

   _____!

Answers on page 244

EINE REISE NACH WIEN UND SALZBURG

SUMMARY

This is the first of five über-lessons that explore two locations within the German-speaking world.

To express that you "like to do" an action, German uses the adverb *gern* (which translates literally to "gladly") with a conjugated verb (e.g., *Ich reise gern*, "I like to travel"; *Du spielst gern Fußball*, "You like to play soccer"; *Wir lernen gern Deutsch*, "We like learning German").

In some verb-noun phrases, the adverb *gern* can also occur after the noun (e.g., *Du spielst Fußball gern*; *Wir lernen Deutsch gern*; *Sie sammelt Insekten gern*).

To negate a verb phrase, adjectival phrase, adverbial phrase, or prepositional phrase, you place the negating particle *nicht* before the phrase you wish to negate (e.g., *Ich koche nicht*; *Das Wetter ist nicht schön*; *Ich jogge nicht schnell*; *Wir gehen nicht in das Konzert*).

To negate a sentence or an action generally, the *nicht* goes at the end (e.g., *Ich spiele Fußball nicht*, "I don't play soccer"; *Ralf arbeitet in München nicht*, "Ralf does not work in Munich"). Otherwise, to negate a specific part of a sentence, you place the *nicht* in front of the element you wish to negate (*Ralf spielt nicht Fußball*, "It's not soccer that Ralf plays" (i.e., it's something else); *Ralf arbeitet nicht in München*, "It's not in Munich where Ralf works" (i.e., it's somewhere else)).

VOCABULARY

Nouns

-r Fiaker -	Viennese coffee drink with rum and whipped cream
-r Liebesroman -e	romance novel
-r Semmelknödel -	bread dumpling
-r Smoking -s	tuxedo
-r Sprachtipp -s	tip about language
-r Stadtplan ¨-e	city map
-e Melange	Austrian coffee drink with steamed milk
-e Sachertorte -n	Austrian chocolate cake
-s Kaffeegetränk -e	coffee drink
-s Kaffeehaus ¨-er	coffeehouse / café

Verbs

bleiben	to stay
denken	to think
schmecken	to taste (as in "it tastes good")
schwitzen	to sweat
stehen	to stand / to be located (as in a building)

Adjectives and Adverbs

ein bisschen	a little (bit)
bestimmt	certainly / surely
entfernt	away (as in distance)
gern	to like to (literally "gladly")
zuerst	first (adv.)

Directions

bis zu … (zur Löwelstraße)	until … / as far as … (Löwelstraße)
geradeaus	straight
gegenüber	across (the way) / on the other side of the street
(die Löwelstraße) … entlang	along … (the Löwelstraße)
rechts	right / to the right
nach rechts	(go) to the right
nach … (Süden)	in the direction of … (south)
links	left / to the left
nach links	(go) to the left
Richtung … (Kirchenplatz)	in the direction of … (Kirchenplatz)
überqueren	to cross (a street)

Das habe ich gern.	I like that.
etwas gern haben	to like something
Du hast Recht.	You're right.
Meine Güte!	My goodness!
Pfui!	Yikes! / Yuck!
Schau mal!	Look!

TEXTS

A. Ralf and Mia in Vienna (Part One)

RALF: Also dann. Wir sind jetzt hier, in der Buchfeldgasse.

MIA: Wir gehen zuerst die Buchfeldgasse entlang, nach Süden.

RALF: Richtung Josefstädterstraße?

MIA: Ja, Richtung Josefstädterstraße. Dann gehen wir nach links in die Josefstädterstraße.

RALF: Und wir gehen zwei Straßen geradeaus.

MIA: Mhm. Dann überqueren wir die Stadiongasse und wir gehen ... eins, zwei, drei, *vier* Straßen geradeaus.

RALF: Richtig. Dann gehen wir nach links in den Universitätsring, und zwei Straßen geradeaus bis zur Löwelstraße.

MIA: Und dann gehen wir rechts in die Löwelstraße.

RALF: Genau. Das Café Landtmann ist links gegenüber.

B. Ralf and Mia in Vienna (Part Two)

MIA: Das Kaffeehaus ist schön.

RALF: Ja. Es ist elegant. Und die Kellner tragen einen Smoking!

MIA: Schau mal. Hier ist die Getränkekarte. Meine Güte! Das sind viele Getränke.

RALF: Na ja. Wir sind in Wien. Die Wiener trinken gern Kaffee.

MIA: Was trinkst du?

RALF: Vielleicht eine Wiener Melange. „Halb Kaffee, halb heiße, geschäumte Milch."

MIA: Eine Melange kostet fünf Euro siebzig.

RALF: Ach ja. Ja, das ist ein bisschen teuer.

MIA: Ein kleiner Brauner kostet nur drei Euro sechzig.

RALF: Hmm ... Vielleicht. Und du? Was trinkst du?

MIA: Ich denke, ein Fiaker schmeckt gut.

RALF: Fiaker ... Wo ist das?

MIA: Hier. „Großer Mokka im Glas, mit Stroh Rum, Schlagobers und Cocktail Kirsche."

RALF: Ja, das schmeckt bestimmt gut.

MIA: Aber?

RALF: Er kostet acht Euro ... Ich finde das ein bisschen teuer.

MIA: Aber, Ralf, wir sind in Wien!

RALF: Du hast Recht. Also dann. Ein Fiaker für dich, und eine Melange für mich.

MIA: Schau mal! Der Kellner kommt!

[Der Kellner bringt die Kaffeegetränke.]

MIA: Mmm ... Der Fiaker schmeckt wunderbar!

RALF: Und die Melange ist auch gut. Schau mal. Ein Glas Wasser dazu.

MIA: Schön. Du trinkst gern Wasser.

RALF: Ja. Wasser ist günstig.

MIA: Und ich trinke gern Kaffee mit Rum und Cocktail Kirschen.

RALF: Das stimmt. Ich glaube, wir haben Wien gern.

C. Ralf and Mia in Salzburg

MIA: Also dann. Wir starten hier, in der Dreifaltigkeitsgasse.

RALF: Wir gehen die Dreifaltigkeitsgasse entlang.

MIA: Gute Idee. Dann gehen wir geradeaus, bis zum Platzl.

RALF: Mhm. Wir überqueren das Platzl. Und dann gehen wir links in
          den Giselakai.

MIA: Genau. Dann gehen wir über die Staatsbrücke bis zur Griesgasse.

RALF: Stimmt. Wir überqueren die Griesgasse, und wir gehen den
          Rathausplatz entlang, bis zur Getreidegasse.

MIA: Genau. Und da finden wir Mozarts Geburtshaus: Getreidegasse 9.

RALF: Richtig. Das Geburtshaus steht rechts.

MIA: Nein, Schatz. Das Haus steht nicht rechts. Es steht links in
          der Getreidegasse.

RALF: Ach so. Stimmt. Du hast recht.

GRAMMAR EXERCISES

A. Add a *gern* to each sentence to express that the subject "likes to do" the action.

1. Die Grubers reisen.

   _____.

2. Ich trinke Kaffeegetränke.

   _____.

3. Maria geht in Kaffeehäuser.

   _____.

4. Ich lese Liebesromane.

   _____.

5. Wir sprechen Deutsch.

   _____.

B. Negate the following sentences.

1. Wir reisen nach Italien.

   _____.

2. Ihr sprecht gern Englisch.

   _____.

3. Mozarts Geburtshaus steht in der Lerchenfelder Straße.

   _____.

4. Ich backe.

   _____.

5. Ich singe in der Dusche (*in the shower*).

   _____.

VOCABULARY EXERCISES

A. Fill in the blank with the appropriate word. Don't forget to conjugate the verbs or to use the correct plural form of a noun where necessary.

1. Mozarts Gerburtshaus _____ in der Getreidegasse.

2. Wir _____ die Brücke und gehen geradeaus bis zum Platzl.

3. A: Nein. Wir gehen nicht nach Rechts. Wir gehen nach links.
   B: Ach so. Ja, _____.

4. Wir lesen gern _____.

5. Ich glaube, ein Fiaker ist _____ zu teuer.

6. Die Grubers _____ im Hotel Graf Stadion.

7. Die Kellner tragen einen _____.

8. Die Grubers gehen in ein Kaffeehaus und bestellen zwei _____.

9. Zuerst gehen wir nach Norden, _____ Kirchenplatz.

10. Die Melange _____ sehr gut!

TRANSLATIONS

A. Translate from German into English.

1. Wir gehen zuerst die Buchfeldgasse entlang, nach Süden.

   _____.

2. Das Café Landtmann steht links gegenüber.

   _____.

3. Das schmeckt bestimmt gut!

   _____.

4. Wir überqueren die Griesgasse, und wir gehen den Rathausplatz entlang, bis zur Getreidegasse.

   _____

   _____.

5. Die Wiener trinken gern Kaffee.

   _____.

B. Translate from English into German.

1. The _Fiaker_ tastes great! I like it/that.

   _____.

2. We cross the _Hauptbrücke_ and go in the direction of _Bahnhofstraße_.

   _____

   _____.

3. First, we go to the left.

   _____.

4. Then, we go three streets until _Buchfeldergasse_.

   _____.

5. I like to drink water!

   _____!

Answers on page 244

ASKING QUESTIONS AND NUMBERS ABOVE 100

SUMMARY

This lesson marks the start of *die zweite Etappe*, "the second stage," in your journey through the German language!

Grammatically, there are two types of questions you can formulate: closed- and open-ended questions.

Closed-ended questions are also called yes-no questions because the answer to them is always *ja* or *nein*. Closed-ended questions in German always begin with a conjugated form of the verb, followed by the subject (e.g., *Kochst du? Bleibst du? Gehen wir?*) and any other information you wish to include in your question, such as adverbs, adjectives, prepositional phrases, and objects (e.g., *Kochst du gern? Bin ich interessant? Kommen Sie aus China? Spielen Sie Fußball?*).

Open-ended questions are answered with specific information, not *ja* or *nein*. Open-ended questions always begin with an interrogative pronoun, followed by a conjugated verb, then the subject, and then any other information you wish to include (e.g., *Wo wohnst du? Wie lange ist das Konzert in München? Wann beginnt das Konzert in München?*).

German is a language that requires its speakers to express directionality through interrogative pronouns, whether it's "where" in terms of location (e.g., *Wo bleiben wir?*), "where from" in terms of origination (e.g., *Woher ist der Wein?*), or "to where" in terms of destination (e.g., *Wohin gehen wir?*).

GRAMMAR

Interrogative Pronouns

wo	where
woher	from where
wohin	to where
wer	who
was	what
wann	when
wie viel	how much
wie viele	how many
warum	why
wie	how, what

VOCABULARY

Nouns

-e Milliarde	billion
-e Million	million

Adjectives and Adverbs

erfreulich	gratifying / pleasant / nice

Talking about the Weather

Der Himmel ist grau.	The sky is gray.
Der Himmel ist klar.	The sky is clear.
Die Sonne scheint.	The sun is shining.
Es blitzt.	There's lightning.
Es donnert.	It's thundering.
Es ist angenehm.	It is pleasant.
Es ist Badewetter!	It's really nice out! (literally "It's bathing weather.")
Es ist bewölkt.	It is cloudy.
Es ist frisch.	It is chilly.
Es ist gar nicht schön.	It is not at all nice.
Es ist heiß.	It is hot.
Es ist heiter.	It is fair.
Es ist Hundewetter!	It's horrible out! (literally "It's dog weather.")
Es ist kalt.	It is cold.

Es ist kühl.	It is cool.
Es ist neblig.	It is foggy.
Es ist regnerisch.	It is rainy.
Es regnet.	It is raining.
Es ist schön.	It is nice/beautiful.
Es ist sonnig.	It is sunny.
Es schneit.	It is snowing.
Es stürmt.	It's storming.
Es ist warm.	It is warm.
Es ist windig.	It is windy.
Wie ist das Wetter?	How is the weather?
Wie viel Grad ist es?	What's the temperature?
Was zeigt das Thermometer?	What does the temperature gauge show?

Phrases

(etwas) macht Spaß	(something) is fun
Fangen wir gleich an!	Let's start right now!
Wissen Sie noch?	Do you still remember?
Zehn Pflanzen in zehn Zimmern macht zehn Zimmerpflanzen.	Ten plants in ten rooms makes ten room plants.

GRAMMAR EXERCISES

A. Formulate a closed-ended question from the following statements.

1. Du kommst aus Österreich.

   _____.

2. Wir lernen Deutsch.

   _____.

3. Ihr seid brav.

   _____.

4. Das Wetter ist schön.

   _____.

5. Sie sprechen gern Deutsch.

   _____.

B. Use the interrogative pronoun in parentheses to formulate an open-ended question from the following statements.

1. Die Oper beginnt. (wann)

   _____.

2. Du lernst gern Deutsch. (warum)

   _____.

3. Eine Flasche Rotwein aus Italien kostet. (wie viel)

   _____.

4. Wir reisen nächste Woche. (wohin)

   _____.

5. Sie wohnen in Deutschland. (wo)

   _____.

C. Fill in the blank with *wo*, *woher*, or *wohin*.

1. _____ übernachten wir?

2. _____ kommt ihr?

3. _____ arbeiten Sie?

4. _____ fliegst du?

5. _____ gehen wir jetzt?

VOCABULARY EXERCISES

A. Read the weather reports below and determine which city's weather is likely being described.

1. Viele Grüße aus dem Süden! Es stürmt und es ist sehr warm. Im Moment ist es 86 Grad Fahrenheit. Das ist 30 Grad Celsius. Es blitzt und donnert, und der Himmel ist dunkel.

   ○ a. Seattle ○ b. Washington DC ○ c. London ○ d. Amsterdam

2. Guten Tag, meine Damen und Herren. Hier spricht Meteorologe James Pfrehm. Ich berichte live und aktuell über das Wetter. Es ist momentan neblig und kühl. Der Thermometer zeigt 12 Grad Celsius. Es regnet auch. Es ist generell Hundewetter.

   ○ a. Bangkok   ○ b. Florida   ○ c. London   ○ d. Honolulu

3. Guten Morgen und viele Grüße aus dem tropischen Paradies. Ich bin wieder live dabei, mit dem aktuellen Wetterbericht. Hier ist es windig aber warm. Es ist 27 Grad Celsius, der Himmel ist blau, und die Sonne scheint. Meine Damen und Herren, hier ist es ist wirklich Badewetter.

   ○ a. Reykjavík   ○ b. Moscow   ○ c. London   ○ d. Honolulu

4. Grüß Gott, liebe Damen und Herren. Hier ist wieder Ihr Meteorloge Nummer Eins. Der Himmel ist bedeckt. Es ist kalt und es schneit. Es ist auch windig. Der Thermometer zeigt null Grad Celsius.

   ○ a. Toronto   ○ b. Cape Town   ○ c. Kairo   ○ d. Buenos Aires

B. Answer the following questions by spelling out the quantities.
   (Note: For simplicity's sake, don't factor in leap years.)

   1. Wie viele Sekunden sind in einem Tag?

      _____

   2. Wie viele Stunden sind in einer Woche (*week*)?

      _____

   3. Wie viele Tage sind in einem Jahrzehnt (*decade*)?

      _____

   4. Wie viele Stunden sind in einem Jahrhundert (*century*)?

      _____

   5. Wie viele Sekunden sind in einem Jahrtausend (*millennium*)?

      _____

   6. Wie viele Kilometer ist es von der Erde (*earth*) bis zum Mond (*moon*)?

      _____

   7. Wie viele Kilometer ist es von der Erde bis zur Sonne (*moon*)?

      _____

   8. Wie viele Kilometer ist es von der Sonne bis zum Planeten Neptune?

      _____

TRANSLATIONS

A. Translate from German into English.

1. In Wien scheint die Sonne und es ist angenehm.

   _____.

2. Übersetzen macht Spaß!

   _____!

3. Es stürmt und es ist gar nicht schön.

   _____.

4. Es schneit und der Himmel ist grau.

   _____.

5. Grammatik ist erfreulich!

   _____!

B. Translate from English into German.

1. It is rainy and foggy.

   _____.

2. Speaking German is fun.

   _____.

3. It's thundering and raining.

   _____.

4. It's horrible weather!

   _____!

5. What's the temperature in Berlin?

   _____?

Answers on page 245

THE NOMINATIVE AND ACCUSATIVE CASES AND *KEIN-*

SUMMARY

The **nominative** is a **grammatical case** that expresses the **subject** in a sentence. The nominative case answers the question, Who or what is doing something?

A **subject** is the person or thing doing the action in a sentence and is conjugated with the verb (e.g., *Der Student geht ins Konzert*).

The **accusative** is a grammatical case that expresses the **direct object** in a sentence. The accusative case answers the question, Who or what is the subject acting on or doing something to?

A direct object is the person or thing that directly receives the subject's action (e.g., *Der Student hat das Buch*; *Die Frau kauft den Pullover*).

The verb *haben* ("to have") is irregular in German and generally takes a direct object (e.g., *Ich habe die Lampe*; *Das Haus hat einen Keller*).

Personal pronouns occur as subjects and direct objects and therefore have nominative and accusative forms.

To negate nouns in German, speakers often use the negating word *kein-*, which takes endings (i.e., gets inflected) according to the number, gender, and case of the noun it precedes (e.g., *Der Student hat kein Buch*; *Das ist kein Pullover, sondern eine Bluse*; *Wir haben keinen Hund*).

GRAMMAR

Conjugation of 'haben'

ich habe [I have]	wir haben [we have]
du hast [you (inform.) have]	ihr habt [you guys (inform.) have]
Sie haben [you (form.) have]	Sie haben [you guys (form.) have]
er/sie/es hat [he/she/it has]	sie haben [they have]

Declensions of Definite and Indefinite Articles

CASE		SINGULAR			PLURAL
		Masc.	Fem.	Neut.	
Nominative (subject)	Def.	der	die	das	die
	Ind.	ein	eine	ein	--
Accusative (direct object)	Def.	den	die	das	die
	Ind.	einen	eine	ein	--

Personal Pronouns

Nominative	Accusative	Nominative	Accusative.
ich [I]	mich [me]	wir [we]	uns [us]
du [you/ informal]	dich [you/ informal]	ihr [you guys/ informal]	euch [you guys/ informal]
Sie [you/ formal]	Sie [you/ formal]	Sie [you guys/ formal]	Sie [you guys/ formal]
er [he]	Ihn [he]	sie [they]	sie [them]
Sie [she]	Sie [she]		
es [it]	es [it]		

Declension of negating word kein-

CASE	GENDER			PLURAL
	Masc.	Fem.	Neut.	
Nominative	kein	keine	kein	keine
Accusative	keinen	keine	kein	keine

Nouns

-r Couchtisch -e	coffee table
-r Dachboden ¨-e	attic
-r Dackel -e	dachshund
-r Fernseher -	television
-r Herd -e	stove / cooker
-r Hund -e	dog
-r Keller -	cellar
-r Kühlschrank ¨-e	refrigerator
-r Ofen ¨-	oven
-r Pappkarton -s	cardboard box
-r Schrank ¨-e	cupboard
-r Spiegel -	mirror
-e Toilette -n	bathroom (with a toilet)
-r Trockner -	dryer
-e Garage -n	garage
-e Hängeleuchte -n	hanging lamp
-e Heizung -en	heater / heating
-e Kommode -n	dresser
-e Küche -n	kitchen
-e Spüle -n	sink
-e Stehlampe -n	floor lamp
-e Treppe -n	stairs / stairway / staircase
-e Wand ¨-e	wall
-e Wanduhr -en	wall clock
-e Waschmaschine -n	washing machine
-e Zimmerpflanze -n	house plant
-s Auto -s	car
-s Badezimmer -	bathroom (with or without a toilet)
-s Bett -en	bed
-s Bild -er	picture
-s Bücherregal -e	bookshelf
-s Einfamilienhaus ¨-er	single-family home
-s Fenster -	window
-s Haus ¨-er	house

-s Licht -er	light
-s Wandregal -e	rack / wall shelf
-s Schlafzimmer -	bedroom
-s Steckregal -e	upright and freestanding shelving unit
-s Wohnzimmer -	living room

Verbs

haben	to have

Adjectives and Adverbs

süß	sweet

Phrases

Jetzt sind Sie daran!	Now you're up! / Now it's your turn!
Natürlich (nicht)!	Of course (not)!
Springen wir gleich ins kalte Wasser!	Let's dive right in!
übrigens	by the way
Wie schreibt man das?	How do you write that?
zum Beispiel	for example

TEXTS

A. Das Einfamilienhaus

Das Haus hat eine Garage, eine Küche, ein Wohnzimmer, ein Badezimmer, ein Schlafzimmer, einen Keller, und einen Dachboden.

Das ist der Keller. Er ist groß. Er hat eine Treppe, eine Heizung, ein Licht, einen Trockner, und eine Waschmaschine.

Und hier ist die Garage. Sie ist ein bisschen klein, aber es gibt ein Auto, ein Wandregal, und ein kleines Steckregal.

Hier ist das Wohnzimmer. Es gibt **ein** Fenster, **ein** Bild, **einen** Fernseher, **eine** Stehlampe, **eine** Couch, und **einen** Couchtisch.

Das ist die Küche. Sie hat eine Zimmerpflanze, einen Kühlschrank, einen Schrank, und eine Mikrowelle. Es gibt auch eine Spüle, einen Herd, und einen Ofen.

Hier ist das Schlafzimmer. Es hat eine Wanduhr, eine Kommode, und ein Bücherregal. Es gibt auch eine Hängeleuchte, und ein Bett.

B. Ralf und Mia sprechen über die Liebe.

RALF: Ich liebe dich sehr.

MIA: Danke, Schatz.

RALF: Und? Liebst du mich auch?

MIA: Natürlich.

RALF: Und die Kinder?

MIA: Ja. Ich liebe sie mit ganzem Herzen.

RALF: Sie lieben uns auch.

MIA: Ich weiß. Ich sage oft, "Kinder, ich liebe euch so sehr."

GRAMMAR EXERCISES

A. Fill in the blank with the correct definite article.

1. _____ Garage hat ein Auto.

2. Ich finde _____ Hund süß.

3. Der Hund findet _____ Katze süß.

4. Wie groß ist _____ Keller?

5. Wir kaufen _____ Bücherregal.

B. Fill in the blank with the correct indefinite article.

1. Was kostet _____ Spiegel bei Walmart?

2. Gibt es _____ Treppe?

3. Ist das _____ Bett von Ikea?

4. Wir brauchen _____ Herd.

5. _____ Kühlschrank steht in der Garage.

C. Fill in the blank with the correct personal pronoun.

1. Das sind meine Kinder. Ich liebe _____ sehr.

2. Das ist meine Tochter. Ich liebe _____ auch sehr.

3. Das ist unser Opa. Wir lieben _____ sehr.

4. Das ist mein Haus. Ich habe _____ gern.

5. Ihr seid gute Menschen! Wir loben (*praise*) _____.

6. Wie heißen Sie? Ich glaube, ich kenne _____.

7. Ralf sagt: „Mia, ich finde _____ toll!"

8. Ralf fragt: „Findest du _____ auch toll?"

D. Negate the following sentences using *kein-*.

1. Ich sehe den Keller.   _____.

2. Wir haben eine Küche.   _____.

3. Es gibt einen Dachboden.   _____.

4. Es gibt Lampen.   _____.

5. Ich kaufe das Haus.   _____.

VOCABULARY EXERCISES

A. Determine which vocabulary word is being described.

1. Hier ist es kühl und es gibt oft Wein in Regalen.   _____.

2. Es ist durchsichtig (*see-through*) und man kann es öffnen (*open*). _____.

3. Das macht Licht und hängt in einem Zimmer.   _____.

4. Hier kann man Tassen und Teller waschen.   _____.

5. Hier parkt man das Auto.   _____.

6. Das macht ein Haus warm. _____.

7. Hier kann man einen Kuchen backen. _____.

8. Das hängt oft in einem Badezimmer über (*above*) der Spüle. _____.

TRANSLATIONS

A. Translate from German into English.

1. Die Kinder finden den Hund süß.

   _____.

2. Es gibt keine Wanduhren.

   _____.

3. Hat das Wohnzimmer eine Hängelampe und ein Bücherregal?

   _____?

4. Wir haben das Badezimmer gern.

   _____.

5. Wir brauchen euch!

   _____!

B. Translate from English into German.

1. There are many mirrors.

   _____.

2. The single-family home has a cellar but no garage.

   _____.

3. We think they are sweet.

   _____.

4. The bedroom has six windows.

   _____.

5. I don't know her.

   _____.

Answers on page 246

TIME IN GERMAN AND POSSESSIVE PRONOUNS

SUMMARY

To express time in German, you first say the hour, followed by the word *Uhr*, and then give the minutes (e.g., *Es ist **elf Uhr zwanzig***).

To avoid any confusion regarding a.m. or p.m., Germans can also use the 24-hour system (e.g., *Es ist **dreiundzwanzig** Uhr zwanzig*).

Just like in English, German also allows you to express time in chunks (e.g., "a quarter after eleven," *Viertel nach elf*; "five till eleven," *fünf vor elf*; and "half past eleven," *halb zwölf*).

Just like in English, the possessive pronouns in German occur before the noun they modify (e.g., "**my** car," ***mein** Wagen*; "**your** cat," ***deine** Katze*; "**her** house," ***ihr** Haus*).

All possessive pronouns in German inflect (i.e., take a grammatical ending) in order to expresses the number, gender, and case of the noun they modify (e.g., *Das ist eur**e** Katze*; *Wo sind unser**e** Kinder?*; *Ich liebe dein**en** Hund*).

In spoken German, it's common to begin with an expression of time like *heute, jetzt*, or *heute Abend*, and when this happens, the verb occurs in the second position, followed by the subject (e.g., ***Jetzt schaue ich** den Film*; ***Heute Abend machen wir** eine Waldwanderung*). This is called **subject-verb inversion**.

GRAMMAR

Possessive Pronouns

mein- [my]	unser- [we]
dein- [your/ informal]	euer- [your guys'/ informal]
Ihr- [your/formal]	Ihr- [your guys'/ formal]
sein- [his]	
ihr- [her]	ihr- [their]
sein- [its]	

Possessive Pronoun Endings

CASE	SINGULAR			PLURAL
	Masc.	Fem.	Neut.	
Nominative (subject)	-	-e	-	-e
Accusative (direct object)	-en	-e	-	-e

VOCABULARY

Nouns

-r Bahnhof ¨-e	train station
-r Fahrplan ¨-e	(train) ticket
-r Maschinenbau	mechanical engineering
-r Name -n	name
-r Schmetterling -e	butterfly
-e Ameise -n	ant
-e Armbanduhr -en	watch
-e einfache Karte	one-way ticket
-e Haltestelle -n	stop
-e Kuckucksuhr -en	cuckoo clock
-e Spinne -n	spider
-e Standuhr -en	grandfather clock
-e Stunde -n	hour (i.e., 60 minutes)
-e Uhrzeit -en	time (i.e., time of day)
-e Umsteigezeit -en	transfer time (i.e., amount of time to change trains)

-e Waldwanderung -en	hike in the forest
-e Zeit -en	time (i.e., "Do we have time?")
-s Frühstück -e	breakfast
-s Geschwister -	siblings
-s Gleis -e	track (i.e., train)
-s Hobby -s	hobby
-s Mal -e	time (i.e., next time, the first time)
-s Tagesprogramm	the day's itinerary

Verbs

essen	to eat
machen	to make/do
reparieren	to repair
sammeln	to collect
schauen	to watch/look
schlafen	to sleep
schwimmen	to swim
singen	to sing

Adjectives and Adverbs

ab	departs (i.e., train or airplane)
an	arrives (i.e., train or airplane)
einmal, zweimal, dreimal, usw.	once, twice, three times, etc.
dann	then
heute	today
heute Abend	this evening
heute in der Früh	early this morning
heute Morgen	this morning
heute Nachmittag	this afternoon
heute Nacht	tonight
jetzt	now
mittelgroß	medium- or moderate-sized
teuer	expensive

Telling Time

Es ist eins/zwei/drei/usw.	It is one/two/three/etc.
Es ist ein/zwei/drei/usw. **Uhr.**	It is one/two/three/etc. o'clock.
Es ist **halb** vier.	It is half past three.
Es ist vier **Uhr** dreiunddreißig.	It is four thirty-three.

Es ist zehn **nach** vier.	It is ten **past** four.
Es ist **Viertel** nach vier.	It is a **quarter** past four.
von zwei Uhr zehn **bis** drei Uhr	**from** two ten **until** three o'clock
fünf **vor** vier Uhr	five **to/till** four

Phrases

Das ist alles!	That's it! / That's everything!
So weit alles gut?	Everything good so far?
Wann fährt der Zug nach	When does the train go to
Wann kommt der Zug in _____ an?	When does the train arrive in _____?
Welche Uhrzeit haben wir?	What is the time? (literally "Which time do we have?")
Wie spät ist es?	What time is it? (literally "How late is it?")
Wie viel Uhr ist es?	What time is it? (literally "How many hour is it?")
Wir machen gute Fortschritte!	We are making good progress!
zum ersten/zweiten/dritten Mal	for the first/second/third time

TEXT

A. Ralf and Mia's First Date

RALF: Hast du eine große Familie?

MIA: Na ja. Meine Familie ist mittelgroß. Ich habe zwei Geschwister, einen Bruder und eine Schwester.

RALF: Wie sind ihre Namen?

MIA: Mein Bruder heißt Jakob. Er ist zwanzig Jahre alt und studiert Maschinenbau.

RALF: Und was sind seine Hobbys?

MIA: Er hat sein Auto gern. Das ist sozusagen sein Hobby. Abends repariert er sein Auto.

RALF: Wo wohnt er?

MIA: Zu Hause.

RALF: Mensch! Ist euer Haus groß?

MIA: Nein, unser Haus ist nicht sehr groß. Aber wir wohnen gerne dort.

RALF: Und wie heißt deine Schwester?

MIA: Sie heißt Stephanie und ist vierzehn Jahre alt.

RALF: Und was macht sie gern?

MIA: Na ja, ihr Hobby ist ein bisschen bizarr.

RALF: Was meinst du mit „bizarr"?

MIA: Sie sammelt gern Insekten.

RALF: Wie bitte?

MIA: Ihre Lieblingsinsekten sind Schmetterlinge, Ameisen und besonders Spinnen.

RALF: Ach so ...

GRAMMAR EXERCISES

A. Fill in the correct possessive pronoun, given in parentheses, with the correct grammatical ending.

1. Wie ist _____ Name? (*your*, formal)

2. Warum esst ihr _____ Frühstück? (*my*)

3. Ist das _____ Zug nach Berlin? (*our*)

4. Wir finden _____ Hobbys sehr interessant. (*your guys'*, informal)

5. _____ Armbanduhr ist teuer. (*his*)

6. Kennst du _____ Bruder? (*their*)

B. Arrange the phrases into a sentence, beginning with the underlined phrase. (Don't forget to conjugate the verb.)

1. ein Museum / <u>heute Nachmittag</u> / besuchen / sie (feminine singular)

   _____

2. ich / nach Deutschland / <u>morgen</u> / fliegen

   _____

3. machen / er / heute in der Früh / ein Kreuzrätsel (*crossword puzzle*)

   _____

4. Kaffee mit Milch / trinken / morgens (*mornings*) / ihr

   _____

5. wir / gern / abends (*evenings*) / lesen / im Bett

   _____

VOCABULARY EXERCISES

A. Fill in the appropriate vocabulary word(s).

1. Meine Lieblingsinsekten sind _____, _____,
   und _____.

2. Wann _____ nach Berlin?

3. Der Zug kommt _____ an; das heißt, in diesem Moment!

4. Meine Schwester studiert _____.

5. Morgens esse ich _____ von 6 Uhr bis halb sieben.

6. Ich bin sehr müde. Also, heute Nacht _____ ich zehn Stunden.

B. Write out the following times, using the 24-hour system to avoid ambiguity.

1. 12:51 p.m.   _____.

2. 11:05 a.m.   _____.

3. 10:50 p.m.   _____.

4. 6:30 a.m.   _____.

5. 3:15 p.m.   _____.

A. Translate from German into English.

1. Findest du meine Hobbys bizarr?

   _____?

2. Jetzt machen wir eine Waldwanderung und dann essen wir Frühstück.

   _____

   _____.

3. Heute Nachmittag üben wir unser Deutsch von vier bis sechs.

   _____.

4. Der Zug kommt um halb neun an.

   _____.

5. Ist unsere Umsteigezeit eine Stunde, eine halbe Stunde, oder nur eine Viertelstunde?

   _____

   _____?

B. Translate from English into German.

1. Do we have enough time?

   _____?

2. She swims three hours in the morning.

   _____.

3. Why do you (formal) sleep from four until six p.m.?

   _____?

4. We like to sing in the evenings.

   _____.

5. They don't like to repair our computer.

   _____.

Answers on page 246

COORDINATING CONJUNCTIONS AND *DER-* WORDS

SUMMARY

Coordinating conjunctions are words that allow you to string phrases and sentences together to create longer utterances.

The coordinating conjunctions in German are as follows: *aber*, "but"; *denn*, "because"; *oder*, "or"; *sondern*, "rather"; *und*, "and." These words unite, or **conjoin**, two or more chunks of language, and they do this **on equal syntactic levels** (i.e., **coordinately**).

> *Ich komme aus den USA, **aber** ich spreche Deutsch.*
> *Ich lerne Deutsch, **denn** es ist interessant.*
> *Ich fliege nach Deutschland **oder** ich fliege nach Österreich.*
> *Ich lerne nicht Italienisch, **sondern** ich lerne Deutsch.*
> *Ich habe Freunde in Deutschland **und** ich spreche gern Deutsch.*

The **general word-position model (WPM) for the German sentence** is a very useful tool for learning how to put together sentences in German. The WPM holds that any sentence in German can comprise up to six spots, or positions, in which a word can occur. For example, consider *Denn ich besuche meine Freunde nächstes Jahr in Wien* ("Because I'm going to visit my friends next year in Vienna"):

0	1	2	3	4	5
Denn	*ich*	*besuche*	*meine Freunde*	*nächstes Jahr in Wien*	X
coordinating conjunction	subject	verb	direct object	elements of time/manner/ place	can be occupied by an infinitive verb, past participle, or separable prefix

Coordinating conjunctions occupy position 0, and the verb remains in position 2, which is standard for all statements.

Der- words are similar to definite articles in that they occur before a noun, modify that noun's contextual meaning, and take particular endings that express the gender, number, and case of the noun they modify (e.g., *Dieses Mädchen heißt Julia*; *Welchen Anzug tragen Sie?*; *Ich liebe alle Tiere*).

The most common *der-* words in German are as follows: ***all-***, "all"; ***dies-***, "this" / "these"; ***jed-***, "each" / "every"; ***welch-***, "which"; ***manch-***, "many" / "many a"; and ***solch-***, "such" / "such a."

GRAMMAR

der -Word Endings

CASE	SINGULAR			PLURAL
	Masc.	**Fem.**	**Neut.**	
Nominative	-er dieser Hund	-e diese Katze	-es dieses Haus	-e diese Leute
Accusative	-en diesen Hund	-e diese Katze	-es dieses Haus	-e diese Leute

VOCABULARY

Nouns

-r Beruf -e	profession
-r Gedankenleser -	mind reader
-r Hausarrest -e	grounded at home
-r Mensch -en	person / human
-e Hauptstadt ¨-e	capital city
-e Person -en	person
-e Strafe -n	punishment
-s Argument -e	argument
-s Handy -s	cell phone

Professions/Jobs

-r Advokat -en	attorney (m.)
-e Advokatin -nen	attorney (f.)
-r Arzt ¨-e	doctor (m.)

-e Ärztin -nen	doctor (f.)
-r Bankangestellter (pl. Bankangestellte)	bank employee (m.)
-e Bankangestellte -	bank employee (f.)
-r Beamter (pl. Beamte)	official (m.)
-e Beamtin -nen	official (f.)
-r Informatiker -	computer scientist (m.)
-e Informatikerin -nen	computer scientist (f.)
-r Krankenpfleger -	nurse (m.)
-e Krankenpflegerin -nen	nurse (f.)
-r Richter -	judge (m.)
-e Richterin -nen	judge (f.)
-r Verkäufer -	salesman
-e Verkäuferin -nen	saleswoman

Verbs

analysieren	to analyze
bekommen	to get/receive
brauchen	to need
schreiben	to write
verstehen	to understand

Adjectives and Adverbs

böse	naughty / angry / wicked / evil
ehrlich	honest
freundlich	friendly
unehrlich	dishonest
unfreundlich	unfriendly

Phrases

Ach so!	Aha!
Alle Leute	all the people / all people
Bescheid wissen	to be in the know
Entschuldigung ...	Beg your pardon ...
Ich hab's!	I've got it!
Ich finde ...	I think ...
Einverstanden!	Agreed!
Recht haben	to be right/correct
von Beruf sein	to be by trade
Was meinst du?	What do you think?

A. Ralf and Mia Discuss Hans's Punishment

MIA: Was meinst du? Zwei Wochen Hausarrest oder zwei Wochen kein Handy?

RALF: Na ja. Er braucht eine Strafe, aber …

MIA: Aber …?

RALF: Zwei Wochen Hausarrest ist zu lang, denn Hans ist doch meistens brav.

MIA: Du hast recht.

RALF: Also dann. Ich finde, Hausarrest ist eine gute Strafe. Aber nicht zwei Wochen lang, sondern nur eine Woche. Was meinst du?

MIA: Einverstanden. Er bekommt eine Woche Hausarrest.

B. Auf der Gedankenleserparty

YOU: Entschuldigung. Wer ist dieser Gedankenleser?

MANN: Welchen Gedankenleser meinen Sie?

YOU: Ich meine diesen Mann da.

MANN: Na ja, jeder Mann auf dieser Party ist Gedankenleser.

YOU: Wie bitte?

MANN: Solche Partys haben viele Gedankenleser.

YOU: Es tut mir leid, aber ich verstehe nicht.

MANN: Das ist eine Gedankenleserparty. Alle Leute hier sind Gedankenleser von Beruf.

A. Select the appropriate coordinating conjunction from the three proposed in parentheses and then use that conjunction to combine the two sentences.

1. Ich bestelle keinen Kaffee. Ich möchte einen Tee. (und / oder / sondern)

   _____.

2. Wir üben Grammatik. Es macht Spaß. (oder / denn / aber)

   _____.

3. Alle Kellner im Kaffeehaus tragen einen Smoking. Ich finde das toll. (und / denn / aber).

   _____
   _____.

4. Der Gedankenleser weiß meinen Namen nicht. Er weiß viel über mich. (und / sondern / aber)

   _____
   _____.

5. Sind Sie Richter von Beruf? Arbeiten Sie als Beamter? (sondern / oder / denn)

   _____?

B. Fill in the blanks with the appropriate *der*-word ending.

1. Was ist dies_____ Frau von Beruf?

2. Wir kennen all_____ Advokaten und Advokatinnen in New York City.

3. Mein Mann findet jed_____ Richter freundlich und fair.

4. Welch_____ Handy finden Sie am besten?

5. Advokaten? Nein ... Solch_____ Menschen sind nicht immer unehrlich, oder?

C. Arrange the phrases into a sentence, beginning with the underlined phrase. (Note: Don't forget to conjugate the verb and to inflect any indefinite articles and *ein-* or *der-* words.)

1. arbeiten / als Bankangestellter / mein- Onkel / in Salzburg

   _____.

2. solch- Spinnen / sammeln / <u>wir</u> / gern

    _____.

3. <u>welch</u>- Beruf / ihr / langweilig / finden?

    _____?

4. bekommen / <u>heute</u> / mein- Kinder / ein- Hund

    _____.

5. ein- Computer / <u>morgens</u> / reparieren / manch- Informatikerin / zu Hause

    _____.

VOCABULARY EXERCISES

A. Which phrase fits best in the situation described? (Note: The pronoun *Sie* refers to you.)

1. Plötzlich (*suddenly*) haben Sie eine Idee. _____.

2. Sie möchten wissen, wo Ihr Nachbar arbeitet. _____.

3. Ihr Freund möchte Sie zu einer Party einladen (*invite*). _____.

4. Sie fragen einen Passanten nach dem Weg (*for directions*). _____.

5. Sie möchten Ihre Meinung (*opinion*) sagen. _____.

B. Fill in the blank with the appropriate vocabulary word. (Don't forget to conjugate the verbs.)

1. Ich bin Milliardär. Also, ich _____ kein Geld.

2. Wenn ich krank bin, besuche ich meinen _____.

3. Hans Gruber ist böse und braucht eine _____.

4. Wie bitte? Ich _____ dich nicht! Ich spreche kein Italienisch.

5. Was _____ unsere Schwester zum Geburtstag?

TRANSLATIONS

A. Translate from German into English.

1. Meine Nichte ist Informatikerin von Beruf.

   _____.

2. Abends spielt der Richter Schach allein zu Hause.

   _____.

3. Jeder Krankenpfleger ist freundlich.

   _____.

4. Manche Leute sprechen gern Deutsch.

   _____.

5. Welchen Hund bekommt dieses Kind zum Geburtstag?

   _____?

B. Translate from English into German.

1. Their father is a salesman by trade.

   _____.

2. This (male) attorney is dishonest and needs a punishment.

   _____.

3. All (female) officials like working in Washington DC.

   _____.

4. Every child gets a cell phone.

   _____.

5. Now we understand you guys.

   _____.

Answers on page 247

MODAL VERBS AND MORE ACCUSATIVE

SUMMARY

Just like modal verbs in English, modal verbs in German often occur with another verb (the main verb), whose meaning the modal verb **modifies** (e.g., "to play" → "I can play," "I must play," "I want to play"; *spielen* → *ich kann spielen, ich muss spielen, ich will spielen*).

There are six modal verbs in German: *dürfen*, "to be allowed"; *können*, "to be able"; *mögen*, "to like"; *müssen*, "to have to / must"; *sollen*, "to ought to / should"; *wollen*, "to want."

The modal verbs have irregular conjugations (see tables that follow).

Modal verbs are conjugated with the subject, and the main verb that it's modifying remains in the infinitive form and is moved to the end of the sentence (e.g., *Wir **wollen** heute Abend ins Konzert **gehen**; Heute **darf** ich eine Waldwanderung **machen***).

Applied to the word-position model (WPM) for German sentences, modal verbs come in position 5:

0	1	2	3	4	5
Denn	*ich*	*will*	*meine Freunde*	*nächstes Jahr in Wien*	*besuchen*
coordinating conjunction	subject	Modal verb	direct object	elements of time, manner, place	Infinitive verb

Modal verbs can also be used alone in a sentence (e.g., *Das **will** ich!*, "I want that!" / "I want to do that!"; *Das **dürfen** wir nicht*, "We're not allowed / We're not allowed to do that"; *Leider **musst** du das*, "Unfortunately, you have to / Unfortunately, you have to do that").

In lieu of the modal verb *mögen*, speakers often use the alternate form ***möchten*** ("would like"), both on its own in a sentence and with a main verb (e.g., *Ich möchte eine Kuckucksuhr*; *Wir möchten Deutsch lernen*).

In addition to expressing the direct object in a sentence, the **accusative** case in German is also used 1) with **certain phrases of time** (e.g., ***den ganzen Tag***; ***diesen Sommer***; ***nächstes Jahr***; ***letzten Monat***) and 2) with certain prepositions, so-called **accusative prepositions**: ***bis***, "until"; ***durch***, "through"; ***entlang***, "along" / "alongside" / "down"; ***für***, "for"; ***gegen***, "against"; ***ohne***, "without"; ***um***, "around" / "at" (e.g., *Wir gehen **durch den Wald**; Sind Sie **für** oder **gegen mich**?; Wir möchten Deutsch nicht **ohne den Professor** lernen!*).

GRAMMAR

dürfen [to be allowed to]

ich **darf** [I am allowed to]	wir **dürfen** [we are allowed to]
du **darfst** [you are allowed to]	ihr **dürft** [you guys are allowed to]
Sie **dürfen** [you are allowed to]	Sie **dürfen** [you guys are allowed to]
er/sie/es **darf** [he/she/it is allowed to]	sie **dürfen** [they are allowed to]

können [to be able to, can

ich **kann** [I am able to, can]	wir **können** [we are able to, can]
du **kannst** [you guys are able to, can]	ihr **könnt** [you are able to, can]
Sie **können** [you guys are able to, can]	Sie **können** [you are able to, can]
er/sie/es **kann** [he/she/it is able to, can]	sie **können** [they are able to, can]

möchten [would like (to)]

ich **möchte** [I would like (to)]	wir **möchten** [we would like (to)]
du **möchtest** [you would like (to)]	ihr **möchtet** [you guys would like (to)]
Sie **möchten** [you would like (to)]	Sie **möchten** [you guys would like (to)]
er/sie/es **möchte** [he/she/it would like (to)]	sie **möchten** [they would like (to)]

mögen [to like]

ich **mag** [I like]	wir **mögen** [we like]
du **magst** [you like]	ihr **mögt** [you guys like]
Sie **mögen** [you like]	Sie **mögen** [you guys like]
er/ sie/ es **mag** [he / she / it likes]	sie **mögen** [they like]

müssen [to have to, must]

ich **muss** [I have to, must]	wir **müssen** [we have to, must]
du **musst** [you have to, must]	ihr **müsst** [you guys have to, must]
Sie **müssen** [you have to, must]	Sie **müssen** [you guys have to, must]
er/sie/es **muss** [he/she/it has to, must]	sie **müssen** [they have to, must]

sollen [to be supposed to, should

ich **soll** [I am supposed to, should]	wir **sollen** [we are supposed to, should]
du **sollst** [you are supposed to, should]	ihr **sollt** [you guys are supposed to, should]
Sie **sollen** [you are supposed to, should]	Sie **sollen** [you guys are supposed to, should]
er/ sie/ es **soll** [he / she / it is supposed to, should]	sie **sollen** [they are supposed to, should]

wollen towantto]

ich **will** [I want]	wir **wollen** [we want]
du **willst** [you want]	ihr **wollt** [you guys want]
Sie **wollen** [you want]	Sie **wollen** [you guys want]
er/sie/es **will** [he / she / it wants]	sie **wollen** [they want]

VOCABULARY

Nouns

-r Apfel ¨-	apple
-r Ausländer -	foreigner (m.)
-r Bierdeckel -	beer coaster

-r Monat -e	month
-r Rasierschaum	shaving cream
-r Spaziergang ¨-e	walk
-r Tag -e	day
-r Teil -e	part
-r Toilettenartikel -	toiletry item
-r Turnschuh -e	gym shoes
-r Wochentag -e	weekday
-r Zweck -e	purpose
-e Anstecknadel -n	pin / badge
-e Ausländerin -nen	foreigner (f.)
-e Ecke -n	corner
-e Gesichtscreme -s	face cream
-e Haarbürste -n	hair brush
-e Jahreszeit -en	season
-e Kleidung -en	clothing / clothes / apparel
-e Rasierklinge -n	razor (i.e., for shaving)
-e Seife -n	soap
-e Welt -en	world
-e Zahnbürste -n	toothbrush
-e Zahnpasta (pl. Zahnpasten)	toothpaste
-s Duschgel -e	shower gel
-s Eis	ice / ice cream
-s Geschenk -e	present
-s Lebensmotto -s	life motto
-s Problem -e	problem
-s Shampoo -s	shampoo
-s Stück	piece (i.e., of pie, of soap, etc.)
-s Taschentuch ¨-er	tissue / handkerchief / Kleenex
-s Vorurteil -e	prejudice
-s Wochenende -n	weekend

Days of the Week

-r Sonntag	Sunday
-r Montag	Monday
-r Dienstag	Tuesday
-r Mittwoch	Wednesday
-r Donnerstag	Thursday
-r Freitag	Friday
-r Samstag	Saturday

Months

-r Januar	January
-r Februar	February
-r März	March
-r April	April
-r Mai	May
-r Juni	June
-r Juli	July
-r August	August
-r September	September
-r Oktober	October
-r November	November
-r Dezember	December

Seasons

-r Frühling -e	spring
-r Herbst -e	fall / autumn
-r Winter -	winter
-r Sommer -	summer

Verbs

angeln	to fish
besorgen	to get/obtain/procure
bleiben	to stay
erklären	to explain
fahren	to drive/ride/go (by vehicle)
fliegen	to fly
lösen	to solve
pflücken	to pick
tragen	to wear
wandern	to hike

Adjectives and Adverbs

alltäglich	everyday / common / mundane
fantastisch	fantastic
ganz	entire / whole
letzt	last
nächst	next
wichtig	important
witzig	funny / humorous

..., oder?	..., right?
Na ja, ...	Well, ...
Was ist los?	What is wrong? / What's the matter?

TEXTS

A. Ralf und Mia planen eine Reise nach Island.

RALF: Was sollen wir für die Reise nach Island kaufen?

MIA: Wir müssen warme Kleidung kaufen.

RALF: Gute Idee.

MIA: Ich brauche eine Jacke und einen Pullover.

RALF: Darf ich auch neue Schuhe bekommen?

MIA: Ja, Ralf, du darfst auch neue Schuhe bekommen.

RALF: Großartig.

MIA: Wir sollen auch ein paar Toilettenartikel besorgen.

RALF: Echt? Was brauchen wir?

MIA: Na ja, ich brauche Zahnpasta, eine Zahnbürste, ein Stück Seife, eine kleine Flasche Shampoo, eine Haarbürste, und Taschentücher. Was brauchst du?

RALF: Hmm ... Ach so! Ja, ich muss auch eine Zahnbürste kaufen. Außerdem brauche ich Rasierklingen, Rasierschaum, Duschgel, und Gesichtscreme.

MIA: Gut. Möchtest du zu Fuß gehen oder mit dem Auto zum Supermarkt fahren?

MIA: Ich möchte zu Fuß gehen.

B. Ein Geschenk für dich

RALF: Ich habe ein Geschenk für dich.

MIA: Für mich?

RALF: Ja. Dieses Geschenk ist aber auch für die ganze Familie. Das ist deine neue Anstecknadel.

MIA: Ralf Gruber!

RALF: Was ist los? Das ist dein Lebensmotto: „Jeder Tag ist ein Geschenk!"

MIA: Ja. Das ist mein Lebensmotto. Aber der letzte Teil?

RALF: Ach so. Ja: „Manchmal ist er nur miserabel verpackt."

MIA: Ralf ...

RALF: Ohne den letzten Teil ist es ...

MIA: Ja ... was?

RALF: ... ein bisschen alltäglich.

MIA: Alltäglich! Willst du sagen, du bist gegen mein Lebensmotto?

RALF: Nein, Schatz. Jeden Morgen höre ich gern: „Weißt du Ralf: Jeder Tag ist ein Geschenk!"

MIA: Ja und? Dieses Motto ist wichtig! Wir sollen es durch jeden Tag, ja durch das ganze Leben tragen.

RALF: Genau ... Und jetzt kannst du dein Lebensmotto jeden Tag auch wirklich tragen.

MIA: Sehr witzig ...

GRAMMAR EXERCISES

A. Choose the modal verb in parentheses that is most likely to fit and conjugate it for the subject.

1. Er _____ Deutsch lernen, denn er reist nach Frankfurt. (können / dürfen / wollen)

2. Ich _____ meinen Wortschatz oft üben. (können / mögen / müssen)

3. Warum _____ ihr mit dem Auto fahren? Ihr _____ auch zu Fuß gehen. (können / dürfen / wollen)

4. Mein Kind! Du bist erst sechszehn Jahre als. Du _____ nicht rauchen! (müssen / dürfen / wollen)

5. Wohin _____ unsere Eltern diesen Sommer fahren? Nach Berlin oder nach Wien? (sollen / wollen / müssen)

B. Fill in the blank with the German translation of the phrase in parentheses.

1. Wir gehen _____ (*around the corner*).

2. Ich bleibe _____ in Berlin (*until this summer*).

3. Sie hat nichts _____ (*against him*).

4. Sie gehen nicht _____ (*without their dog*).

5. Was machst du _____ zum Geburtstag (*for your child*)?

C. Arrange the phrases into a sentence, beginning with the underlined phrase. (Note: Don't forget to conjugate the modal verb and to inflect any indefinite articles and *ein-* or *der-* words.)

1. müssen / die Eltern / ihr- Sohn / bestrafen / jetzt

   _____.

2. dies- Winter / du / besorgen / sollen / ein- Heizung

   _____.

3. dürfen / schwimmen / jed- Sommer / ich / im Meer

   _____.

4. können / nächst- Monat / Sie / besuchen / mich / in Berlin?

   _____?

5. ein- Smoking / möchten / in der Arbeit / er / tragen / jed- Freitag

   _____.

A. Fill in the blank with the appropriate vocabulary word.

1. Der Komiker ist sehr _____.

2. Wir müssen dieses Problem _____.

3. Die Monate vom _____ sind März, April, und Mai.

4. Im Sommer esse ich gern _____.

5. Mein Bruder bekommt viele _____ zum Geburtstag.

6. Meine Freunde und ich haben keine _____ gegen Ausländer.

7. Ein Bierdeckel hat mehr als nur (*more than just*) einen _____.

8. Heute Abend sollen wir einen _____ durch den Park machen.

9. Es gibt sieben _____: Sontag, Montag, Dienstag, usw.

10. _____ hat nur zwei Tage: Samstag und Sonntag.

TRANSLATIONS

A. Translate from German into English.

1. Wohin fahrt ihr nächstes Wochenende?

   _____?

2. Sie muss Taschentücher und Kleidung für die Reise besorgen.

   _____.

3. Meine Witze können manchmal alltäglich sein.

   _____.

4. Er kann alle Matheaufgaben ohne Probleme lösen.

   _____.

5. Warum möchtest du durch den Wald wandern?

   _____?

B. Translate from English into German.

1. Our favorite season is fall.

   _____.

2. Our mother has to work the entire day.

   _____.

3. You (formal) are allowed to fish this evening, right?

   _____?

4. I should get shampoo and soap for this trip.

   _____.

5. They are going to stay an entire month in Vienna this winter.

   _____

   _____.

Answers on page 248

EINE REISE NACH MÜNCHEN UND ROTHENBURG OB DER TAUBER

SUMMARY

There are two verbs that express "to know" in German:

>*Wissen* means "to know" as in knowledge, facts, or information and has an irregular conjugation (e.g., *Ich **weiß** die Antwort*; ***Wissen** Sie meinen Namen?*; *Ihr **wisst** alles*); and

>*Kennen* means "to know" as in "to be familiar with" and has a regular conjugation (*Ich **kenne** den Film* Das Boot; ***Kennst** du Augsburg?*; *Wir **kennen** ihn gut*).

German has a number of so-called **stem-vowel-changing** verbs, which are verbs whose main vowel changes when you conjugate it for a second-person or third-person singular subject (e.g., *ich gebe → du **gibst**; ihn nehmt → du **nimmst**; wir fahren → er/sie/es **fährt**; sie laufen → das Kind **läuft***).

Unfortunately, a verb's infinitive form doesn't indicate whether that verb is a stem-vowel-changing verb; you just have to learn these verbs.

kennen [to know (be familiar with)]

ich **kenne** [I know]	wir **kennen** [we know]
du **kennst** [you know]	ihr **kennt** [you guys know]
Sie **kennen** [you know]	Sie **kennen** [you guys know]
er / sie / es **kennt** [he / she / it knows]	sie **kennen** [they know]

wissen [to know]

ich **weiß** [I know]	wir **wissen** [we know]
du **weißt** [you know]	ihr **wisst** [you guys know]
Sie **wissen** [you know]	Sie **wissen** [you guys know]
er / sie / es **weiß** [he / she / it knows]	sie **wissen** [they know]

fahren [to drive, to go]

ich **fahre** [I drive, I go]	wir **fahren** [we drive, we go]
du **fährst** [you drive, you go]	ihr **fahrt** [you guys drive, you guys go]
Sie **fahren** [you drive, you go]	Sie **fahren** [you guys drive, you guys go]
er / sie / es **fährt** [he / she / it drives, he / she / it goes]	sie **fahren** [they drive, they go]

tragen [to carry, to wear]

ich **trage** [I carry, I wear]	wir **tragen** [we carry, we wear]
du **trägst** [you carry, you wear]	ihr **tragt** [you guys carry, you guys wear]
Sie **tragen** [you carry, you wear]	Sie **tragen** [you guys carry, you guys wear]
er / sie / es **trägt** [he / she/ it carries, he / she / it wears]	sie **tragen** [they carry, they wear]

laufen [to walk or run]

ich **laufe** [I walk, I run]	wir **laufen** [we walk, we run]
du **läufst** [you walk, you run]	ihr **lauft** [you guys walk, you guys run]
Sie **laufen** [you walk, you run]	Sie **laufen** [you guys walk, you guys run]
er / sie / es **läuft** [he /she / it walks, he / she / it runs]	sie **laufen** [they walk, they run]

ich **gebe** [I give]	wir **geben** [we give]
du **gibst** [you give]	ihr **gebt** [you guys give]
Sie **geben** [you give]	Sie **geben** [you guys give]
er/ sie/ es **gibt** [he / she / it gives]	sie **geben** [they give]

sehen [to see]

ich **sehe** [I see]	wir **sehen** [we see]
du **siehst** [you see]	ihr **seht** [you guys see]
Sie **sehen** [you see]	Sie **sehen** [you guys see]
er/ sie / es **sieht** [he / she / it sees]	sie **sehen** [they see]

nehmen [to take]

ich **nehme** [I take]	wir **nehmen** [we take]
du **nimmst** [you take]	ihr **nehmt** [you guys take]
Sie **nehmen** [you take]	Sie **nehmen** [you guys take]
er/ sie/ es **nimmt** [he / she / it takes]	sie **nehmen** [they take]

VOCABULARY

Nouns

-r Biergarten ¨-	beer garden
-r Eichstrich -e	measurement pour line on a liter beer mug
-r Gast ¨-e	guest / patron / visitor
-r Henkel -	handle
-r Hopfen -	hops
-r Innenhof ¨-e	inner courtyard
-r Knödel -	dumpling
-r Liter -	liter
-r Maßkrug ¨-e	liter beer mug
-r Netzplan ¨-e	subway map
-r Senf -e	mustard
-r Turm ¨-e	tower

-e Gerste -n	barley
-e Hefe -n	yeast
-e Kleinstadt ¨-e	small city
-e Kneipe -n	bar / tavern
-e Jugendherberge -n	youth hostel
-e Maß -	a liter of beer
-e Mauer -n	wall (outside of a building; i.e., not part of a room)
-e Speisekammer -n	dining room
-e Stadtmauer -n	city wall
-e U-Bahn -en	subway / underground
-e Unterkunft ¨-e	accommodations
-e Wanderung -en	hike
-e Weißwurst ¨-e	Bavarian veal sausage
-e Wissenschaft -en	science
-s Bierzelt -e	beer tent
-s Bild -er	picture
-s Blaukraut	red cabbage (Bavarian)
-s Dach ¨-er	roof
-s Geländer -	railing
-s Gemüse	vegetables
-s Fahrrad ¨-er	bicycle
-s Foltergerät -e	torture device
-s Fleisch	meat
-s Reinheitsgebot	German purity law for beer
-s Wasser	water
-s Zweibettzimmer -	room with two beds

Regular Verbs

beginnen	to begin
holen	to fetch
Hunger haben	to be hungry (literally "to have hunger")
klingen	to sound (e.g., "That sounds good!")
mälzen	to malt
mieten	to rent
probieren	to try
übernachten	to stay the night

Stem-Vowel-Changing Verbs

(a → ä)

backen (bäckst)	to bake
fahren (fährst)	to ride/travel/go (by vehicle)
fallen (fällst)	to fall
fangen (fängst)	to catch
graben (gräbst)	to dig
halten (hältst)	to hold/stop (vehicle)/keep
lassen (lässt)	to let
Rad fahren (fährst)	to ride a bike
schlafen (schläfst)	to sleep
tragen (trägst)	to wear/carry
wachsen (wächst)	to grow (intransitive)
waschen (wäschst)	to wash

(e → i)

brechen (brichst)	to break
essen (isst)	to eat
geben (gibst)	to give
helfen (hilfst)	to help
nehmen (nimmst)	to take
sprechen (sprichst)	to speak
sterben (stirbst)	to die
treffen (triffst)	to meet/run across/hit (i.e., where you're aiming)
treten (trittst)	to kick/step
unternehmen (unternimmst)	to undertake
vergessen (vergisst)	to forget
werfen (wirfst)	to throw

(e → ie)

empfehlen (empfiehlst)	to recommend
geschehen (geschieht)	to happen/occur
lesen (liest)	to read
sehen (siehst)	to see
stehlen (stiehlst)	to steal

(au → äu)

laufen (läufst)	to walk/run
saufen (säufst)	to drink heartily/souse

Adjectives and Adverbs

beides	both
bestimmt	certainly / surely
empfehlenswert	recommendable
fast	almost
gefährlich	dangerous
gemütlich	comfortable
lecker	tasty
lieber	rather (as in preference)
manchmal	sometimes
nass	wet
günstig	convenient / low in price / reasonable (price)
richtig	correct / right
schnell	fast

Phrases

das ____ Jahrhundert (neunzehnte, zwanzigste, usw.)	the _____ century (nineteenth, twentieth, etc.)
Das können Sie mir glauben!	Believe me!
der Meinung sein	to be of the opinion
dort drüben	over there
Ein letztes Mal!	one last time
Ich hätte gern eine Maß.	I would like a liter.
Ich nehme eine Maß.	I'll take a liter.
inklusive Frühstück	breakfast included
Ja, Schatz.	Yes, dear.
Für mich eine Maß, bitte.	For me, a liter, please.
mit dem Rad	by bike
Prost!	Cheers! (Bavarian/southern German)
Tja.	Well then.
Wie bitte?	Beg your pardon?
Wie schön!	How nice! / How lovely!
Wie weit ist _____ von hier?	How far is _____ from here?
Zum Wohl!	Cheers!

A. Ralf und Mia in der Jugendherberge München-Park

PROF. PFREHM: Jetzt gehen wir nach München! München ist eine Großstadt in Bayern mit circa 1,5 Millionen Menschen. Ralf und Mia übernachten in der Jugendherberge München-Park. Sie haben ein Zweibettzimmer inklusive Frühstück.

MIA: Wie weit ist das Oktoberfest von hier?

RALF: Vier Kilometer.

MIA: Gut. Wir können zu Fuß gehen.

RALF: Na ja ... Ich bin der Meinung, das ist zu weit.

MIA: Willst du Fahrräder mieten?

RALF: Ich weiß nicht ...

MIA: Was? Vier Kilometer mit dem Rad ist zu weit für dich?

RALF: Nein. Du weißt, ich fahre gern Rad. Aber heute Abend soll es regnen.

MIA: Kein Problem. Ich trage meinen Regenmantel und du trägst deine Jacke.

RALF: Aber meine Turnschuhe! Sie sind neu. Sie werden bestimmt nass.

MIA: Tja. Dann müssen wir die U-Bahn nehmen.

RALF: Gute Idee! Kennst du die U-Bahn hier?

MIA: Nein. Aber es gibt einen Netzplan an der Rezeption im Foyer.

RALF: Toll. Ich gehe schnell zur Rezeption und hole einen Plan.

B. Ralf und Mia beim Oktoberfest

MIA: Ich habe Hunger. Wir sollen etwas essen.

RALF: Möchtest du lieber Fleisch oder Gemüse haben?

MIA: Beides!

RALF: In Ordnung. Weißt du, die Weißwurst mit Senf ist sehr empfehlenswert.

MIA: Ja, das klingt appetitlich. Willst du auch eine Weißwurst?

RALF: Ich denke, ich möchte lieber ein Wiesnhendl.

MIA: Lecker! Mit Knödeln und Blaukraut?

RALF: Natürlich.

MIA: Darf ich dein Hendl dann probieren?

RALF: Ja, Schatz. Natürlich darfst du es probieren.

MIA: Danke! Jetzt brauchen wir ein Bierzelt.

RALF: Gute Idee. Dort drüben gibt es ein Bierzelt.

MIA: Also dann. Los geht's!

C. Ralf und Mia in Rothenburg ob der Tauber

PROF. PFREHM: Rothenburg ob der Tauber ist eine Kleinstadt in Bayern. Sie liegt circa zweihundertdreißig Kilometer nordwestlich von München, und circa hundertsechzig Kilometer südöstlich von Frankfurt. Ralf und Mia finden eine günstige Unterkunft in der Altstadt. Sie übernachten im Gasthof Butz. Der Gasthof hat einen schönen Innenhof und eine gemütliche Speisekammer.

RALF: Heute möchte ich eine Radtour machen.

MIA: Ich weiß nicht. Manchmal fährst du zu schnell.

RALF: Vielleicht sollen wir eine Wanderung durch die Stadt unternehmen.

MIA: Das ist eine gute Idee!

RALF: Wir können einen Spaziergang auf der alten Stadtmauer machen.

MIA: Wie bitte?

RALF: In Rothenburg ob der Tauber gibt es eine mittelalterliche Stadtmauer. Sie ist fast zwei Kilometer lang. Es gibt auch die originellen Türme.

MIA: Ich weiß nicht ... Eine mittelalterliche Stadtmauer? Alte Türme? Ist das nicht gefährlich?

RALF: Nein. Es gibt Geländer und die Mauer hat ein Dach.

MIA: Aber manchmal läufst du zu schnell. Vielleicht sollen wir ein Museum besuchen.

RALF: Gute Idee! Wir können in das Mittelalterliche Kriminalmuseum gehen. Es gibt viele interessante Foltergeräte und viele Bilder.

MIA: Ja ... Das ist ... Na ja ... Das ist bestimmt interessant ...

GRAMMAR EXERCISES

A. Fill in the blank with a conjugated form of either *kennen* or *wissen*.

1. Mein Mann _____ die Adresse nicht.

2. _____ du, wann das Oktoberfest beginnt?

3. Wir _____ die Gäste aus Augsburg gut! Sie heißen Ralf und Mia.

4. Die Politikerin _____ die Antworten auf unsere Fragen.

5. _____ Sie den neuen Videokurs von The Great Courses? Er heißt *Learning German*.

B. Fill in the blank with the correct conjugated form of the stem-vowel-changing verb given in parentheses.

1. Wie oft _____ du Rad? (fahren)

2. Meine Kusine _____ gern Marathon. (laufen)

3. Der Kriminelle _____ Autos. (stehlen)

4. Der Hund _____ die Katze nicht. (sehen)

5. Was _____ hier? (geschehen)

6. Im Frühling _____ das Gras schnell (wachsen).

7. Manchmal _____ ihr zu viel. (helfen)

8. Mancher Gast _____ gern beim Oktoberfest. (saufen)

9. Ralf Gruber _____ gern Knödel. (essen)

10. Was _____ ihr gern? (lesen)

VOCABULARY EXERCISES

A. Fill in the blank with the appropriate vocabulary word.

1. Es regnet und wir werden _____.

2. Du empfiehlst den Sauerbraten? Nein, danke. Ich bin Vegetarier. Ich esse
   kein _____, sondern nur _____.

3. Das Reinheitsgebot erlaubt nur _____, _____
   und _____.

4. Möchten Sie ein Bier, oder trinken Sie _____ Wein?

5. Ich studiere Biologie. Das ist eine _____.

6. Diese Weißwurst ist lecker! Möchtest du sie _____?

B. Which phrase fits best for the situation?

1. You didn't understand something that was just said to you.

   _____

2. You're about to take a sip from your first beer at Oktoberfest.

   _____

3. You're in a discussion about a political issue.

   _____

4. Your best friend has just told you that he or she is retiring.

   _____

5. You're ordering a beer at Oktoberfest.

   _____

TRANSLATIONS

A. Translate from German into English.

1. Habt ihr Hunger?

   _____?

2. Die Stadtmauer und die Treppen sind nicht gefährlich, denn es gibt Geländer.

   _____

   _____.

3. Sollen wir zu Fuß gehen, oder willst du Fahrräder mieten?

   _____

   _____?

4. Das Bierzelt hat kein Dach, aber ich finde es gemütlich.

   _____.

5. Warum wirft der Gast den Senf und das Blaukraut?

   _____?

B. Translate from English into German.

1. She eats both meat and vegetables.

   _____.

2. Your (informal) nephew likes to speak German.

   _____.

3. He wears a tuxedo almost every day.

   _____.

4. This bar is recommendable because it has an inner courtyard and a liter of beer is reasonable.

   _____

   _____.

5. Sometimes our guest reads all night and sleeps all day.

   _____.

Answers on page 249

PRESENT PERFECT AND *DA-* AND *WO-* COMPOUNDS

SUMMARY

This lesson marks the start of *die dritte Etappe* ("the third stage") in your journey through the German language!

Da- and *wo-* compounds are words that comprise the word *da* or *wo* paired with a preposition (e.g., ***wogegen***, ***wofür***, ***worum***, ***dagegen***, ***dafür***, ***darum***) or a particle (e.g., ***wohin***, ***dahin***).

If the preposition with which the *wo* or *da* is coupled begins with a vowel, you insert an *r* (e.g., *wo + um → worum*; *wo + in → worin*; *da + um → darum*; *da + in → darin*).

Wo- compounds initiate a question (e.g., ***Wofür** zahlst du?* "**What** are you paying **for**?"; ***Wogegen** bist bist?* "**What** are you **against**?"; ***Wohin** geht ihr?* "**Where** are you guys going (**to**)?"), whereas *da-* compounds are used in statements or responses (e.g., *Ich zahle **dafür**,* "I'm paying for that"; *Ich bin **dagagen**,* "I'm against that"; *Wir gehen **dahin**,* "We're going (to) there").

Da- compounds are especially context-dependent; the speaker you use them with must know what you're referring to with the *da-* compound (e.g., Person A: *Bist du für oder gegen den Kapitalismus?* Person B: *Hmm ... Ich bin **dafür**, aber meine Kinder sind **dagagen**).

Da- and *wo-* compounds are used to refer to objects, not to humans (e.g., Person A: ***Wofür** zahlst du?* Person B: *Ich zahle für **die Weißwurst**.* Person A: *Zahlst du für **das Bier**?* Person B: *Nein, ich zahle nicht **dafür**, sondern für die Weißwurst).

When you use a preposition to ask a question about a person, you begin with the preposition and follow it with the interrogative pronoun *wen* for the accusative case (e.g., *Für **wen** bist du?*; *Gegen **wen** sprichst du?*) and with the interrogative pronoun *wem* for the dative case (e.g., *Mit **wem** gehst du ins Restaurant?*; *Zu **wem** sprechen Sie?*).

German grammar does not allow the preposition to come at the end of the sentence as English grammar does (e.g., "Who are you **against**?"; "Who are you talking **to**?").

The **present perfect** is a grammatical tense that is used to express actions and events that took place in the past (e.g., *Ich **habe** den Videokurs* Learning German ***gekauft**, "I **bought** the video course *Learning German*" / "I **have bought** the video course *Learning German*" / "I **was buying** the video course *Learning German*" / "I **did buy** the video course *Learning German*").

The present perfect in German is only a **tense, not an aspect**—that is, it **doesn't express how the action unfolded in the past** (i.e., whether the action "happened," "was happening," "has happened," or "did happen"). Speakers use adverbs or context to indicate this information.

The present perfect is the most common way of expressing the past tense in everyday spoken German.

The present perfect is constructed with the helping verb *haben*, conjugated with the subject, and a past participle of the main verb, placed at the end of the sentence (e.g., *Wir **haben** Fußball **gespielt**; Du **hast** eine Lederhose auf dem Oktoberfest **gekauft***).

The past participle of **regular verbs** (also called weak verbs) is formed by dropping the *-en* suffix from the infinitive (e.g., *machen → mach-; spielen → spiel-; kaufen → kauf-*), adding a *-t* or *-et* **suffix** (e.g., *macht, spielt, kauft*) and a *ge-* **prefix** (e.g., *gemacht, gespielt, gekauft, geredet*).

If a verb's infinitive form **is not stressed on the first syllable, then its past participle does not take a *ge-* prefix** (*reparieren → repariert; probieren → probiert; spekulieren → spekuliert*).

VOCABULARY

Nouns

-r Bundeskanzler -	federal chancellor (m.)
-r Weltfrieden	world peace
-r Witz -e	joke
-e Bundeskanzlerin -nen	federal chancellor (f.)
-e Etappe -n	stage (i.e., of a plan, journey, etc.)
-e Gegenwartsform -en	present tense form
-e Vergangenheitsform -en	past tense form
-e Zeitung -en	newspaper
-s Gespräch -e	conversation

Verbs

abonnieren	to subscribe to
aktualisieren	to update (i.e., technology)
chatten	to chat (i.e., on a computer, etc.)
emailen	to email
fragen	to ask
googeln	to google
gratulieren	to congratulate
joggen	to jog
jonglieren	to juggle
modernisieren	to modernize
reden	to talk
sagen	to say
spekulieren	to speculate
sprinten	to sprint
qualifizieren	to qualify
werden	to become

Adjectives and Adverbs

bekanntlich	as is well known / known to be / famously
darum ...	that's why ...
höflich	courteous
gestern	yesterday
leider	unfortunately
respektvoll	respectful
stundenlang	for hours
unbedingt	definitely

Phrases

Hier steht's ...	It says here ... (i.e., in a printed or written source)
Seit wann ...?	Since when ...?
Sind Sie bereit?	Are you ready?

TEXT

A. Ralf and Mia Discuss Politics in the *Schrebergarten*

RALF: Welche Zeitung liest du da?

MIA: Die *FAZ*.

RALF: Ach so. Seit wann abonnieren wir die *Frankfurter Allgemeine Zeitung*?

MIA: Warum? Was hast du dagegen?

RALF: Ich habe nichts dagegen. Aber die *FAZ* ist bekanntlich teuer.

MIA: Na ja, darum ist sie auch die beste Zeitung!

RALF: Woher hast du sie?

MIA: Ich habe sie heute Morgen in der Bäckerei gekauft.

RALF: Also dann. Was gibt's Neues in der Welt?

MIA: Die Bundeskanzlerin macht eine große internationale Reise.

RALF: Ist das alles?

MIA: Nein. Hier steht's: „Arnold Schwarzenegger will nächster deutsche Bundeskanzler sein."

RALF: Wie bitte?

MIA: Ja. Und? Bist du für oder gegen ihn?

RALF: Du machst wohl Witze, oder?

MIA: Natürlich ist das ein Witz! Was denkst du?

RALF: Gut. Und der Weltfrieden? Was steht da darüber?

MIA: Leider nichts. Aber ich bin definitiv dafür.

A. Fill in the blank with the appropriate *da-* or *wo-* compound or with the appropriate preposition and interrogative pronoun *wen* or personal pronoun.

1. A: _____ gehen Sie jetzt?
   B: Nach Hause.

2. A: Hast du für oder gegen das neue Gesetz gestimmt (*voted*)?
   B: Ich habe _____ gestimmt. Ich finde es gut.

3. A: Ich möchte nicht durch den dunklen Park gehen.
   B: Tja. Dann gehe ich allein _____.

4. A: _____ hast du gestimmt?
   B: Ich habe für den Kandidaten aus Ohio gestimmt.

5. A: _____ soll die Menschheit etwas unternehmen?
   B: Gegen den Welthunger.

B. Rewrite the following sentences in the present perfect.

1. Der Junge sammelt Schmetterlinge.

   _____.

2. Jeden Tag üben wir unser Deutsch.

   _____.

3. Meine Mutter repariert den Kühlschrank.

   _____.

4. Sein Vater arbeitet viele Jahre bei Boeing.

   _____.

5. Aktualisierst du schon dein neues Handy?

   _____?

6. Die Chefin redet heute Morgen stundenlang über das neue Geschäftsmodell.

   _____
   _____.

VOCABULARY EXERCISES

A. Fill in the blank with the appropriate vocabulary word.

1. Das ist jetzt die dritte _____ in unserer Reise durch die deutsche Sprache!

2. Ich habe leider kein Geld. _____ kann ich diesen Winter nicht nach Hawaii fliegen.

3. A: Ach so! _____: „Studien zeigen: Deutsch ist die tollste Sprache in ganz Europa."
   B: Das ist schön! Welche Zeitung liest du?

4. Unsere Kinder sind sehr brav. Sie sind _____ und _____.

5. Sonntagmorgens lese ich gern _____.

6. KIND: Eines Tages (*one day*) möchte ich Professor für Deutsch _____.
   VATER: Wie bitte? Spinnst du?

TRANSLATIONS

A. Translate from German into English.

1. Was gibt's Neues in der Welt?

   _____?

2. Warum hast du heute Morgen vier Zeitungen in der Bäckerei gekauft?

   _____?

3. Als Kind habe ich stundenlang allein in meinem Zimmer jongliert.

   _____.

4. Wir haben gestern Abend ein schönes Gespräch gehabt.

   _____.

5. Die Bundeskanzlerin hat eine große internationale Reise gemacht.

   _____.

B. Translate from English into German.

1. I googled my name yesterday.

   _____.

2. Today we learned a past tense form.

   _____.

3. Who are you (formal) voting for this year?

   _____?

4. What did your (informal) boss say yesterday?

   _____?

5. Do you guys (informal) have something against it?

   _____?

Answers on page 249

ICH HAB' MEIN HERZ IN HEIDELBERG VERLOREN

SUMMARY

In terms of their past participle, German verbs fall into three categories: **weak**, **strong**, and **mixed**.

> Weak verbs take a *-t* suffix and have no vowel change (e.g., *gefragt, gemacht, geredet*)
>
> Strong verbs take an *-en* suffix and sometimes have a vowel change (e.g., *gesehen, getragen, getrunken*)
>
> Mixed verbs take a *-t* suffix and have a vowel change (e.g., *gekannt, gedacht, gewusst*)

For the most part, you have to memorize whether a verb is weak, strong, or mixed.

Strong verbs can be categorized according to their stem-vowel pattern—that is, what their infinitive stem vowel changes to in the past participle (e.g., *sehen → gesehen; schneiden → geschnitten; treiben → getrieben; ziehen → gezogen, schwimmen → geschwommen, usw.*).

There are **seven categories of strong verbs** (see tables that follow).

Modal verbs can also be used on their own (i.e., without modifying a main verb) in the present perfect (e.g., *Wir haben dich **gemocht**; Das habe ich nicht **gewollt**; Das hat sie **gemusst***).

Modal verbs are either weak or mixed: *können* → **gekonnt**; müssen → **gemusst**; dürfen → **gedurft**; *mögen* → **gemocht**; *sollen* → **gesollt**; *wollen* → **gewollt**.

GRAMMAR

Category 1: Strong Verbs e → o

INFINITIVE	PAST PARTICIPLE	ENGLISH
helfen	geholfen	to help
sprechen	gesprochen	to speak
nehmen	genommen	to take
sterben	gestorben	to die
werden	geworden	to become

Category 2: Strong Verbs ei → ie

INFINITIVE	PAST PARTICIPLE	ENGLISH
treiben	getrieben	to do, to propel
leihen	geliehen	to loan
schreien	geschrien	to scream, to shout
scheinen	geschienen	to shine
schreiben	geschrieben	to write

Category 3: Strong Verbs in → un

INFINITIVE	PAST PARTICIPLE	ENGLISH
finden	gefunden	to find
zwingen	gezwungen	to force, to compel
binden	gebunden	to tie, to bind
springen	gesprungen	to jump

CATEGORY 4: Strong Verbs inn → onn

INFINITIVE	PAST PARTICIPLE	ENGLISH
beginnen	begonnen	to begin
gewinnen	gewonnen	to win, earn
sinnen	gesonnen	to ponder, muse
spinnen	gesponnen	to spin, to weave

CATEGORY 5: No Vowel Change in Their Past Participle

INFINITIVE	PAST PARTICIPLE	ENGLISH
geben	gegeben	to give
sehen	gesehen	to see
tragen	getragen	to carry, to wear
kommen	gekommen	to come
fahren	gefahren	to drive
essen	gegessen	to eat
lesen	gelesen	to read
laufen	gelaufen	to run
schlafen	geschlafen	to sleep

CATEGORY 6: Strong Verbs ie → o

INFINITIVE	PAST PARTICIPLE	ENGLISH
fliegen	geflogen	to fly
riechen	gerochen	to smell
verlieren	verloren	to lose
ziehen	gezogen	to pull, drag

CATEGORY 7: Strong Verbs ei → i

INFINITIVE	PAST PARTICIPLE	ENGLISH
greifen	gegriffen	to grab
beißen	gebissen	to bite
streiten	gestritten	to argue, bicker
schneiden	geschnitten	to cut

VOCABULARY

Nouns

-r Grundschullehrer -	primary school teacher
-r Lehrer -	teacher (m.)
-r Schuljahrbeginn	start of the school year
-r Universitätsstudent -en	university student

-e Entscheidung -en	decision
-e Erziehungswissenschaft -en	pedagogy / education science
-e Lehrerin -nen	teacher (f.)
-e Liebesgeschichte -n	love story
-e Party -s	party
-e Vorspeise -n	appetizer
-s Getränk -e	drink / beverage
-s Sommerkleid -er	summer dress

Verbs

beißen (gebissen)	to bite
binden (gebunden)	to tie/bind
brennen (gebrannt)	to burn
bringen (gebracht)	to bring
greifen (gegriffen)	to grab/grasp
helfen (geholfen)	to help
kommen (ist gekommen)	to come
lächeln	to smile
leihen (geliehen)	to loan
nennen (genannt)	to name
rennen (ist gerannt)	to run
riechen (gerochen)	to smell
schneiden (geschnitten)	to cut
schreien (geschrien)	to scream
springen (gesprungen)	to jump
streiten (gestritten)	to argue
studieren	to study (i.e., at university)
treiben (getrieben)	to do/drive/propel/drift
trinken (getrunken)	to drink
verlieren (verloren)	to lose
verändern	to change
ziehen (gezogen)	to pull
zwingen (gezwungen)	to force/compel

Adjectives and Adverbs

aufregend	exciting / thrilling
eigenständig	independent (i.e., a person)
fertig	done / ready / finished / completed
hinreißend	gorgeous / ravishing
vor allem	above all

Genau!	Exactly!
Hoppla!	Whoops!
Liebe auf den ersten Blick	love at first sight
Nicht vergessen!	Don't forget!
Versprochen!	Promise!

TEXTS

A. Eine Liebesgeschichte in Heidelberg (Teil eins)

PROF. PFREHM: Das Jahr ist 1910. Helmut Richter ist Universitätsstudent in Heidelberg. Er möchte Grundschullehrer werden.

HELMUT RICHTER: Im Sommer 1910 bin ich 22 Jahre alt gewesen. Ich habe Erziehungswissenschaft an der Universität in Heidelberg studiert. Meine Eltern haben das nicht gewollt, aber ich habe die Entscheidung getroffen.

PROF. PFREHM: Gisela wohnt bei ihren Eltern, aber sie will eigenständig sein. Vor allem möchte sie um die Welt reisen.

GISELA KLEIN: Der Sommer vom Jahr 1910 hat mein Leben verändert. Mein Vater hat eine Party für die neuen Lehrer und Lehrerinnen gegeben. Ich habe Vorspeisen und Getränke gebracht. Dort habe ich Helmut gesehen.

B. Eine Liebesgeschichte in Heidelberg (Teil zwei)

HELMUT RICHTER: Zum Schuljahrbeginn hat der Schuldirektor eine Party gegeben. Und da hab' ich Gisela zum ersten Mal gesehen. Sie hat ein schönes Sommerkleid getragen und ich habe sie hinreißend gefunden. Ich habe gedacht: „Wer ist diese Frau?"

GISELA KLEIN: Helmut hat allein dort gestanden, aber er hat kein Getränk gehabt. Deshalb bin ich zu ihm gegangen und habe gefragt: „Möchten Sie ein Getränk?" Er hat gelächelt und gesagt: „Gerne. Ich heiße Helmut. Und wie heißen Sie?" Und so hat alles begonnen. Es war Liebe auf den ersten Blick!

GRAMMAR EXERCISES

A. For each verb, give the second-person and third-person present tense conjugation and the past participle.

infinitive	2nd per. present	3rd per. present	past participle
1. sehen	_____	_____	_____
2. fahren	_____	_____	_____
3. dürfen	_____	_____	_____
4. kennen	_____	_____	_____
5. trinken	_____	_____	_____
6. treiben	_____	_____	_____
7. ziehen	_____	_____	_____
8. schneiden	_____	_____	_____
9. binden	_____	_____	_____
10. wollen	_____	_____	_____
11. vergessen	_____	_____	_____
12. verlieren	_____	_____	_____
13. treffen	_____	_____	_____
14. bringen	_____	_____	_____
15. müssen	_____	_____	_____

B. Rewrite the following sentences in the present perfect tense.

1. Das Kind wirft den Ball über das Dach.

   _____.

2. Warum isst du kein Gemüse?

   _____?

3. Unsere Fußballmannschaft gewinnt jedes Spiel.

   _____.

4. Beißt du deinen Bruder?

   _____?

5. Wie nennt ihr euer Kind?

   _____?

VOCABULARY EXERCISES

A. Fill in the blank with the appropriate vocabulary word. (Note: Watch out for verbs that need to be conjugated and verbs that need to be in past participle form.)

1. Kinder: _____! Heute geht ihr zum Zahnarzt.

2. Die junge Frau in dem Sommerkleid ist _____.

3. Ich _____ nicht zur Schule, sondern ich laufe langsam.

4. Im Restaurant bestellt sie immer eine _____.

5. Und? Haben Sie eine _____ getroffen?

6. Wo hast du gelernt, diese Knoten zu _____?

7. Ich will nicht mehr bei meinen Eltern im Keller wohnen.
   Ich möchte _____ sein!

8. Hoppla! An der Tür steht's „_____" und nicht „drücken."

9. Das Kind ist glücklich und _____.

10. Die Entscheidung hat mein ganzes Leben _____.

TRANSLATIONS

A. Translate from German into English.

1. Helmut hat allein dort gestanden, aber er hat kein Getränk gehabt.

   _____.

2. Gisela hat ein schönes Sommerkleid getragen und ich habe sie hinreißend gefunden.

   _____

   _____.

3. Ich habe Erziehungswissenschaft studiert. Meine Eltern haben das nicht gewollt, aber das habe ich gemacht.

   _____

   _____.

4. Der Sommer vom Jahr 1910 hat mein Leben verändert.

   _____.

5. Gisela hat von einer Weltreise geträumt. Aber das hat sie nicht gedurft, denn sie hat noch bei ihren Eltern gewohnt.

   _____

   _____.

B. Translate from English into German.

1. As a university student, I studied German and education sciences.

   _____.

2. The dog smelled the cat.

   _____.

3. The cat didn't like the dog.

   _____.

4. Our baseball team lost the game and we screamed.

   _____.

5. Whoops! We brought only beverages, but you guys wanted veal sausage and mustard.

   _____

   _____.

Answers on page 250

SEPARABLE-PREFIX VERBS

SUMMARY

Some verbs in German take *sein* as a helping verb in the past tense:

> verbs whose meaning involves a change in state, condition, or location from one place to another (e.g., *Wir **sind** früh **aufgestanden**; Ich **bin** Grundschullehrer **geworden**; Du **bist** nach Hause **gegangen**; Meine alte Katze **ist** gestern **gestorben***); and

> two verbs that you have to memorize as taking *sein* in the present perfect: *bleiben* and *sein* (e.g., *Sie **sind** den ganzen Sommer in Berlin **geblieben**; Ich **bin** damals zwanzig Jahre alt **gewesen***).

It's common to use the verb *gehen* as a secondary verb with a main verb to express "go + -ing," "going + -ing," or "went + -ing" (e.g., *Ich **gehe** jeden Tag **schwimmen***, "I **go swimming** every day"; *Heute gehe ich **schwimmen***, "I'm **going swimming** today"; *Ich **bin** gestern **schwimmen gegangen***, "I went swimming yesterday").

When *gehen* is used as a secondary verb with a main verb and is expressed in the present perfect tense, you 1) conjugate the helping verb *sein* with the subject, 2) place the past participle *gegangen* at the end of the sentence, and 3) insert the main verb in infinitive form in front of *gegangen* (e.g., *Wir **sind** heute morgen **einkaufen gegangen**; Sie **sind** heute in der Früh **angeln gegangen**; **Bist** du letztes Wochenende Rad **fahren gegangen**?*).

In southern Germany and Switzerland and in all of Austria, speakers often use the present perfect tense with modal verbs that are also modifying a main verb. This construction involves conjugating the subject with the helping verb *haben* and then placing at the end of the sentence the main verb followed by the modal verb, both in their infinitive forms (e.g., *Ich **habe** nach Hause **gehen müssen***, "I had to go home"; *Er **hat** Erziehungswissenschaft **studieren wollen***, "He wanted to study education sciences"; ***Haben** Sie Arbeit in Berlin **finden können**?* "Were you able to find work in Berlin?").

One common type of verb in German are separable-prefix verbs, which are verbs with a prefix that detaches when conjugated in the present tense and is moved to the end of the sentence. The root verb is conjugated with the subject and remains in the second position for statements and open-ended questions (e.g., *Ich **rufe** meine Mutter heute Abend **an**,* "I'm going to call my mother tonight"; *Wann **rufst** du deine Mutter **an**?* "When are you going to call your mother?") and in the first position for yes-no questions (*Rufst du deine Mutter heute Abend an?* "Are you going to call your mother tonight?").

Past participles of separable-prefix verbs take a *-ge-* between the prefix and the root verb (e.g., *an**ge**rufen, aus**ge**gangen, ein**ge**schlafen*).

VOCABULARY

Nouns

-r Abfall ¨-e	garbage / refuse
-r Bekannte -n	acquaintance
-r Fisch -e	fish
-r Knochen -	bone
-r Restmüll	unrecyclable garbage
-r Sommerschlussverkauf ¨-e	summer seasonal sale
-r Straßenpassant -en	pedestrian (m.)
-e Blume -n	flower
-e Damenabteilung -en	women's department (i.e., in a store)
-e Herrenabteilung -en	men's department (i.e., in a store)
-e Kleidung	clothing
-e Konservendose -n	tin can
-e Müllsortierung	garbage sorting (for recycling)
-e Mülltonne -n	garbage bin
-e Mülltrennung	garbage separation (for recycling)
-e Packung -en	package / packaging
-e Pflanze -n	plant
-e Plastik	plastic
-e Schokomilch	chocolate milk
-e Stimme -n	voice
-e Straßenpassantin -nen	pedestrian (f.)
-e Tonne -n	bin
-e Werbung -en	advertisement
-s Kaufhaus ¨-er	department store

-s Milchprodukt -e	dairy product
-s Obst	fruit
-s Stadtbad ¨-er	municipal (public) pool
-s Studentenwohnheim -e	student dorm
-s Styropor	Styrofoam
-s Verpackungsmaterial -ien	packaging material

Department Store Items

-r Anzug ¨-e	suit
-e Bluse -n	blouse
-r BH -s	bra
-e Brieftasche -n	wallet
-er Büstenhalter -	brazier
-r Gürtel -	belt
-e Halskette -n	necklace
-e Handtasche -n	handbag / purse
-s Hemd -en	shirt
-e Hose -n	pants
-e Jeans	jeans
-s Kleid -er	dress
-e Krawatte -n	tie
-r Ohrring -e	earring
-r Ring -e	ring
-r Schlips -e	tie
-r Schmuck	jewelry
-r Slip -s	panties
-e Socke -n	sock
-e Strumpfhose -n	pantyhose
-s T-Shirt -s	T-shirt
-e Unterwäsche -n	undergarments / underwear

Verbs

entsorgen	to dispose of
etwas essen gehen	to go eat something
etwas trinken gehen	to go drink something
joggen gehen	to go jogging
Rad fahren gehen	to go bicycling
spazieren gehen	to go for a walk
Ski laufen gehen	to go skiing

abfahren	to depart (i.e., a vehicle)
ankommen	to arrive
anprobieren	to try on (i.e., clothing)
anrufen	to call
anziehen	to put on (i.e., clothing) / to attract
aufgehen	to rise (i.e., the sun)
aufstehen	to get up (i.e., in the morning)
auschecken	to check out (i.e., of a hotel)
ausgeben	to spend (i.e., money)
ausgehen	to go out
ausloggen	to log out
aussehen	to look like/appear
ausziehen	to take off (i.e., clothes) / to move out (i.e., of a building)
einchecken	to check in (i.e., to a hotel)
einkaufen	to shop
einladen	to invite
einloggen	to log in
einschlafen	to fall asleep
fernsehen	to watch TV
umziehen	to change (i.e., clothes) / to move (i.e., from one place to another)

Adjectives and Adverbs

einfach	simple / simply / just
gestern	yesterday
gestern Abend	yesterday evening / last night
gestern Nachmittag	yesterday afternoon
kompostierbar	compostable
konfus	confused / bewildered
leer	empty
umweltbewusst	environmentally conscious
umweltfreundlich	environmentally friendly / green

Phrases

auf dem Heimweg	on the way home

TEXT

A. Hamdi's anecdote about *die Müllsortierung*

Ich bin heute einkaufen gegangen. Auf dem Heimweg habe ich eine Schokomilch getrunken. Natürlich habe ich die leere Packung richtig entsorgen wollen. Aber es gibt vier verschiedene Mülltonnen! Ich habe nicht verstanden! Ich bin einfach konfus geblieben.

Dann habe ich eine freundliche Stimme gehört: „Kann ich Ihnen vielleicht helfen?" Es ist eine Straßenpassantin gewesen. Sie hat die Mülltonnen erklärt. Und weißt du was? Meine Schokomilchpackung ist in die gelbe Tonne gekommen. Die Menschen in Deutschland sind so freundlich!

GRAMMAR EXERCISES

A. Put the following sentences into the past perfect.

1. Im Sommer fliegen wir nach Deutschland.

   _____ .

2. Im Jahr 1975 seid ihr erst (*only*) acht Jahre alt.

   _____ .

3. Wann ziehst du nach Berlin um?

   _____ ?

4. Das Baby schläft immer im Auto ein.

   _____ .

5. Warum darf ich im Restaurant nicht rauchen?

   _____ ?

6. Unser Chef geht diesen Winter auf Hawaii schnorcheln.

   _____
   _____ .

7. Gisela sieht in dem Sommerkleid hinreißend aus.

   _____
   _____ .

B. Arrange the phrases into a sentence, beginning with the underlined phrase. (Note: Don't forget to conjugate the verbs and to inflect any words with a hyphen.)

1. anrufen / heute Abend / sein- Mutter / <u>mein Mann</u>.

   _____.

2. morgen / gehen / du / etwas essen / in der Stadt / <u>wollen</u>?

   _____.

3. dies- Anzug / schnell / anprobieren / <u>ich</u> / in der Umkleidungskabine.

   _____.

4. in Zürich / <u>der Zug</u> / ankommen / um zehn vor zehn.

   _____.

5. die Sonne / <u>wann</u> / morgen / aufgehen?

   _____.

6. an der Rezeption / <u>zuerst</u> / einchecken / sollen / du.

   _____.

VOCABULARY EXERCISES

A. Fill in the blank with the appropriate vocabulary word. Remember to conjugate any verbs or give the correct past participle.

1. Abends _____ ich meistens eine Stunde _____, bevor ich ins Bett gehe. Lieblingsprogramm. Mein Lieblingsprogramm ist *Tatort München.*

2. Ist dieses Verpackungsmaterial _____? Wir sind sehr _____ und möchten sie recyceln.

3. Der Kühlschrank ist fast _____. Wir müssen einkaufen gehen.

4. Heute Morgen ist Ralf um fünf Uhr _____.

5. Diese Hose ist ein bisschen zu groß. Ich brauche einen_____.

6. Schau dir diese _____ an! Da steht's: „Heute beginnt der Sommerschlussverkauf!"

7. Hmm … In welche _____ soll ich diese Packung werfen …?

8. Soll ich eine _____ mit diesem Anzug tragen?

9. Unsere Freunde haben uns zur Party _____.

10. Als Universitätsstudent habe ich im _____ gewohnt.

TRANSLATIONS

A. Translate from German into English.

1. Natürlich habe ich die leere Packung richtig entsorgen wollen.

   _____.

2. Die Leute in Deutschland sind sehr umweltfreundlich gewesen.

   _____.

3. Auf dem Heimweg habe ich eine Schokomilch getrunken.

   _____.

4. Gestern haben wir den ganzen Tag im Studentenwohnheim ferngesehen.

   _____.

5. Um wie viel Uhr haben Sie im Hotel eingecheckt?

   _____?

B. Translate from English into German.

1. Our son fell asleep at a quarter past eight last night.

   _____.

2. They were able to log in quickly.

   _____.

3. Her brother looks confused.

   _____.

4. You guys spend a lot of money in the summer.

   _____.

5. We went for a walk, and then we correctly disposed of our tin cans.

   _____.

Answers on page 251

SUBORDINATE AND INFINITIVE CLAUSES

SUMMARY

There are two basic types of clauses in German: **independent** and **dependent** clauses. Whereas independent clauses can stand on their own (e.g., *Ich finde es großartig*, "I think it's wonderful"), dependent clauses need, or depend on, an independent clause—also called the **main clause**—for context (e.g., *dass du Deutsch bei mir lernst*, "that you're learning German with me").

Subordinating conjunctions are grammatical words that are used to conjoin dependent clauses with independent clauses; this type of dependent clause is then called a **subordinate** clause, and **the verb moves from position 2 to the end of the clause:**

(main) independent clause	(subordinate) dependent clause				
	1	2	3	4	5
Ich finde es großartig,	*dass*	*du*	*Deutsch*	*bei mir*	*lernst*
	subordinating conjunction	subject	direct object	elements of time/ manner/ place	conjugated main verb

When you use a **modal verb in a subordinate clause**, the conjugated form of the modal verb occurs at the end of the clause and is preceded by the main verb in infinitive form:

(main) independent clause	(subordinate) dependent clause				
	1	**2**	**3**	**4**	**5**
Ich finde es großartig,	*dass*	*du*	*Deutsch*	*bei mir*	***lernen willst***
	subordinating conjunction	subject	direct object	elements of time/ manner/ place	conjugated main verb and modal verb

When you use the **present perfect tense in a subordinate clause**, the conjugated form of the auxiliary verb occurs at the end of the clause and is preceded by the past participle of the main verb:

(main) independent clause	(subordinate) dependent clause				
	1	**2**	**3**	**4**	**5**
Ich finde es großartig,	*dass*	*Sie*	*Deutsch*	*bei mir*	***gelernt haben***
	subordinating conjunction	subject	direct object	elements of time/ manner/ place	past participle and helping verb

When you use a **separable-prefix verb in a subordinate clause**, the conjugated form of the verb occurs at the end of the clause and you do not separate the prefix from the root verb:

(main) independent clause	(subordinate) dependent clause				
	1	**2**	**3**	**4**	**5**
Ich finde es großartig,	*dass*	*du*	*deine Mutter*	*jede Woche*	***anrufst***
	subordinating conjunction	subject	direct object	elements of time/ manner/ place	conjugated separable-prefix verb (prefix still attached)

Three of the most commonly used subordinating conjunctions are **dass** ("that"), **weil** ("because"), and **wenn** ("if" / "when" / "whenever").

When a dependent clause is headed up by an interrogative pronoun (e.g. *wann, warum, wo, wie, usw.*), the clause is called an **indirect question**:

(main) independent clause	(subordinate) dependent clause (indirect question)				
	1	2	3	4	5
Weißt du,	*wann*	*Oma*	*die Kinder*	*von der Schule*	***abholt?***
	interrogative pronoun	subject	direct object	elements of time/manner/place	conjugated main verb

Another type of dependent clause is **infinitive** *zu* clauses. Unlike subordinate clauses, *zu* clauses don't contain a subject; rather, the subject from the main clause carries over into the *zu* clause. However, the verb still occurs in the final position, but preceded by a *zu* particle:

(main) independent clause	(infinitive) dependent clause		
Ich habe keine Zeit,	*die Kinder*	*heute Morgen zur Schule*	***zu bringen***
	direct object	elements of time/manner/place	*zu* infinitive phrase

When you use a separable-prefix verb in an infinitive clause, the *zu* particle occurs between the separable prefix and the root verb:

(main) independent clause	(infinitive) dependent clause		
Ich habe keine Zeit,	*die Kinder*	*heute Nachmittag von der Schule*	***abzuholen***
	direct object	elements of time/manner/place	*zu* infinitive phrase

The preferred word order in German clauses is **TMP**—i.e. **time** first, **manner** second, and **place** third (e.g., *Ich fliege **morgen allein nach Berlin**; Ich hoffe, dass wir dich **nächstes Jahr in Berlin** besuchen können*).

VOCABULARY

Nouns

-r Chef -s	boss (m.)
-r Roman -e	novel
-e Chefin -nen	boss (f.)
-e Hälfte -n	half
-e Überraschung -en	surprise
-s Büro -s	office

Verbs

dabeibleiben	to stick with it/stick around
herausfinden	to find out
kosten	to cost
überreden (hat überredet)	to convince
versuchen	to attempt/try
vorhaben (hat vorgehabt)	to have planned/to intend

Adjectives and Adverbs

mitternachts	at midnight
halb wach	half awake

Interrogative Pronouns

ob	whether / if (i.e., a question)
wann	when
warum	why
was	what
wen	who(m) (accusative)
wer	who (nominative)
wie viel	how much
wie viele	how many
wo	where
woher	from where
wohin	(to) where

Phrases

Abgemacht!	Deal! / Settled!
Echt?	Really?
Ende gut, alles gut.	All's well that ends well.
(keine) Lust haben (etw. zu tun)	to (not) have a desire (to do something)
Mist!	Crap!
Was ist los?	What's wrong? / What's the matter?
Was tun?	What to do?

A. In welches konzert sollen wir gehen? (Teil eins)

MIA: Hallo, Schatz. Und? Hast du einen schönen Tag gehabt?

RALF: Na ja ... Heute Morgen ist der Chef in mein Büro gekommen ...

MIA: Dein Chef?

RALF: Ja. Er ist gekommen, weil er eine Überraschung für mich gehabt hat.

MIA: Das klingt interessant.

RALF: Du weißt, dass ich Herbert Grönemeyer gern habe.

MIA: Ja ...

RALF: Und weißt du, wer dieses Wochenende ein Konzert in München gibt?

MIA: Herbert Grönemeyer.

RALF: Richtig! Mein Chef hat zwei Tickets für das Konzert, aber er kann selbst nicht hingehen.

MIA: Und jetzt hast *du* die Tickets.

RALF: Genau! *Ich*, Ralf Gruber, habe jetzt zwei Tickets für das Grönemeyer Konzert!

B. In welches konzert sollen wir gehen? (Teil zwei)

RALF: Genau! Ich, Ralf Gruber, habe jetzt zwei Tickets für das Grönemeyer Konzert!

MIA: Und weißt du, wann das Konzert ist?

RALF: Samstagabend.

MIA: Ach so ... Samstagabend ...

RALF: Was ist los?

MIA: Diesen Samstag ist auch das Konzert von Annemarie.

RALF: Echt?

MIA: Und weißt du, wo Annemarie ihr Konzert gibt?

MIA: Auch in München?

RALF: Nein. In Stuttgart.

RALF: Ach. Mist!

MIA: Tja. Was tun ...?

C. In welches konzert sollen wir gehen? (Teil drei)

MIA: Tja. Was tun ...?

RALF: Meine Tickets haben nichts gekostet.

MIA: Gut. Aber ich habe keine Lust, in das Grönemeyer-Konzert zu gehen.

RALF: Was kann ich tun, um dich zu überreden?

MIA: Ich weiß nicht ... Moment mal. Wie ist das Datum am Samstag?

RALF: Der zehnte Mai. Warum?

MIA: Ach so! Annemarie spielt am siebzehnten Mai.

RALF: Prima! Dann können wir dieses Wochenende ins Grönemeyer-Konzert gehen.

MIA: Richtig. Aber nächsten Samstag, also am siebzehnten Mai, da gehen wir ins Annemarie-Konzert.

RALF: Abgemacht!

GRAMMAR EXERCISES

A. Use the subordinating conjunction or interrogative pronoun given in parentheses to conjoin the two sentences.

1. Die Chefin ist heute nicht im Büro. Heute Morgen hat sie ein Meeting in München. (weil)

   _____

   _____ .

2. Weißt du? Wo haben die Kinder Deutsch gelernt? (wo)

   _____ .

3. Ich habe nicht gewusst. Du kannst so schnell einschlafen. (dass)

   _____ .

4. Ich habe keine Ahnung. Wer holt die Kinder heute von der Schule ab? (wer)

   _____

   _____ .

5. Ihr sollt es aufschreiben. Ihr vergesst meine Telefonnummer immer. (wenn)

   _____

   _____ .

B. Rewrite the following sentences using a *zu* clause. Note: The main clause that you'll begin with is underlined.

1. Ich möchte im Sommer nach Deutschland fliegen, aber <u>ich habe keine Zeit</u>.

   _____

   _____ .

2. <u>Es ist wichtig</u>, dass man heutzutage eine Fremdsprache lernt.

   _____ .

3. Ich soll meinen Chef heute Abend anrufen, aber <u>ich habe keine Lust</u>.

   _____

   _____ .

4. Was <u>hast du vor</u>? Willst du einen Spaziergang im Wald machen.

   _____

   _____ .

5. Ich will mein Haus ohne einen Immobilienmakler verkaufen, und <u>ich versuche es</u>.

   _____

   _____ .

VOCABULARY EXERCISES

A. Fill in the blank with the appropriate vocabulary word.

1. A: _____? Du siehst ganz gestresst aus.
   B: Ja. Ich habe ein großes Problem. Ich habe meine Kreditkarte verloren.

2. Morgens um fünf bin ich immer nur _____.

3. A: Was _____ du Freitagabend _____?
   B: Ich glaube, ich bleibe zu Hause und lese einen Liebesroman.

4. Ach so! Du bist tatsächlich zur Party gekommen! Das ist eine
   schöne _____.

5. Mein Freund _____, eine Grunge-Band zu gründen.

TRANSLATIONS

A. Translate from German into English.

1. Heute Morgen ist der Chef in mein Büro gekommen, weil er eine Überraschung für mich gehabt hat.

   _____

   _____.

2. Weißt du, wo Annemarie ihr Konzert gibt?

   _____?

3. Wir versuchen, unsere Eltern zu überreden.

   _____.

4. Ach Mist! Warum hast du nicht gesagt, dass du Country Musik nicht gern hast?

   _____

   _____?

5. Ihr müsst mich anrufen, wenn ihr herausfinden wollt, wann meine Party beginnt.

   _____

   _____.

B. Translate from English into German.

1. We have no desire to eat only fruit and vegetables.

   _____.

2. Should I try to repair this car, or should I simply sell it ...? What to do?

   _____

   _____?

3. Crap! She knows that I have a surprise for her.

   _____.

4. Ralf can't go to the concert because he didn't buy any tickets.

   _____.

5. He doesn't have time to try on every suit.

   _____.

Answers on page 252

MORE INFINITIVE CLAUSES AND THE DATIVE CASE

SUMMARY

The particle pairs *um ... zu* ("in order to ..."), *ohne ... zu* ("without ..."), and *statt ... zu* ("instead of ...") are frequently used to construct dependent infinitive clauses.

To construct a dependent infinitive clause with *um ... zu, ohne ... zu,* or *statt ... zu,* you begin the clause with the *um, ohne,* or *statt,* include your additional sentence information (i.e., direct object, time, manner, place), and end the clause with a *zu* participle and the main verb in its infinitive form:

(main) independent clause	(infinitive) dependent clause			
Ich bleibe im Bett	*statt*	*die Kinder*	*heute Morgen zur Schule*	***zu bringen***
	particle	direct object	elements of time/ manner/place	*zu* infinitive phrase

The dative case expresses the **indirect object** in a sentence—that is, the dative case expresses **to whom** or **for whom** (e.g., *Ich kaufe **meiner Tochter** einen Schokoriegel,* "I'm buying a chocolate bar **for my daughter**"; *Wir bringen **den Kindern** diese Bücher,* "We're bringing these books **to/for the children**").

GRAMMAR

	SINGULAR			PLURAL		
	nom.	**acc.**	**dat.**	**nom.**	**acc.**	**dat.**
1st per.	ich	mich	mir	wir	uns	uns
2nd per. informal	du	dich	dir	ihr	euch	euch
2nd per. formal	Sie	Sie	Ihnen	Sie	Sie	Ihnen
3rd per. masc.	er	ihn	ihm			
3rd per. fem.	sie	sie	ihr	sie	sie	ihnen
3rd per. neut.	es	es	ihm			

Possessive Pronoun Endings

CASE	SINGULAR			PLURAL
	Masc.	**Fem.**	**Neut.**	
Nominative (subject)	der	die	das	die
Accusative (direct object)	den	die	das	die
Dative (indirect object)	dem	der	dem	den (+n)

VOCABULARY

Nouns

-r Christkindlesmarkt	Christmas market
-r Glühwein	mulled/spiced wine
-r Heiligabend	Christmas Eve
-r Kuss ¨-e	kiss
-e Achterbahn -en	roller coaster
-e Erinnerung -en	memory
-e Rute -n	rod / switch
-e Süßigkeit -en	candy / treat
-s Spielzeug -e	toy
-s Weihnachtslied -er	Christmas song

Verbs

beibringen	to teach
besorgen	to get/acquire
feiern	to celebrate
wünschen	to wish

aufregend	exciting
herrlich	superb / glorious / gorgeous
schließlich	after all / finally / eventually
zuverlässig	reliable

Phrases

Alles Gute zum Nikolaustag!	Happy St. Nicholas Day!
Alles Gute zu Weihnachten!	Merry Christmas!
Das ist schlimm!	That's bad!
Kenntnisse von ...	knowledge or skills of ...
Meine Zeit ist um.	My time is up.
Oje!	Oh boy!
Viel Erfolg!	May you do well! / I wish you much success!
Viel Spaß!	Have fun!

TEXTS

A. Sankt Nikolaus

Guten Tag, meine Damen und Herren. Oder besser gesagt: Viele warme Grüße zum Nikolaustag! Ich heiße Sankt Nikolaus. Professor Pfrehm hat mich in die siebzehnte Lektion eingeladen, um den sechsten Dezember mit Ihnen zu feiern.

Nun, was ist der sechste Dezember? Alle Kinder in Deutschland wissen, dass der sechste Dezember der Nikolaustag ist.

Und jetzt möchte ich Ihnen ein Weihnachtslied beibringen. Das Lied ist sehr schön. Es heißt „Kling, Glöckchen":

Kling, Glöckchen, klingelingeling, kling, Glöckchen, kling!

Lasst mich ein, ihr Kinder, ist so kalt der Winter,
öffnet mir die Türen, lasst mich nicht erfrieren!

Kling, Glöckchen, klingelingeling, kling, Glöckchen, kling!

Danke schön. Danke schön.

Also dann. Wie ich schon gesagt habe: Mein Name ist Sankt Nikolaus. Jedes Jahr am sechsten Dezember besuche ich die Kinder in Deutschland. Ich schenke den braven Kindern Süßigkeiten und Spielzeuge. Aber die bösen Kinder bekommen eine Rute.

Also dann. Was habe ich für Sie...?

Zum Nikolaustag bekommen Sie Kenntnisse von der deutschen Sprache!

Schauen Sie: In dieser Lektion lernen Sie mehr Infinitivsätze, und Sie lernen den Dativ! Das ist aufregend!

Nun. Meine Zeit ist leider um. Ihr Professor ist gleich wieder da. Aber ich wünsche Ihnen viel Spaß und viel Erfolg. Und alles Gute zum Nikolaustag!

B. Ralf und Mia auf dem Christkindlesmarkt

MIA: Ach! Ich liebe den Christkindlesmarkt! Es ist herrlich!

RALF: Ich auch. Hast du Lust auf einen Glühwein?

MIA: Gerne!

RALF: Gut. Ich hole dir einen Glühwein.

MIA: Danke. Aber nur einen Glühwein. Schließlich müssen wir den Kindern noch Geschenke besorgen.

RALF: Alles klar. Du suchst Geschenke, und ich bringe uns zwei Glühwein. Bis gleich.

GRAMMAR EXERCISES

A. Combine the two short sentences using the particle pair given in parentheses.

1. Das Kind ist eingeschlafen. Es weint nicht. (ohne ... zu)

   _____.

2. Man muss arbeiten. Man verdient Geld. (um ... zu)

   _____.

3. Ich erzähle eine Geschichte. Ich bringe dir ein Weihnachtslied bei. (statt ... zu)

   _____

   _____.

4. Ihr braucht einen Plan. Ihr gewinnt das Spiel. (um ... zu)

   _____

   _____.

5. Dieses Jahr schenken wir den Kindern Bücher. Wir besorgen ihnen Spielzeuge. (statt ... zu)

   _____

   _____.

B. Identify the subject (nominative), direct object (accusative), and indirect object (dative) in each sentence.

1. Der Professor schenkt uns Kenntnisse von der deutschen Sprache.

   _____

2. Sankt Nikolaus hat den Studenten ein Weihnachtslied beigebracht.

   _____

3. Wo haben die Eltern ihren Kindern diese Geschenke gekauft?

   _____

4. Seiner Frau hat der Chef einen Glühwein gebracht.

   _____

5. Wir wünschen Ihnen alles Gute zu Weihnachten!

   _____

C. Fill in the blanks with the correct grammatical ending.

1. St. Nikolaus schenkt mein_____ Sohn eine Rute!

2. Hast du dein_____ Oma alles Gute zum Geburtstag gewünscht?

3. Mein_____ Kollegen und Kolleginnen sind zuverlässig.

4. Nein. Dies_____ Gedankenlesern schenken wir nichts zu Weihnachten, denn sie wissen schon im Voraus (*ahead of time*), was sie bekommen!

5. Jed_____ Kind bekommt ein Geschenk, aber jed_____ Politiker schenken wir eine Rute.

D. Fill in the blanks with the appropriate personal pronoun.

1. Ich wünsche _____ alles Gute zum Nikolaustag! (*you*, singular, informal)

2. Seine Tochter hat _____ einen Kuss auf die Wange gegeben. (*him*)

3. Wir bringen _____ ein Kinderlied bei. (*them*)

4. Was hast du _____ für den Picknick besorgt? (*us*)

5. Ihr Bruder schenkt _____ einen neuen iPhone zu Weihnachten. (*her*)

VOCABULARY EXERCISES

A. Fill in the blank with the appropriate vocabulary word.

1. A: Mein Chef hat mich heute gefeuert.
   B: _____!

2. A: Morgen fängt das neue Schulsemester an.
   B: _____!

3. Unsere Freunde sind _____. Sie kommen immer sofort, wenn wir Hilfe brauchen.

4. Manche Leute finden es _____, Achterbahn zu fahren, aber ich finde es furchtbar.

5. Also dann, meine Damen und Herren: _____ Das heißt, ich muss „Auf Wiedersehen und bis gleich" sagen.

TRANSLATIONS

A. Translate from German into English.

1. Schließlich müssen wir den Kindern noch Geschenke besorgen.
   _____.

2. Professor Pfrehm hat mich in die siebzehnte Lektion eingeladen, um den sechsten Dezember mit Ihnen zu feiern.
   _____
   _____.

3. Hast du Lust auf einen Glühwein? Ich hole dir einen, wenn du willst.
   _____
   _____.

4. Warum haben Sie ihnen Geld gegeben, ohne es mir zu sagen?
   _____
   _____?

5. Man muss oft üben und viel Geduld haben, um eine Fremdsprache zu lernen.
   _____
   _____.

B. Translate from English into German.

1. We bought our grandmother a car for Christmas.

   _____

   _____.

2. Did you (singular, informal) get me razors and shaving cream?

   _____

   _____?

3. How many years did you (singular, formal) have to study to become a professor?

   _____

   _____?

4. This dog is reliable! He brings us the paper every morning.

   _____

   _____.

5. Oh boy. Unfortunately, there is no time to teach you (plural, formal) a Christmas song.

   _____

   _____.

Answers on page 252

EINE REISE NACH ZÜRICH UND ZERMATT

SUMMARY

Ein- words and *der-* words also take dative endings to express the indirect object-ness of the noun they're modifying (e.g., *Ich kaufe meiner Tochter einen Schokoriegel*; *Er schenkt jedem Kind einen iPad*).

German syntax is fairly specific when it comes to the order of nominative, accusative, and dative nouns in a sentence: **The indirect object always comes before the direct object, unless the direct object is in pronoun form**
(e.g., A: *Kaufen wir dem Jungen Süßigkeiten?* "Are we going to buy the boy sweets?"
B: *Vielleicht sollen wir ihm einen Schokoriegel kaufen.*
"Maybe we should buy him a chocolate bar." A: *Gut. Dann kaufen wir ihn ihm!* "Good. Then let's buy it for him!" / "Let's buy him it!").

GRAMMAR

ein -Word Endings (by example of possessive pronoun unser-)

CASE	SINGULAR			PLURAL
	Masc.	Fem.	Neut.	
Nominative (subject)	unser	unsere	unser	unsere
Accusative (direct object)	unser**en**	unsere	unser	unsere
Dative (indirect object)	unser**em**	unser**er**	unser**em**	unser**en** + n

der -Word Endings: dies-

CASE	SINGULAR			PLURAL
	Masc.	Fem.	Neut.	
Nominative (subject)	dieser	diese	dieses	diese
Accusative (direct object)	diesen	diese	dieses	diese
Dative (indirect object)	diesem	dieser	diesem	diesen + n

VOCABULARY

Nouns

-r Bergpionier -e	mountaineer
-r Einwohner -	inhabitant / resident
-r Gründer -	founder
-r Kanton -e	canton (i.e., a state in Switzerland)
-r Pferdestall ¨-e	horse stall
-r Prinz -en	prince
-r Schokoriegel -	chocolate bar
-r Traumjob -s	dream job
-e Alphütte -n	alpine hut
-e Eingangshalle -n	foyer / lobby
-e Fabrik -en	factory / plant / manufactory
-e Hütte -n	hut / shack / cottage / cabin
-e Milchschokolade	milk chocolate
-e Prinzessin -nen	princess
-e Sitzbank ¨-e	bench / seat
-e Zartbitterschokolade	dark (bitter) chocolate
-s Abenteuer -	adventure
-s Bundesland ¨-er	state (in Germany and Austria)
-s Pferd -e	horse

Verbs

anbieten	to offer (something to someone)
bauen	to build
bieten	to offer (in general)
tief durchatmen	to take a deep breath
vererben	to hand down/leave/bequeath
verkaufen	to sell

Adjectives and Adverbs

beeindruckend	important
besonders	especially / particularly
eben	just / now / even / level
eigen-	own
eines Tages	one day
rund	around / approximately

Phrases

Grüezi mitenand!	Greetings! (in Switzerland)
Machen Sie sich bereit!	Get ready!
So weit, so gut?	So far, so good?

TEXTS

A. Ralf und Mia in Zürich (Teil eins)

MIA: Das Hotel ist sehr schön. Du hast gut gemacht, Ralf.

RALF: Natürlich. Ich biete meiner Prinzessin nur das Beste.

MIA: Danke, mein Prinz. Und jetzt zum Plan.

RALF: Gut. Was möchtest du machen?

MIA: Ich möchte eine Schweizer Schokoladenfabrik besuchen.

RALF: Toll. Also dann. Los geht's.

B. Ralf und Mia in Zürich (Teil zwei)

RALF: Hier ist die Eingangshalle. Sehr schön.

MIA: Die Sitzbank sieht wie ein Schokoriegel aus.

RALF: Und das ist der Gründer von der Schokoladenfabrik.

MIA: Ich möchte diesem Mann einen großen Kuss geben, denn Schokolade macht mich glücklich.

RALF: Wirklich? Und welchen anderen Angestellten möchtest du einen Kuss geben?

MIA: Das muss ein Traumjob sein ... Schau mal! Der Schoko-Shop.

RALF: Willst du ein paar Süßigkeiten kaufen?

MIA: Natürlich. Ich kaufe unseren Kindern ein Dutzend Schokoriegel.

RALF: Und was kaufst du deinem Prinzen?

MIA: Wem?

RALF: Na, mir! Welche Süßigkeiten kaufst du deinem Prinzen?

MIA: Ach so ... Ja, ich kaufe dir—ich meine, ich kaufe meinem Prinzen auch einen Schokoriegel.

RALF: Danke.

C. Ralf und Mia in Zermatt

MIA: Schau mal. Das Museum heißt Zermatlantis.

RALF: Interessant. Gehen wir hinein.

RALF: Das ist beeindruckend. Schau mal. Das ist eine Alphütte für die Pferde.

MIA: Wirklich? Die Bergpioniere haben den Pferden ihre eigenen Hütten gebaut?

RALF: Bitte?

MIA: Du hast eben gesagt, dass sie ihnen Alphütten gebaut haben.

RALF: Nein.

MIA: Also, sie haben sie ihnen nicht gebaut.

RALF: Nein. Sie haben ihnen Ställe gebaut.

MIA: Also, keine Pferdehütten?

RALF: Nein. Pferdeställe.

GRAMMAR EXERCISES

A. Fill in the blanks with the appropriate ending.

1. Wir bieten unser____ Angestellten die besten Löhne (*salaries*).

2. Die Bergpioniere bauen jed____ Pferd ein____ Hütte.

3. Die Prinzessin hat ihr____ Prinzen kein____ Schokoriegel gebracht.

4. Die Fabrik finanziert all____ Gründer____ ein____ Haus am See.

5. Das Bundesland ermöglicht (*makes possible*) manch____ Einwohner sein____ Traumjob.

6. Welch_____ Familienmitglied (*family member*) sollen wir unser_____ Geld vererben (*to hand down/leave/bequeath*)?

B. Arrange the phrases into a sentence, beginning with the underlined phrase. (Don't forget to conjugate the verbs.)

1. <u>dieses Jahr</u> / wir / eine Reise / finanzieren / unserem Sohn / nach Berlin

   _____ .

2. es / schenken / <u>ich</u> / ihr / zum Geburtstag

   _____ .

3. dürfen / er / ihnen / keine iPads / <u>dieses Jahr zu Weihnachten</u> / kaufen

   _____ .

4. geboten / der Chef / dem Angestellten / haben / eine Lohnerhöhung / <u>gestern</u>

   _____ .

5. euch / sie / wir / bringen / <u>heute Abend</u>

   _____ .

VOCABULARY EXERCISES

A. Fill in the blank with the appropriate vocabulary word. (Note: Don't forget to conjugate the verbs.)

1. Wie bitte? Was haben Sie _____ gesagt?

2. Die Arbeiterin kündigt, weil die Fabrik keine guten Löhne _____.

3. Entschuldigung? Können Sie mir sagen, wo die _____ ist? Ich kenne das Gebäude nicht.

4. Also dann. Das Abenteuer beginnt. _____ !

5. Zermatt hat _____ sechstausend Einwohner.

6. A: Wie viele _____ gibt es in der Schweiz: fünfundzwanzig oder sechsundzwanzig?
   B: Es gibt sechsundzwanzig.

7. Ich finde die Ausstellungen (*displays*) in diesem Museum sehr _____ .

8. Manchmal muss man eine Pause machen und _____ , wenn man im Stress ist.

A. Translate from German into English.

1. Ich biete meiner Prinzessin nur das Beste.

   _____.

2. Ich möchte diesem Mann einen großen Kuss geben, denn Schokolade macht mich glücklich.

   _____

   _____.

3. Du hast eben gesagt, dass sie ihnen Alphütten gebaut haben.

   _____.

4. Soll ich ihm diesen Zartbitter oder diesen Milchschokoladenriegel kaufen?

   _____

   _____?

5. Der Prinz hat der Prinzessin ein großes Abenteuer versprochen.

   _____.

B. Translate from English into German.

1. Do we have to give our female cousin money for her birthday?

   _____?

2. When did they offer you (formal) more money?

   _____?

3. Why didn't you guys buy your parents any chocolate in Zürich?

   _____

   _____?

4. That's her piano, but she wants to pass it down to me one day.

   _____

   _____.

5. Which child should I sell my bicycle to?

   _____?

Answers on page 253

REFLEXIVE VERBS AND PRONOUNS

SUMMARY

This lesson marks the start of *die vierte Etappe* in your journey through the German language!

Reflexive verbs take a reflexive pronoun object when conjugated; each personal pronoun has a corresponding accusative reflexive form (e.g., **Ich** *fühle* **mich** *wohl*, **Du** *fühlst* **dich** *wohl*, *er fühlt* **sich** *wohl*, etc.).

The infinitive form of reflexive verbs always includes the reflexive pronoun *sich* (e.g., **sich** *fühlen*, "to feel"; **sich** *aufregen*, "to get upset"; **sich** *umsehen*, "to look around"; etc.).

Many reflexive verbs involve a physical or emotional action that a person or thing goes through on its own or does to itself (e.g., *sich anmelden*, "to register or announce oneself"; *sich erholen*, "to recover"; *sich aufregen*, "to get excited / worked up"). This is also why the reflexive pronouns of these verbs are in the accusative case because, in a sense, **the subject is acting on itself**, **making itself a direct object**, rather than acting on something or someone else and making that its direct object.

In both statements and questions, the subject and its reflexive pronoun generally occur either directly adjacent to one another or on either side of the conjugated verb (e.g., *Fühlen* **Sie sich** *wohl?*; *Wie fühlen* **Sie sich** *heute?*; *Heute fühlt* **sie sich** *wohl.*; *Warum hast* **du dich** *gestern Abend aufgeregt?*).

GRAMMAR

	SINGULAR	PLURAL
1st per.	mich	uns
2nd per. informal	dich	euch
2nd per. formal	sich	sich
3rd per. masc./fem./neut.	sich	sich

VOCABULARY

Nouns

-r Arm -e	arm
-r Fuß ¨-e	foot
-r Fußknöchel -	ankle
-r Hals ¨-e	neck / throat
-r Husten	cough
-r Kopf ¨-e	head
-r Kopfschmerzen	headache
-r Körper -	body
-r Körperteil -e	body part
-r Mund -ër	mouth
-r Nacken -	neck / nape
-r Po -s	tush / butt / fanny
-r Rücken -	back
-r Schenkel -	thigh
-r Schnupfen -	cold / sniffles
-r Stress	stress
-r Zeh -en	toe
-e Augenbraue -n	eyebrow
-e Erholung	recovery / rest / recuperation
-e Erkältung -en	cold
-e Glatze -n	bald head
-e Grippe -n	flu
-e Lippe -n	lip
-e Nase -n	nose
-e Schaufensterpuppe -n	mannequin

-e Schulter -n	shoulder
-e Spannung -en	suspense / tension
-e Sprechstunde -n	doctor consultation / office hour
-e Wade -n	calf
-e Wange -n	cheek
-e Wimper -n	eyelash
-s Auge -n	eye
-s Bein -e	leg
-s Fieber -	fever
-s Gesäß -e	bottom / buttocks
-s Gesicht -er	face
-s Haar -e	hair
-s Kinn -e	chin
-s Knie -	knee
-s Ohr -en	ear
-s Rezept	prescription / recipe
-s Symptom -e	symptom

Verbs

krank schreiben	to give someone a sick note
vorstellen	to introduce
wehtun	to hurt (literally "to do pain")

Reflexive Verbs

sich anhören	to sound (intransitive)
sich anmelden	to announce/register oneself
sich anziehen	to get dressed
sich aufregen	to get upset
sich ausruhen	to rest
sich ausziehen	to get undressed
sich baden	to bathe
sich beeilen	to hurry
sich duschen	to shower
sich entspannen	to relax
sich entschuldigen	to excuse oneself
sich erholen	to rest/recuperate/recover
sich erinnern	to remember
sich erkälten	to catch a cold
sich freuen	to be glad
sich fühlen	to feel (intransitive)
sich hinlegen	to lie down
sich rasieren	to shave (intransitive)

sich setzen	to sit down/seat oneself
sich umsehen	to look around
sich umziehen	to change clothes
sich verkühlen	to catch a cold (Austrian)

Adjectives and Adverbs

heiser	hoarse
kahl	bald
mies	lousy
möglich	possible
oben	above / at the top / upstairs
sofort	immediately
unten	below / at the bottom / downstairs

Phrases

beim Arzt	at the doctor's
Machen wir weiter.	Let's keep going. / Let's continue.

TEXT

A. Ralf beim Arzt

Dr.: Also dann, Herr Gruber. Wie fühlen Sie sich?

RALF: Seit einer Woche fühle ich mich mies.

Dr: Das hört sich nicht gut an. Was haben Sie für Symptome?

RALF: Ich habe Kopfschmerzen und mein Rücken tut weh.

Dr.: Haben Sie auch Fieber gehabt?

RALF: Nein.

Dr.: Haben Sie einen Husten, oder einen Schnupfen?

RALF: Nein.

Dr.: Dann ist es keine Grippe oder Erkältung. Und wie schlafen Sie?

RALF: Nicht gut. Aber ich habe viel Stress.

Dr.: Ich glaube, Ihr Körper braucht Erholung.

RALF: Brauche ich ein Rezept?

Dr.: Nein, aber ich schreibe Sie für einen Tag krank. Sie müssen sich ausruhen, Ralf.

RALF: Ich verstehe. Danke, Doktor Schmetterling.

GRAMMAR EXERCISES

A. Fill in the blanks with the appropriate reflexive pronoun.

1. Wir fühlen _____ gar nicht wohl.

2. Warum habt ihr _____ aufgeregt?

3. Haben Sie _____ erkältet?

4. Ich muss _____ eine Stunde hinlegen.

5. Sie kann _____ nicht erinnern.

6. Die Kinder wollen _____ nicht baden.

7. Der Hund freut _____ sehr, wenn wir ihm einen Kochen geben.

8. Kannst du _____ dieses Wochenende erholen?

B. Arrange the phrases into a sentence, beginning with the underlined phrase.
   (Note: Don't forget to conjugate the reflexive verbs and to include the appropriate reflexive pronoun.)

1. sich duschen / morgens / die Kinder / gern

   _____.

2. dürfen / ich / sich setzen?

   _____?

3. Meine Frau / zu Hause / sich ausruhen / heute

   _____.

4. sich entspannen / in ihrer Alphütte / unsere Großeltern / am Wochenende

   _____
   _____.

5. sofort / auf der Konferenz / der Professor / sich anmelden

   _____.

VOCABULARY EXERCISES

A. Which of the following words does not fit.

1. ○ Nase, ○ Kinn, ○ Fußknöchel, ○ Augenbraue

2. ○ Grippe, ○ sich erkälten, ○ Schnupfen, ○ sich umziehen

3. ○ sich entspannen, ○ sich beeilen, ○ sich ausruhen, ○ sich erholen

4. ○ das Auge, ○ der Zeh, ○ die Wade, ○ der Schenkel

5. ○ wehtun, ○ der Kopfschmerzen, ○ mies, ○ sofort

B. Fill in the blank with the appropriate vocabulary word.

1. Ich habe keine Haare mehr. Das heißt, ich habe eine _____.

2. Wie heißt deine Tochter nochmal? Ich kann mich nicht _____.

3. Ich habe meine Stimme verloren. Das heißt, ich bin _____.

4. Ach Mist! Wir sind spät dran. Wir müssen uns _____.

5. Können Sie mich bitte _____? Ich kenne die Leute da nicht.

6. Das ist eine prima Idee. Das _____ sich gut _____!

TRANSLATIONS

A. Translate from German into English.

1. Ich habe Kopfschmerzen und mein Rücken tut weh.

   _____.

2. Ich freue mich, dass du dich erholen kannst.

   _____.

3. Seit einer Woche fühle ich mich mies.

   _____.

4. Wir haben uns im Kaufhaus umgesehen, aber wir haben nichts gekauft.

   _____

   _____.

5. Unser Sohn muss sich für ein paar Tage zu Hause ausruhen, weil er sich erkältet hat.

   _____

   _____.

B. Translate from English into German.

1. Are you (informal, plural) going to relax this weekend?

   _____.

2. They feel lousy because they didn't rest yesterday.

   _____.

3. We want to lie down for an hour, but it is not possible.

   _____

   _____.

4. I changed my clothes quickly.

   _____.

5. In the mornings he likes to shave, but he doesn't like to shower.

   _____

   _____.

Answers on page 254

MORE DATIVE AND SUBORDINATING CONJUNCTIONS

SUMMARY

In addition to expressing the indirect object in a sentence, the dative case in German also occurs with a select number of verbs (e.g., *Wir **helfen dir***; *Ich **gratuliere Ihnen***; *Hast du **deinem Onkel** gedankt?*), with adjectives (e.g., ***Mir** ist **heiß***; *Das ist **uns** zu **teuer***; *Die Musik ist **ihnen** zu **laut***), and after a select number of prepositions (e.g., *Sie wohnt **bei uns***; *Kommst du **mit mir**?*).

The dative verb *gefallen* roughly means "to please" and is used frequently in the sense of "to like." However, unlike in English—in which the subject is liking someone or something else—in German, the subject "pleases" someone or something and is therefore conjugated with *gefallen*. Thus, *Das Auto gefällt mir* and *Gefallen Ihnen diese Blumen?* literally mean "The car pleases me" and "Please you these flowers?"; however, these utterances are translated in English as "I like the car" and "Do you like these flowers?".

The dative preposition *bei* is commonly contracted with the definite article *dem* (e.g., ***beim** Arzt*, ***beim** Bäker*, ***beim** Friseur*), and the dative preposition *zu* is commonly contracted with the definite articles *dem* and *der* (e.g., ***zum** Arzt*, ***zum** Frühstück*, ***zur** Schule*, ***zur** Arbeit*).

In addition to the subordinating conjuctions *dass*, *weil*, and *wenn*, there are several subordinating conjunctions that express the concept of time (e.g., ***während**, **bis**, **sobald**, **bevor**, **nachdem***) and causality, condition, or purpose (e.g., *obwohl, da, falls, indem*).

GRAMMAR

Dative Reflexive Pronouns

	SINGULAR	PLURAL
1st per.	mir	uns
2nd per. informal	dir	euch
2nd per. formal	sich	sich
3rd per. masc./fem./neut.	sich	sich

Subordinating Conjunctions expressing time	Subordinating Conjunctions expressing causality, condition, or purpose
bevor [before]	dass [that]
nachdem [after]	weil [because]
wenn [whenever]	wenn [if]
während [while]	indem [by...-ing]
sobald [as soon as]	da [since, because]
bis [until]	falls [in case]
seit, seitdem [since]	damit [if]
	obwohl [although]

VOCABULARY

Nouns

-r Alltag -e	everyday life / day to day
-r Außerirdische -n	alien (i.e., extraterrestrial)
-r Lärm	noise
-r Übergang ¨-e	transition
-e Aktivität -en	activity
-e Alltagsroutine -n	daily routine
-e Erklärung -en	explanation
-e Eselsbrücke -en	mnemonic device
-e Gewohnheit -en	habit

Verbs

sich (etwas) anhören	to listen to something
gehören	to belong to
sich (etwas) brechen	to break something (e.g., your arm)
entführen	to abduct
sich die Haare kämmen	to comb one's hair
kochen	to cook
sich (etwas) kochen	to cook oneself something
leihen	to loan
sich (etwas) leihen	to borrow something
sich (etwas) leisten	to afford something
sich schminken	to put on makeup
sich (etwas) putzen	to clean something (e.g., your teeth)
sich unterhalten	to converse/have a talk
sich (etwas) vorstellen	to imagine something
sich (etwas) waschen	to wash something (e.g., your hands)

Dative Verbs

antworten	to answer
danken	to thank
folgen	to follow
gehören	to belong to
gefallen	to please
glauben	to believe
gratulieren	to congratulate
helfen	to help
passen	to fit
schmecken	to taste
verzeihen	to excuse

Adjectives and Adverbs

angenehm	pleasant
unangenehm	unpleasant
bekannt	known
unbekannt	unknown
behilflich	helpful
unbehilflich	unhelpful
dankbar	thankful
undankbar	unthankful

leicht	easy / light
plausibel	feasible / plausible
schwer	hard (i.e., difficult) / heavy
unendlich	endless
tagtäglich	on a daily basis

Accusative Prepositions

bis	until
durch	through
entlang	along
für	for
gegen	against
ohne	without
um	at / around

Dative Prepositions

aus	out / out of / from (i.e., material)
außer	except for
bei	at / by / near
mit	with
von	from
seit	since
nach	after / to
zu	to / at / for

Phrases

Das ist mir/dir/ihm/ihnen egal.	I/you/he/they don't/doesn't care.
bei der Arbeit	at work
bei mir/dir/euch/ihnen	at my/your/your guys'/their place
beim Zahnarzt	at the dentist (office)
eine Frage stellen	to ask a question
Nicht wahr?	Isn't that true?
zum Geburtstag	for someone's birthday
zum Frühstück	for breakfast
zum Schluss	in the end / ultimately
zu der Arbeit	to work
zu der Zeit	at that time
zu diesem Zeitpunkt	at that/this point in time
zu mir/dir/euch/ihnen	to my/your/your guys'/their place
zum Zahnarzt	to the dentist (office)

A. Mias Alltag (Teil eins)

Ich stehe meistens um halb sieben auf. Ich wasche mir das Gesicht, schminke mich und ziehe mich an.

Ralf steht meistens um Viertel vor sieben auf. Er singt gern Popmusik, während er sich duscht. Das heißt, ich muss mir diesen Lärm zehn Minuten lang anhören. Das scheint mir manchmal unendlich.

Danach rasiert er sich und kämmt sich die Haare.

Um Viertel nach sieben kochen wir uns einen Kaffee, und wir unterhalten uns ein bisschen, bis die Kinder aufstehen.

B. Mias Alltag (Teil zwei)

Abends ist es bei uns zu Hause sehr angenehm. Nach dem Abendessen lese ich gern. Krimis gefallen mir am besten. Bevor ich ins Bett gehe, dusche ich mich. Ich wasche mir die Haare und rasiere mir die Beine. Danach putze ich mir die Zähne. Im Bett lese ich weiter, solang es Ralf nicht stört.

GRAMMAR EXERCISES

A. Fill in the blank with the appropriate dative reflexive pronoun.

1. Die Kinder müssen _____ die Zähne putzen.

2. Letzten Sommer hat sie _____ den Arm gebrochen.

3. Moment mal! Ich wasche _____ schnell die Hände.

4. Ihr könnt _____ leider keinen neuen Mercedes leisten.

5. Kochst du _____ jeden Morgen um fünf einen Kaffee?

B. Select the appropriate conjunction from those given in parentheses and then use that preposition to conjoin the two sentences.

1. Ich lerne meinen Wortschatz für Deutsch. Ich esse Frühstück. (solang, da, während)

   _____

   _____ .

2. Wir haben neue iPhones gekauft. Wir haben kein Geld gehabt.
(da, wenn, obwohl)

_____

_____.

3. Du musst mich anrufen. Du kommst in Berlin an. (da, sobald, falls)

_____.

4. Sie lernt Deutsch. Sie kann eine Stelle bei Deutsche Bank bekommen.
(obwohl, damit, da)

_____

_____.

5. Der Arzt hat uns seine Nummer gegeben. Wir fühlen uns nächste Woche
plötzlich mies. (wenn, da, falls)

_____

_____.

C. Fill in the blank with the appropriate grammatical ending.

1. Obwohl der Mercedes mein_____ Vater zu teuer ist, ist der Preis mein_____
Mutter egal, denn sie sagt: „Ich muss einen Mercedes haben."

2. Welch_____ Leuten sollen wir danken?

3. Ihr Chef kommt zu jed_____ Party, weil es ihm Spaß macht.

4. Unsere Tochter wohnt bei ihr_____ Großeltern.

5. Deine alten Schuhe passen dies_____ Kind nicht.

6. Meine Erklärung hat unser_____ Chefin unangenehm geschienen.

VOCABULARY EXERCISES

A. Fill in the blank with the appropriate dative verb.

1. Mein Freund hat sein Diplom gemacht und ich möchte
ihm _____.

2. Mist! Das habe ich wirklich nicht beabsichtigt (_intended_). Kannst du mir
bitte _____.

3. Diese Krawatte _____ mir nicht! Sie ist zu bunt.

4. A: Und? Wie _____ der Kuchen?

   B: Er _____ uns sehr, danke! (Note: It's the same verb twice.)

5. Ich habe ihr eine Frage gestellt, aber sie hat mir nicht _____.

B. Fill in the blank with the appropriate dative preposition.

1. Ich möchte nicht ewig (*forever*) _____ meinen Eltern wohnen.

2. _____ dem Frühstück mache ich gern einen Spaziergang.

3. Bevor Sie eine Entscheidung treffen, sollen Sie _____ Ihren Kollegen sprechen.

4. Ich komme nicht _____ einer reichen Familie.

5. _____ mir sind alle zur Party gegangen.

C. Which reflexive verb would work best for the nouns given?

1. das Gesicht, die Hände   _____

2. die Zähne, die Nase   _____

3. einen Porsche, ein eigenes Flugzeug   _____

4. die Zukunft, ein Leben als Popstar   _____

5. Geld, ein Auto   _____

6. Musik, Lärm   _____

7. einen Kaffee, Abendessen   _____

8. den Arm, das Bein   _____

A. Translate from German into English.

1. Abends ist es bei uns zu Hause sehr angenehm.

    _____.

2. Ralf singt gern Popmusik, während er sich duscht, und diesen Lärm muss ich mir zehn Minuten lang anhören.

    _____

    _____.

3. Wir unterhalten uns ein bisschen, bis die Kinder aufstehen.

    _____.

4. Krimis gefallen mir am besten.

    _____.

5. Im Bett lese ich weiter, solang es Ralf nicht stört.

    _____.

B. Translate from English into German.

1. She likes learning German. (Note: Use *gefallen*.)

    _____.

2. They like to wash their hands, as long as there is enough soap.

    _____

    _____.

3. This car belongs to you (formal, singular), in case you have forgotten.

    _____.

4. He likes to go to the dentist, although he seldom (*selten*) cleans his teeth.

    _____

    _____.

5. She relaxes at home after her birthday.

    _____

    _____.

Answers on page 255

THE SIMPLE PAST

SUMMARY

In addition to the present perfect tense, German has another tense for expressing events in the past: the simple past tense.

The simple past tense stems of *haben*, *sein*, and *geben* are **hatt-**, **war-**, and **gab-** (see tables that follow for conjugational endings).

The simple past stems of the modal verbs are **musst-**, **konnt-**, **wollt-**, **sollt-**, **mocht-**, and **durft-** (see table that follows for conjugational endings).

Unlike other languages, such as French, Spanish, and Italian—which have various past tenses that express different meanings or aspects of a verb—there are no major differences in meaning between a verb expressed in the present perfect and a verb expressed in the simple past (e.g., *Gestern Abend **war** ich zu Hause*, "Last night I was at home"; *Gestern Abend **bin** ich zu Hause **gewesen***, "Last night I was at home"; *Als Kind **musste** er sein Zimmer nie aufräumen*, "He never had to clean his room as a child"; *Als Kind **hat** er sein Zimmer nie **aufräumen müssen***, "He never had to clean his room as a child").

However, in the southern regions of Germany and in Austria, speakers often prefer to use the present perfect in spoken, informal interactions, whereas in central and northern Germany, speakers tend to more frequently use the simple past of the verbs *haben*, *sein*, *geben*, *tun*, and the modal verbs in many spoken interactions.

Regardless of geography, the simple past tense of all verbs (i.e., not just *sein*, *haben*, *geben*, and the modal verbs) is widely used in written texts and in more formal spoken domains.

There are two words for "when" in German: The conjunction **als** is used to express "when" in the past (e.g., *Als ich Kind war*, "When I was a kid"; *Als wir kein Geld hatten*, "When we had no money"; *Als du mit uns noch ausgehen durftest*, "When you were still allowed to go out with us"), whereas the interrogative pronoun **wann** denotes a point in time, whether past, present, or future (e.g., ***Wann** fährt der Zug ab?*, "When does the train depart?"; ***Wann** mussten Sie gestern aufstehen?*, "When did you have to get up yesterday?").

The conjunction *als* works just like a subordinating conjunction in that it causes the main verb, helping verb, or modal verb to occur at the end of the sentence (e.g., *Ich habe oft am Wochendende ins Büro gehen müssen,* **als** *ich bei Siemens* **gearbeitet habe**; *Mein Sohn hat seine Hausaufgaben immer gemacht,* **als** *er auf der Uni* **war**).

GRAMMAR

Simple Past of haben

ich hatt**e**	wir hatt**en**
du hatt**est**	ihr hatt**et**
Sie hatt**en**	Sie hatt**en**
er/sie/es hatt**e**	sie hatt**en**

Simple Past of sein

ich war	wir war**en**
du war**st**	ihr war**t**
Sie war**en**	Sie war**en**
er / sie / es **war**	sie war**en**

Simple Past of geben

ich gab	wir gab**en**
du gab**st**	ihr gab**t**
Sie gab**en**	Sie gab**en**
er / sie / es gab	sie gab**en**

Conjugational Endings for Modal Verbs in Simple Past by example of [wollen]

ich	**-e** woll**e**	wir	**-en** woll**en**
du	**-est** woll**est**	ihr	**-et** woll**et**
Sie	**-en** woll**en**	Sie	**-en** woll**en**
er / sie / es	**-e** woll**e**	sie	**-en** **wollten**

VOCABULARY

Nouns

-r Bleistift -e	pencil
-r Engel	angel
-r Kugelschreiber -	pen
-r Kuli -s	pen (clipped form)
-r Ostdeutsche -n	East German
-r Ossi -s	East German (clipped form)
-r Professionelle -n	professional
-r Profi -s	professional (clipped form)
-r Pullover -	sweater / jumper
-r Pulli -s	sweater / jumper (clipped form)
-r Studierende -n	student
-r Studi -s	student (clipped form)
-r Westdeutsche -n	West German
-r Wessi -s	West German (clipped form)
-r Zivildienstleistende -n	conscientious objector doing civil service
-r Zivi -s	conscientious objector doing civil service (clipped form)
-e Hausaufgabe -n (usually used in plural)	homework
-e Mikrowelle -n	microwave
-e Mikro -s	microwave (clipped form)
-e Wahrheit -en	truth
-s Deodorant -s	deodorant
-s Deo -s	deodorant (clipped form)
-s Kinematograf -en	movies / cinema
-s Kino -s	movies / cinema (clipped form)

Verbs

aufräumen	to clean up
schwören	to swear

Adjectives and Adverbs

artig	good / courteous / polite
brav	good / well-behaved
extrovertiert	extroverted
frech	sassy / cheeky
gesprächig	talkative
gut erzogen	well-bred / well-educated
höflich	courteous / polite

redefreudig	talkative / chatty
schüchtern	shy
schweigsam	quiet
schwierig	difficult

Phrases

Ärger geben	to cause or be trouble
Das habe ich gesagt.	That's what I said.
Es ist schön, Sie wiederzusehen.	It's nice to see you again.
Jetzt weiß ich's wieder!	Now I remember!
reinen Tisch machen	to wipe the slate clean
So war ich als Kind.	That/This is what I was like as a child.
Wie waren Sie als Kind?	What were you like as a child?

GRAMMAR EXERCISES

A. Rewrite the sentences in the simple past.

1. Der Junge ist redefreudig und kann nicht schweigsam sein.

   _____.

2. Es gibt oft Ärger, weil ich frech bin.

   _____.

3. Dürft ihr ins Kino gehen, wenn ihr Geld habt?

   _____?

4. Sie sind schüchtern und wollen nicht reden.

   _____.

5. Du hast Durst, aber du willst kein Bier trinken, denn du magst es nicht.

   _____.

B. Fill in the blank with *als* or *wann*.

1. Wissen Sie, _____ das Fußballspiel heute Abend anfängt?

2. _____ ich fünf war, durfte ich jeden Morgen allein zu Fuß zur Schule gehen.

3. Wir haben viele nette Leute kennengelernt, _____ wir in Salzburg gewohnt haben.

4. Ich habe keine Ahnung, _____ die Kinder gestern Abend nach Hause gekommen sind. Aber ich glaube, es war gegen Mitternacht.

5. Unser Sohn hat gearbeitet, _____ er in Frankfurt studiert hat.

VOCABULARY EXERCISES

A. Fill in the blanks with the appropriate vocabulary word.

1. Als Kind war ich ein bisschen schwierig. Ich war unartig und frech. Aber eines Tages habe ich mir gesagt: _____! Und seitdem bin ich ein Engel.

2. Jeden Samstag musste das Mädchen ihr Zimmer _____.

3. Wo ist mein _____? Ich brauche ihn, um meine _____ zu machen. Die Lehrerin ist bestimmt böse, wenn ich ihr diese Lösungen nicht gebe.

4. Wir wollten die Spaghetti nicht kalt essen. Darum (*that's why*) haben wir sie mit dem _____ aufgewärmt.

5. A: Können Sie _____, dass Sie nur die _____ sprechen?
   B: Ja. Ich _____, dass ich nicht lüge.

B. Give the antonym for each word.

1. böse   _____

2. respektvoll   _____

3. gesprächig   _____

4. der Soldat   _____

5. introvertiert _____

6. der Amateur   _____

7. leicht, unproblematisch _____

8. der Schweiß   _____

TRANSLATIONS

A. Translate from German into English.

1. Sie musste ihr Zimmer jedes Wochenende aufräumen.

   _____.

2. Als wir jung waren, sollten wir artig und höflich sein.

   _____
   _____.

3. Statt in die Armee zu gehen, wollte er Zivi sein.

   _____
   _____.

4. Als ich Kind war, durfte ich nicht frech sein.

   _____.

5. Es gab ein bisschen Ärger, weil ihr immer Hunger hattet.

   _____
   _____.

B. Translate from English into German.

1. She was often shy when she was a child.

   _____.

2. We had to clean the kitchen every day at our house.

   _____.

3. I wanted to congratulate the professional because he was successful. (Note: Use _Erfolg haben_.)

   _____
   _____.

4. Our female friend wasn't able to find a pen since there were only pencils.

   _____
   _____.

5. Were you (informal, singular) supposed to do your homework every day when you were staying at home last week?

   _____
   _____?

Answers on page 255

BÄUERIN BÄRBEL UND DIE ROTBÄRTIGEN ZWERGE

SUMMARY

The simple past in German is sometimes also referred to as the preterit; however, it is not the same as the preterit found in other languages, such as Spanish, French, and Italian. Remember that there is no significant difference in meaning between the simple past and the present perfect in German.

Every verb in German can be expressed in the simple past and therefore has a simple past root.

Whereas weak verbs take a -t suffix and no vowel change, **all strong verbs take a vowel change in the simple past, but no -t suffix**.

There are **seven categories of strong verbs**, each classified by the vowel mutation from present infinitive to simple past to past participle (see tables that follow). Note that category 5 strong verbs are further broken down into categories 5a, 5b, and 5c.

GRAMMAR

CATEGORY 1: Strong Verbs with e → a → o vowel pattern

INFINITIVE	SIMPLE PAST	PAST PARTICIPLE
helfen	half	geholfen
sprechen	sprach	gesprochen
nehmen	nahm	genommen

CATEGORY 2: Strong Verbs with ei → ie → ie vowel pattern

INFINITIVE	SIMPLE PAST	PAST PARTICIPLE
treiben	trieb	getrieben
leihen	lieh	geliehen
schreien	schrie	geschrien

CATEGORY 3: Strong Verbs with in → an → un vowel pattern

INFINITIVE	SIMPLE PAST	PAST PARTICIPLE
zwingen	zwang	gezwungen
binden	band	gebunden
springen	sprang	gesprungen

CATEGORY 4: Strong Verbs with inn/imm → ann/ann → onn/omm vowel pattern

INFINITIVE	SIMPLE PAST	PAST PARTICIPLE
gewinnen	gewann	gewonnen
sinnen	sann	gesonnen
schwimmen	schwamm	geschwommen

Category 5a: Strong Verbs with a in Simple Past and No Vowel Change in Past Participle

INFINITIVE	SIMPLE PAST	PAST PARTICIPLE
essen	aß	gegessen
sehen	sah	gesehen
lesen	las	gelesen

CATEGORY 5b: Strong Verbs with ie or i in simple past and no vowel change in past participle

INFINITIVE	SIMPLE PAST	PAST PARTICIPLE
lassen	ließ	gelassen
schlafen	schlief	geschlafen
rufen	rief	gerufen

CATEGORY 5c: Strong Verbs with u in the simple past and no vowel change in past participle

INFINITIVE	SIMPLE PAST	PAST PARTICIPLE
fahren	fuhr	gefahren
wachsen [to grow]	wuchs	gewachsen
laden [to load, charge]	lud	geladen

CATEGORY 6: Strong Verbs with ie → o → o vowel pattern

INFINITIVE	SIMPLE PAST	PAST PARTICIPLE
ziehen [to pull]	zog	gezogen
verlieren	verlor	verloren
fliegen	flog	geflogen

CATEGORY 7: Strong Verbs with ei → i → i vowel pattern

INFINITIVE	SIMPLE PAST	PAST PARTICIPLE
greifen [to grab]	griff	gegriffen
beißen [to bite]	biss	gebissen
streiten [to argue]	stritt	gestritten

VOCABULARY

Nouns

-r Bauer -	farmer (m.)
-r Ehemann ¨-er	husband
-r Graben ¨-	grave
-r König -e	king

-r Lappen -	rag
-r Krieg -e	war
-r Sonnenaufgang ¨-e	sunrise
-r Zwerg -e	dwarf
-e Axt ¨-e	axe
-e Aufgabe -n	task
-e Bäuerin -nen	farmer (f.)
-e Erde	earth / ground
-e Erzählung -en	tale / story
-e Gesellschaft -en	society
-e Hausarbeit -en	housework
-e Königin -nen	queen
-e Lehre -e	lesson (i.e., that you learn)
-e Moral -en	moral
-e Pfeife -n	pipe
-e Schaufel -n	shovel
-e Scheune -n	barn
-e Wiese -n	meadow
-s Gebüsch -e	bushes
-s Fabelwesen -	fictional creature
-s Geräusch -e	sound
-s Körperglied -er	body limb
-s Märchen -	fairytale
-s Morgenlicht	first light / early light
-s Tier -e	animal

Verbs

abschneiden (schnitt … ab, abgeschnitten)	to cut off
ahnen	to suspect/sense/anticipate
annehmen (nahm … an, angenommen)	to accept/adopt/assume
ausbrechen (brach … aus, ist ausgebrochen)	to break out
beißen (biss … gebissen)	to bite
betreiben (betrieb, betrieben)	to operate/conduct/manage/run
sich befassen mit	to occupy oneself with/attend to/ consider
erschrecken (erschrak, ist erschrocken)	to become scared/alarmed (intransitive)
greifen (griff, gegriffen)	to grip/grab
heben (hob, gehoben)	to lift
lassen (ließ, gelassen)	to let/allow
rufen (rief, gerufen)	to call (i.e., using your voice)

vergehen (verging, ist vergangen)	to pass (i.e., time)
vergraben (vergrub, vergraben)	to bury
sich verstecken	to hide oneself
sich etwas wünschen	to wish something for oneself
zurückkehren	to return/come back

Adjectives and Adverbs

abermals	once again
abgeschnitten	severed / cut off
diesmal	this time
einsam	lonely
erschöpft	exhausted
fiktiv	fictional / fictitious
fromm	devout / pious
hoffnungsvoll	hopeful
gesellschaftlich	social / socially
gewalttätig	violent / violently
gleich	same / similar / equal
grün	green
hell	light / bright
muffig	musty / stuffy
nach wie vor	as before
schimmernd	shimmering / iridescent / gleaming
sprechend	speaking
tagsüber	during the day
taufeucht	moist with dew
verheiratet	married
verstorben	deceased
verzweifelt	despaired
wochenlang	for weeks

Phrases

Aber hallo!	Heck yeah! / You bet!
Achtung!	Attention! / Look out!
Du liebe Zeit!	Dear me! / Good heavens!
einerseits ... andererseits	on the one hand ... on the other (hand)
es schaffen	to do it / achieve it
Etwas stimmt nicht.	Something's not right.
Mal sehen.	We'll (just) have to wait and see.
Was fehlt dir/Ihnen?	What's wrong (with you)? / What's ailing you?

A. Bäuerin Bärbel und die rotbärtigen Zwerge (Teil eins)

Es war einmal eine junge, schöne Bäuerin. Sie hieß Bärbel. Bärbel hatte lange blonde Haare und schimmernde grüne Augen.

Bäuerin Bärbel war mit einem Bauer verheiratet. Er hieß Hans, und er liebte Bärbel sehr.

Während Hans tagsüber auf dem Feld arbeitete, blieb Bärbel zu Hause und machte die Hausarbeit. Sie sang gerne das Lieblingslied von ihrer Mutter:

> *Es gibt wohl nichts schöner*
> *als das Morgenlicht.*
> *Es scheint so warm und hell*
> *auf des Frommen Gesicht.*

Eines Tages geschah es, dass der Krieg im Land ausbrach. Der König brauchte Soldaten. Hans wurde Soldat und ging in den Krieg. Leider starb er im ersten großen Gefecht.

Bäuerin Bärbel weinte wochenlang. Ihr Mann war tot, und jetzt musste sie den Bauernhof ganz allein betreiben. Jeden Abend fiel sie traurig und erschöpft ins Bett. Und jede Nacht träumte sie von ihrem verstorbenen Mann.

So verging die Zeit. Aus Tagen wurden Wochen. Aus Wochen wurden Monate. Und aus Monaten wurden Jahre.

Eines schönen Sommermorgens ging sie zum Graben von ihrem Mann. Sie setzte sich ins Gras und begann zu weinen. So sehr vermisste sie ihren Hans.

Da hörte sie ein Geräusch im Gebüsch. „Wer versteckt sich dort?" schrie sie.

B. Bäuerin Bärbel und die rotbärtigen Zwerge (Teil zwei)

„Wer versteckt sich dort?" schrie sie.

Drei Zwerge traten aus dem Gebüsch. Sie sahen alle gleich aus. Jeder war klein und rotbärtig, und jeder rauchte eine Pfeife. Sie trugen Lappen und rochen muffig.

Als Bärbel die Zwerge sah, erschrak sie. Die Zwerge sprachen: „Sie sollen keine Angst haben."

Bärbel sagte: „Mein Mann ist im Krieg gefallen, und ich muss den Bauernhof ganz allein betreiben."

Der erste Zwerg kam auf sie zu und sagte: „Wir können Ihnen helfen."

Nun, Bärbel war ein bisschen skeptisch. Aber sie fühlte sich so einsam und verzweifelt, dass Sie die Hilfe von den Zwergen annahm.

„Wie können Sie mir helfen?" fragte sie.

Der erste Zwerg antwortete: „Bei Sonnenaufgang müssen Sie sich einen Daumen abschneiden. Dann müssen Sie den Daumen in der taufeuchten Wiese vergraben. Am Abend sollen Sie zu der Stelle zurückkehren, denn dort finden Sie einen netten, starken Ehemann.“

Bärbel rannte zurück nach Hause und begann ihre Pläne zu machen. In der Scheune fand sie eine Axt und eine Schaufel. Und am nächsten Morgen stand sie auf und ging zu der Wiese. Sie nahm die Axt und die Schaufel mit. Und als die Sonne aufging, tat sie, wie ihr geheißen. Sie schnitt sich einen Daumen ab und vergrub ihn in der taufeuchten Erde.

Und am Abend kehrte sie glücklich und hoffnungsvoll zu der Wiese zurück.

C. Bäuerin Bärbel und die rotbärtigen Zwerge (Teil drei)

Aber da fand sie niemanden. Es gab keinen Ehemann.

Sie lief zum Grab von ihrem Mann und setzte sich wieder ins Gras. Wieder fing sie zu weinen an.

Da hörte sie wieder ein Geräusch im Gebüsch, und die drei rotbärtigen Zwerge erschienen. „Was fehlt Ihnen, schönes Fräulein?“ fragten Sie.

„Ich habe alles getan,“ erzählte Bärbel, “aber kein Ehemann ist erschienen.“

Diesmal kam der zweite Zwerg auf sie zu und sagte: „Bestimmt haben Sie etwas Falsches gemacht ... Sie sollen morgen zurück zur Wiese gehen, sich den anderen Daumen abschneiden und ihn auch vergraben.“

Am nächsten Tag schnitt sie sich den anderen Daumen ab und vergrub ihn auch in der Erde. Aber am Abend fand sie wieder keinen Ehemann.

Sie wusste nicht, was sie tun sollte. Deshalb lief sie wieder zum Grab von ihrem Mann, setzte sich ins Gras und weinte.

Da hörte sie wieder ein Geräusch im Gebüsch ...

D. Bäuerin Bärbel und die rotbärtigen Zwerge (Teil vier)

Abermals erschienen die Zwerge. „Was fehlt Ihnen, schönes Fräulein?“ fragten sie.

„Ich habe wieder alles getan,“ erzählte Bärbel, „und da ist wieder kein Ehemann erschienen.“

Diesmal kam der dritte Zwerg auf sie zu und sagte: „Bestimmt haben Sie wieder etwas Falsches gemacht. Morgen sollen sie ein drittes Mal zu der Wiese gehen ... Aber diesmal müssen Sie sich einen Arm abschneiden und ihn vergraben.“

Nun, Bärbel ahnte, dass etwas nicht stimmte. Aber sie war so einsam und verzweifelt ...

Und am nächsten Morgen stand sie früh auf und holte wieder die Axt und die Schaufel. Und bei Sonnenaufgang stand sie wieder auf der Wiese.

Sie weinte. Einerseits wollte sie sich den Arm nicht abschneiden; andererseits wünschte sie sich so sehr einen Ehemann.

Sie hob langsam die Axt und schloss die Augen ...

GRAMMAR EXERCISES

A. Select the appropriate strong verb from the three given in parentheses and then fill in the blank with the correct simple past form of that strong verb.

1. Gestern _____ mein Hund den Nachbarn. (greifen / beißen / streiten)

2. Ich _____ an der Tür aber sie ging nicht auf. (ziehen / lassen / nehmen)

3. Das Mädchen _____ der älteren Damen, als sie die Straße überquerten. (helfen / sehen / schreien)

4. Am Wochenende _____ wir im See, weil es Badewetter war. (nehmen / schwimmen / wachsen)

5. Die arme Bäuerin Bärbel _____ ihre abgeschnittenen Finger in der Wiese. (vergessen / vergraben / versehen)

B. Rewrite the sentences in the simple past.

1. Bärbel bleibt wochenlang verzweifelt, aber sie betreibt den Bauernhof weiterhin.

   _____
   _____.

2. Bärbel läuft zum Graben von ihrem Mann und ruft seinen Namen.

   _____
   _____.

3. Bärbel nimmt die Axt und schneidet sich einen Finger ab.

   _____.

4. Der Bauer hebt die Schaufel und greift nach der Mistgabel (*pitchfork*).

   _____.

5. Die Zwerge schlafen im Gebüsch, tragen alte Lappen, und riechen muffig.

   _____
   _____.

VOCABULARY EXERCISES

A. Fill in the blank with the appropriate vocabulary word.

1. A: _____?
   B: Ich fühle mich schlecht und habe nicht viel geschlafen.

2. Bärbel war so _____, dass sie wochenlang weinte.

3. Im Jahr 1939 ist _____ in Europa ausgebrochen.

4. Wissen Sie, ob die Chefin _____ ist? Wenn ja, wie heißt ihr Ehemann?

5. Es riecht _____ in diesem Zimmer. Wir sollen es lüften (*ventilate*)?

6. Wenn Menschen zusammenleben und es Gesetze gibt, nennt man das eine _____.

B. Which word in each series does not fit with the others?

1. ○ sprechende Tiere, ○ Fabelwesen, ○ Scheune, ○ Zwerge

2. ○ Axt, ○ Geräusch, ○ Hammer, ○ Schaufel

3. ○ gewalttätig, ○ verstorben, ○ verzweifelt, ○ hoffnungsvoll

4. ○ Erzählung, ○ Wiese, ○ Märchen, ○ Geschichte

5. ○ heben, ○ vergraben, ○ ahnen, ○ betreiben

TRANSLATIONS

A. Translate from German into English.

1. Einerseits wollte sie sich den Arm nicht abschneiden; anderseits wünschte sie sich einen neuen Ehemann. Sie hob die Axt und schloss die Augen.

   _____

   _____.

2. Eines Tages geschah es, dass der Krieg ausbrach.

   _____.

3. Nun, Bärbel ahnte, dass etwas nicht stimmte. Aber sie war sehr einsam und verzweifelt.

   _____

   _____.

4. Die Sonne schien auf das taufeuchte Gras, die Vögel sangen, und kein einziges (*not a single*) Tier erschrak.

   _____

   _____.

5. Den ganzen Tag schwang ich die Axt und grub in der Erde, und am Abend fiel ich erschöpft ins Bett und schlief stundenlang.

   _____

   _____.

B. Translate from English into German. (Note: Use the simple past.)

1. Bärbel buried her fingers in the meadow and ran to the grave of her husband.

   _____

   _____.

2. Did you (informal, singular) win the game on Saturday night?

   _____?

3. What happened last night, and why were you (formal, singular) carrying an axe?

   _____

   _____.

4. The dwarf had two brothers, smoked a pipe, and looked very old.

   _____

   _____.

5. Dear me! Yesterday my husband drank two liters of beer, ate five sausages, and rode ten kilometers by bike.

   _____

   _____.

Answers on page 256

MORE SIMPLE PAST AND RELATIVE PRONOUNS

SUMMARY

There is a small number of strong verbs that don't fit into categories 1 through 7: *kommen* (*kam*, *ist gekommen*), *gehen* (*ging*, *ist gegangen*), *tun* (*tat*, *getan*), *lügen* (*log*, *gelogen*), and *betrügen* (*betrog*, *betrogen*).

Just like their past participle form, the simple past of **mixed verbs** take a *-t* suffix **and** a stem-vowel change (e.g., *kennen*, *kannte*, *gekannt*; *denken*, *dachte*, *gedacht*; *bringen*, *brachte*, *gebracht*; *usw.*)

Relative pronouns are grammatical words that refer back to a specific noun—called the **antecedent**—in the main clause:

(antecedent) (rel. pr.)
Dieser Mann liefert **das Gemüse**, **das** vom Bauerhof kommt.
[This man delivers the vegetables that come from the farm.]

(antecedent) (rel. pr.)
Das ist **ein Mann**, **der** Sachen aus Holz baut.
[This is a man who builds things out of wood.]

Relative pronouns reflect 1) **the number and gender of their antecedent in the main clause** and 2) **the grammatical relations in the relative clause:**

(antecedent) (rel. pr.)
(masc. sing. nom.) (masc. sing. acc.)
Wo ist **der Computer**, **den ich** neulich gekauft habe?
Where is **the computer** **that I** recently bought have?
[Where's the computer that I recently bought?]

(antecedent) (rel. pr.)
(pl. acc.) (pl. nom.)
Der Chef sucht **die Unterlagen**, **die auf seinem Bürotisch waren**.
The boss seeks **the documents** **that on his desk were**
[The boss is looking for the documents that were on his office desk.]

There are 16 relative pronouns in German, one for each gender, number, and case; however, you will only learn 12 of them in this lesson (see table that follows).

Relative pronouns always head up a relative clause and work like subordinating conjunctions in that the verb (i.e., main, helping, or modal) gets moved to the end of the clause:

(Main Clause)   (Relative) Clause)
                    ante.   relative pronoun
                    (pl.)   (subj.)
Das Unternehmen hat viele **Angestellte**, **die** dort gern arbeiten.
[The company has a lot of employees who like to work there.]

GRAMMAR

Mixed Verbs

INFINITIVE	SIMPLE PAST	PAST PARTICIPLE
rennen	rannte	gerannt
kennen	kannte	gekannt
denken	dachte	gedacht
bringen	brachte	gebracht
brennen	brannte	gebrannt
nennen	nannte	genannt

Relative Pronouns

Case	Singular			Plural
	Masc.	Fem.	Neut.	
Nominative (subject)	der	die	das	die
Accusative (direct object)	den	die	das	die
Dative (indirect object)	dem	der	dem	denen

VOCABULARY

Nouns

-r Arbeitsplatz ¨-e	workplace
-r Auftrag ¨-e	order / assignment / errand / task
-r Grabstein -e	gravestone
-r Jäger -	huntsman / hunter (m.)
-r Pfeil -e	arrow
-e Armbrust ¨-e	crossbow
-e Jägerin -nen	huntswoman / hunter (f.)
-e Unterlage -n (mostly used in plural)	document
-s Gehirn -e	brain
-s Happyend -s	happy ending

Professions

-r Advokat -en	attorney (m.)
-e Advokatin -nen	attorney (f.)

-r Altenpfleger -	geriatric nurse (m.)
-e Altenpflegerin -nen	geriatric nurse (f.)
-r Apotheker -	pharmacist (m.)
-e Apothekerin -nen	pharmacist (f.)
-r Architekt -en	architect (m.)
-e Architektin -nen	architect (f.)
-r Bauarbeiter -	construction worker (m.)
-e Bauarbeiterin -nen	construction worker (f.)
-r Briefträger -	mail carrier (m.)
-e Briefträgerin -nen	mail carrier (f.)
-r Busfahrer -	bus driver (m.)
-e Busfahrerin -nen	bus driver (f.)
-r Chef -s	boss (m.)
-e Chefin -nen	boss (f.)
-r Dachdecker -	roofer (m.)
-e Dachdeckerin -nen	roofer (f.)
-r Dirigent -en	music conductor (m.)
-e Dirigentin -nen	music conductor (f.)
-r Elektriker -	electrician (m.)
-e Elektrikerin -nen	electrician (f.)
-r Feuerwehrmann ¨-er	firefighter (m.)
-e Feuerwehrfrau -en	firefighter (f.)
-r Fleischer -	butcher (m.)
-e Fleischerin -nen	butcher (f.)
-r Fotograf -en	photographer (m.)
-e Fotografin -nen	photographer (f.)
-r Koch ¨-e	chef (m.)
-e Köchin -nen	chef (f.)
-r Künstler -	artist (m.)
-e Künstlerin -nen	artist (f.)
-r Immobilienmakler -	realtor (m.)
-e Immobilienmaklerin -nen	realtor (f.)
-r Ingenieur -	engineer (m.)
-e Ingenieurin -nen	engineer (f.)
-r Kellner -	server (m.) / waiter
-e Kellnerin -nen	server (f.) / waitress
-r Klempner -	plumber (m.)
-e Klempnerin -nen	plumber (f.)
-r Lieferant -en	supplier / deliverer / distributor (m.)

-e Lieferantin -nen	supplier / deliverer / distributor (f.)
-r Maler -	painter (m.)
-e Malerin -nen	painter (f.)
-r Mauerer -	mason (m.)
-e Maurerin -nen	mason (f.)
-r Mechaniker -	mechanic (m.)
-e Mechanikerin -nen	mechanic (f.)
-r Müllmann ¨-er	garbage collector (m.)
-e Müllfrau -en	garbage collector (f.)
-r Musiker -	musician (m.)
-e Musikerin -nen	musician (f.)
-r Pilot -en	pilot (m.)
-e Pilotin -nen	pilot (f.)
-r Polizist -en	police officer (m.)
-e Polizistin -nen	police officer (f.)
-r Redakteur -en	editor (m.)
-e Redakteurin -nen	editor (f.)
-r Regisseur -e	film or stage director (m.)
-e Regisseurin -nen	film or stage director (f.)
-r Richter -	judge (m.)
-e Richterin -nen	judge (f.)
-r Sänger -	singer / vocal performer (m.)
-e Sängerin -nen	singer / vocal performer (f.)
-r Schauspieler -	tailor (m.)
-e Schauspielerin -nen	tailor (f.) / seamstress
-r Schneider -	actor (m.)
-e Schneiderin -nen	actor (f.)
-r Sekretär -en	administrative assistant (m.)
-e Sekretärin -nen	administrative assistant (f.)
-r Tischler -	carpenter / cabinetmaker (m.)
-e Tischlerin -nen	carpenter / cabinetmaker (f.)
-r Verkäufer -	salesman
-e Verkäuferin -nen	saleswoman

Verbs

anvertrauen	to entrust/confide
aufspringen (sprang ... auf, ist aufgesprungen)	to jump up
betrügen (betrog, betrogen)	to deceive/betray/cheat
erscheinen (erschien, ist erschienen)	to appear

erschießen (erschoss, erschossen)	to shoot to death
lügen (log, gelogen)	to lie (i.e., not tell the truth)
werden (wurde, geworden)	to become

Adjectives and Adverbs

bald	soon
darauf	thereafter / after that
wütend	angry

Phrases

Und wenn sie nicht gestorben sind, so leben sie noch heute.	And they lived happily ever after.

TEXT

A. Bärbel und die rotbärtigen Zwerge (Teil fünf)

Bärbel hob die Axt und schloss die Augen ...

Aber bevor sie die Axt schwang, sang sie das Lieblingslied von ihrer Mutter:

Es gibt wohl nichts schöner

als das Morgenlicht.

Es scheint so warm und hell

auf des Frommen Gesicht.

Nun, an diesem Morgen gab es einen jungen Jäger im Wald. Er hörte das Singen und dachte sich, „Das ist eine wunderschöne Stimme!"

Er sah Bärbel mit der Axt und schrie: „Was machen Sie da, schönes Fräulein?"

Bärbel ließ die Axt fallen. Sie erzählte von den Zwergen, und der Jäger wurde wütend. Er wusste, dass sie Bärbel betrogen.

„Ich habe eine Idee," sagte der Jäger. „Sie sollen Ihren Arm im Hemd verstecken. Ich verstecke mich hinter dem Grabstein. Und wenn die bösen Zwerge kommen, erschieße ich sie mit meiner Armbrust."

Also, Bärbel versteckte ihren Arm im Hemd und der Jäger versteckte sich hinter dem Grabstein. Wieder fing Bärbel an zu weinen. Und wieder erschienen die drei Zwerge.

In diesem Moment sprang der Jäger auf und erschoss alle drei mit einem Pfeil.

Bald darauf heirateten Bärbel und der Jäger.

Und wenn sie nicht gestorben sind, so leben sie noch heute.

A. Identify the simple past forms in the following news reports and then give the corresponding infinitive and past participle form of each.

Tier-Chaos in der Großstadt

Heute morgen entkamen drei Zebra aus einem Brüsseler Tiergarten. Die Polizei konnte die Tiere, die mehr als eine Stunde durch die Straßen von Brüssels liefen, nach mehreren Versuchen (*after several attempts*) einfangen (*capture / trap*). Bisher (*as yet*) ist nicht bekannt, ob die Tiere von alleine (*on their own*) entkamen, oder ob jemand sie absichtlich (*intentionally*) befreite.

_____

_____

_____

_____

_____

_____

_____

Schmutziges Geld

Als eine Bankangestellte gestern in einer Bank in Genf (*Geneva*) auf die Toilette ging, entdeckte (*discovered*) sie zwanzig Fünfhunderteuroscheine im Toilettenbecken. Die Banknoten, die man aus dem Wasser holte und reinigte (*cleaned*), waren unbeschädigt (*undamaged*). Wann und warum das Geld ins Klobecken kam, ist bisher nicht bekannt. Die aufrechte (*upstanding*) Angestellte, die die Scheine sofort meldete (*reported*), durfte das Geld nicht behalten.

_____

_____

_____

_____

_____

_____

_____

Gewagter Sprung

Es war vorgestern in San Francisco kein gewöhnlicher (*normal*) Besuch beim Stadtaquarium. Als ein dreißigjähriger Mann zum berühmten (*famous*) Haifischbecken (*shark tank*) kam, zog er sich plötzlich aus und sprang ins Wasser. Der Mann, dem die Polizei eine Strafzettel (*ticket*) aushändigte (*handed*), verbrachte zehn Minuten nackt (*naked*) im Wasser mit den Haifischen. Als die Polizei ihn hinterher (*afterward*) fragte, was er mit seiner riskanten Aktion (*risky action*) erreichen (*achieve*) wollte, sagte er: „Haifische sind sensible Wesen (*sensitive beings*), genau wie (*exactly like*) wir Menschen. Sie gehören ins Meer, nicht in ein künstliches Gefängnis (*artificial prison*). Das ist doch Tierquälerei (*animal abuse*)! Und wenn ich sehe, dass Haifische eingeschlossen (*locked up*) sind, muss ich etwas dagegen unternehmen."

_____

_____

_____

_____

_____

_____

_____

_____

_____

B. First, fill in the blank with the correct relative pronoun. Then, rewrite the sentence in the simple past.

1. Das Kind kennt das Märchen, _____ Professor Pfrehm schreibt.

   _____.

2. Die Leute, _____ Deutsch lernen, sehen intelligent aus.

   _____.

3. Wo ist der Pfeil, _____ der Jäger für seine Armbrust braucht?

   _____?

4. Ich will die Altenpflegerin kennen lernen, _____ älteren Menschen hilft.

   _____.

5. Das ist die Richterin, _____ du danken sollst.

   _____.

6. Wir wollen den Auftrag, _____ die andere Firma nicht bekommen hat.

   _____.

7. Ich rufe die Immobilienmaklerin an, _____ dir am besten gefällt.

   _____.

8. Wir entdecken die Unterlagen, _____ sie verstecken.

   _____.

9. Ich wünsche mir einen Arbeitsplatz, _____ freundliche Mitarbeiter hat.

   _____.

10. Der Jäger erschießt die Zwerge, _____ Bärbel betrügen.

    _____.

11. Die Studenten, _____ die Lehrerin schlechte Noten (*grades*) gibt, werden wütend.

    _____
    _____.

12. Die Klempner, _____ wir finden, erscheinen sofort.

    _____.

VOCABULARY EXERCISES

A. Which vocabulary word does each series of words suggest?

1. der Schrank, die Kommode, der Regal_____

2. gleich, sofort, demnächst _____

3. die Leber, das Herz, die Lunge _____

4. der Ärger, der Hass, aggressiv _____

5. Der Schwindler, täuschen, der Lover _____

B. Fill in blank with the appropriate vocabulary word.

1. Ich habe die _____ im Büro gelassen. Aber die Chefin braucht sie für das Meeting!

2. _____ hat unseren Wasserhahn repariert.

3. Die Zwerge _____, wenn Bärbel weint.

4. Er hat ein Geheimnis, das er nur seiner Frau _____.

5. Mein Opa starb letztes Jahr, und jeden Sonntag lege ich Blumen auf seinen _____.

TRANSLATIONS

A. Translate from German into English.

1. Bald darauf heirateten Bärbel und der Jäger.

   _____ .

2. Bärbel ließ die Axt, die sie in der Hand hielt, sofort fallen.

   _____ .

3. Sie erzählte von den Zwergen, die sie betrogen, und der Jäger wurde wütend.

   _____

   _____ .

4. Die aufrechte Angestellte, die die Scheine sofort meldete, durfte das Geld nicht behalten.

   _____

   _____ .

5. Der Mann, dem die Polizei eine Strafzettel gab, verbrachte zehn Minuten nackt im Wasser mit den Haifischen.

   _____

   _____ .

B. Translate from English into German.

1. Do you guys know the (male) distributors who brought the beer?

   _____ .

2. They deceived the (male) hunter who helped them.

   _____ .

3. Where is the (male) construction worker who got angry yesterday?

   _____ .

4. That is the table that the (female) carpenter built.

   _____ .

5. I know the (female) geriatric nurse you (formal, singular) bought these flowers for.

   _____

   _____ .

Answers on page 257

EINE REISE NACH HAMBURG UND CUXHAVEN

SUMMARY

There are **three grammatical moods in German**: the **indicative**, the **subjunctive**, and the **imperative**.

> The **indicative** mood is used **to express things that are generally accepted to be true or realistic** (e.g., *Die Grubers fliegen nach Hamburg*; *Wohin fliegen die Grubers?*; *Fliegen die Grubers nach Hamburg?*).
>
> The **subjunctive** mood is used **to express the possibility of events**, as opposed to the reality of events. For example, instead of saying *Die Grubers fliegen nach Hamburg,* which represents a realistic condition, you can also use the subjunctive mood to express the event in **hypothetical terms**, as in *Wenn die Grubers nach Hamburg **fliegen würden**, ...*" ("If the Grubers **flew/were to fly** to Hamburg ...").
>
> The **imperative** mood is used to express commands.

There are four ways in German to construct the imperative form of a given verb (see tables that follow), according to whether you're addressing

> **a single person formally** (e.g., ***Sprechen Sie** lauter, bitte*);
> **a single person informally** (e.g., ***Sprich** lauter, bitte*);
> **more than one person formally** (e.g., ***Sprechen Sie** lauter, bitte*); or
> **more than one person informally** (e.g., ***Sprecht** lauter, bitte*).

You build the imperative for the singular and plural formal address by using the infinitive form and adding the formal pronoun *Sie* (e.g., ***Gehen Sie** nach Hause*; ***Fragen Sie** den Chef*; ***Probieren Sie** die Weißwurst*).

You build the imperative for the singular informal address by conjugating the verb with the **second-person singular personal pronoun** *du* (e.g., *gehst, fragst, probierst*), removing the *-st* suffix and dropping the pronoun (e.g., ***Geh** nach Hause;* ***Frag** den Chef;* ***Probier** die Weißwurst*).

You build the imperative for the plural informal address by conjugating the verb with the **second-person plural pronoun** *ihr* (e.g., *geht, fragt, probiert*) and then dropping the pronoun (e.g., ***Geht** nach Hause;* ***Fragt** den Chef;* ***Probiert** die Weißwurst*).

When you use the imperative with a separable-prefix verb, you still separate the prefix from the root verb and move it to the end of the imperative clause (e.g., ***Nehmen** Sie bitte den Auftrag **an**,* "Please accept this assignment/order"; ***Räumt** euer Zimmer sofort **auf**,* "Clean up your room right now").

When you use the single-person informal imperative with a stem-vowel-changing verb that takes an umlaut in its second- and third-person conjugation forms (e.g., *du **fährst**, er/sie/es **läuft***), you **drop the umlaut** in the imperative (e.g., ***Fahr** bitte sofort nach Hause;* *Bitte **lauf** nicht so schnell*).

The imperative forms of *sein* are slightly irregular (see table that follows).

When a relative pronoun is modified by a preposition (e.g., "The woman [who] I work **with**"; "The building that I work **in**," etc.), the way you have to construct the relative clause is analogous to the more proper-sounding construction in English (e.g., *Die Frau, **mit der** ich arbeite,* "The woman **with whom** I work"; *Das Gebäude, **in dem** ich arbeite,* "The building **in which** I work"). In other words, the preposition heads up the relative clause and is followed immediately by the relative pronoun:

(Independent Clause)   Dependent (Relative) Clause

ante.   rel. pr.
(pl.)   (pl. acc.)
Wo sind **die Robben** **für** **die** wir gekommen sind?
(acc. prep.)
Where are the seals for which we come are?
[Where are the seals we came for?]

(Independent Clause)   Dependent (Relative) Clause

ante.
(sing. fem.)   (dat. prep.)
Das ist die Firma, **bei** **der** ich zwanzig Jahre gearbeitet habe.
rel. pr.
(sing. fem. dat.)
That is the company, for which I worked for twenty years.
[That's the company that I worked for for twenty years.]

GRAMMAR

Imperative Mood aufstehen

Sing. Informal	Plural Informal	Sing. Formal	Plural Formal
Steh auf!	Steht auf!	Stehen Sie auf!	Stehen Sie auf!

Imperative Mood sein

Sing. Informal	Plural Informal	Sing. Formal	Plural Formal
Sei vorsichtig!	Seid vorsichtig!	Seien Sie vorsichtig!	Seien Sie vorsichtig!

VOCABULARY

Nouns

-r Befehl -e	command / order
-r Flug ¨-e	flight
-r Flugbegleiter -	flight attendant (m.)
-r Passagier -e	passenger
-r Rückflug ¨-e	return flight
-r Theatergänger -	theatergoer
-r Typ -en	guy / type / fellow
-r Wurm ¨-e	worm
-e Befehlsform -en	imperative
-e Firma -en	company
-e Flugdauer	flight duration
-e Flugbegleiterin -nen	flight attendant (f.)
-e Fluggesellschaft -en	airline
-e Krabbe -n	crab
-e Muschel -n	mussel
-e Passagierin -nen	passenger
-e Reihe -n	row
-e Robbe -n	seal
-e Seelandschaft -en	seascape
-e Wahrheit -en	truth
-e Zwischenlandung -en	stopover flight / layover
-s Flugticket -s	airplane ticket
-s Stück -e	play (i.e., theater)

Verbs

aufhören	to stop / quit (i.e., an activity)
ausdrucken	to print out
beschimpfen	to scold/berate
beschließen (beschloss, beschlossen)	to decide (i.e., to do something)
einscannen	to scan (in)
eintippen	to type/enter (i.e., on a keyboard)
erwischen	to catch (i.e., a train or bus)
genießen (genoss, genossen)	to enjoy
sich interessieren für	to be interested in
nachsehen (sah nach, nachgesehen)	to go see/check
übertreiben (übertrieb, übertrieben)	to exaggerate
vorschlagen (schlug vor, vorgeschlagen)	to suggest (i.e., an idea or plan)

Adjectives and Adverbs

anderthalb (anderthalb Stunden)	one and a half
einzigartig	unique
empfehlenswert	recommendable
frühlingshaft	springlike
geduldig	patient(ly)
hartnäckig	persistent(ly)
herrlich	gorgeous
immer	always
überheblich	arrogant
vorsichtig	careful(ly) / cautious(ly)

Phrases

das Stück	a piece
Halt die Augen offen.	Keep your eyes open.
sich dem Ende zuneigen	to near its end

TEXTS

A. Professor Pfrehm's Introduction to Hamburg

Es ist der erste frühlingshafte Tag in Augsburg. Ralf und Mia beschließen, eine Reise nach Norddeutschland zu unternehmen. Mia möchte die Großstadt Hamburg besuchen, aber Ralf interessiert sich für die norddeutsche Seelandschaft.

B. Ralf und Mia in Hamburg (Teil eins)

RALF: Rahel! Hans! Hört bitte damit auf!

MIA: Seid bitte vorsichtig!

RALF: Soll ich nachsehen?

MIA: Nein. Bleib hier und hilf mir mit den Flugtickets.

RALF: Schau mal. Bei Eurowings gibt es viele Möglichkeiten.

MIA: Von München nach Hamburg?

RALF: Ja.

MIA: Direkt oder mit Zwischenlandung?

RALF: Direkt. Mit einer Flugdauer von anderthalb Stunden.

MIA: Toll! Wie viel kosten die Tickets?

RALF: Neunundvierzig Euro das Stück.

MIA: Ich schlage vor, wir fliegen für eine Nacht nach Hamburg. Danach fahren wir mit dem Zug an die Nordsee.

RALF: Großartig! Die Stadt Cuxhaven liegt direkt an der Nordsee und ist nicht zu weit von Hamburg.

MIA: Gut. Wir bleiben eine Nacht in Cuxhaven. Dann fahren wir zurück zum Hamburger Flughafen und erwischen unseren Rückflug.

C. Ralf und Mia in Hamburg (Teil zwei)

RALF: Also dann. Was willst du machen?

MIA: Heute Abend habe ich Lust auf Theater.

Ralf: Echt?

Mia: Ja. Nicht weit von hier steht das Deutsche Schauspielhaus. Es ist das größte Theaterhaus in Deutschland.

Ralf: Hmm ... Ich weiß nicht ...

MIA: Was ist?

RALF: Erinnerst du dich an unseren letzten Theaterabend in München?

Mia: Ja. Wir haben ein Stück von Arthur Miller gesehen.

RALF: *Die Hexenjagd.*

MIA: Genau. Das war super.

Ralf:	Tja. Für dich war's super. Aber der überhebliche Typ, der in der Reihe vor uns gesessen hat, hat mich sehr geärgert.
MIA:	Es war nicht so schlimm.
RALF:	Doch! Er hat mich mehrmals beschimpft: „Seien Sie leise!" „Hören Sie mit dem Husten auf." „Treten Sie nicht gegen meinen Sitz!"
MIA:	Ach. Du übertreibst ...
RALF:	Nein. Ich sage immer nur die Wahrheit.
MIA:	Aber natürlich ...

D. Ralf und Mia in Cuxhaven

RALF:	Ach. Ist dieser Anblick nicht herrlich?
MIA:	Ja. Diese Wattwanderung war eine gute Idee. Aber wo sind die Robben, von denen du mir erzählt hast?
RALF:	Keine Ahnung.
MIA:	Ich habe nur Wattwürmer, Muscheln, und Krabben gesehen. Aber keine Robben ...
RALF:	Halt die Augen offen.
MIA:	Schau mal! Dort drüben ist eine!
RALF:	Wo?
MIA:	Da. Auf dem Sand.
RALF:	Ach so! Hallo, Robbe! Wie geht's dir?

GRAMMAR EXERCISES

A. Rephrase the following questions as commands using the imperative.

1. Können Sie bitte leiser sein?

   _____.

2. Könnt ihr bitte diese Unterlagen einscannen?

   _____.

3. Kannst du brav sein?

   _____.

4. Kannst du bitte gleich nachsehen?

   _____.

5. Können Sie bitte die Krabben probieren?

   _____.

6. Könnt ihr bitte mit dem Schreien aufhören?

   _____.

7. Kannst du bitte meine Freunde zur Party am Freitagabend einladen?

   _____.

8. Kannst du bitte morgen allein nach Hause fahren?

   _____.

B. Combine the sentences using a relative pronoun modified by a preposition.

1. Wo sind die Leute? Ich bin mit ihnen aufgewachsen.

   _____.

2. Wir kennen den Wald. Ihr wandert durch diesen Wald.

   _____.

3. Das ist die Frau. Ich muss von ihr erzählen.

   _____.

4. Sie sind mit dem Mann verheiratet. Ich habe früher bei ihm gewohnt.

   _____.

5. Ist das die Chefin? Mein Bruder arbeitet für sie.

   _____.

6. Dort drüben steht das Haus. Der Hund ist aus diesem Haus herausgerannt.

   _____
   _____.

VOCABULARY EXERCISES

A. Fill in the blank with the appropriate vocabulary word.

1. A: Vati, wo sind die Robben? Ich sehe sie nicht?
   B: _____. Die Robben verstecken gern. Man muss gut
   aufpassen, um sie zu sehen.

2. Ach! Das sind prima Sitzplätze für das Konzert! Wir sind in der
ersten _____!

3. Meine Frau lügt nie. Sie sagt immer nur _____.

4. Wir haben _____, nächstes Jahr eine Reise nach Österreich
zu machen.

5. Können Sie bitte diese Unterlagen für mich _____? Ich brauche
Hardcopys für das Meeting.

6. A: Die Konzertkarten kosten hundert Euro _____.
B: Mensch! Das ist mir viel zu teuer!

7. Dieser Flug ist direkt; das heißt, es gibt keine _____.

8. Ich finde den neuen Chef _____. Er glaubt, er ist besser und
intelligenter als wir.

9. Wo soll ich meinen Usernamen und mein Password _____?

10. Boeing ist eine _____, bei der ich arbeiten möchte.

TRANSLATIONS

A. Translate from German into English.

1. Ralf und Mia beschließen, eine Reise nach Norddeutschland zu unternehmen.

   _____

   _____.

2. Ich schlage vor, dass wir für eine Nacht nach Hamburg fliegen. Danach fahren
wir mit dem Zug an die Nordsee.

   _____

   _____.

3. Der überhebliche Typ, der in der Reihe vor uns gesessen hat, hat mich sehr
geärgert.

   _____

   _____.

4. Erinnerst du dich an unseren letzten Theaterabend in München?

   _____

   _____.

5. Er hat mich mehrmals beschimpft: „Seien Sie leise!" „Hören Sie mit dem Husten auf." „Treten Sie nicht gegen meinen Sitz!"

   _____

   _____.

6. Bleib geduldig und sieh nach, wann der nächste Zug nach Berlin abfährt.

   _____

   _____.

B. Translate from English into German.

1. The play lasted an hour and a half, but we enjoyed it.

   _____

   _____.

2. We have to catch the train that arrives at five tomorrow morning.

   _____

   _____.

3. Do you (formal, singular) want to berate the (male) boss that you told me about?

   _____

   _____?

4. Be careful (informal, plural)! I didn't exaggerate when I told you guys that the seals are very angry.

   _____

   _____

   _____.

5. Ralf, stay here and help me with the plane tickets. This is the airline we should fly with.

   _____

   _____.

Answers on page 259

TWO-WAY PREPOSITIONS AND VERBS THAT USE THEM

SUMMARY

In addition to accusative and dative prepositions, German has nine prepositions that take **either the accusative or the dative case**, depending on the semantics of **location** or **movement/destination**.

These prepositions are called **two-way prepositions** (*Wechselpräpositionen*), and they include *an, auf, in, hinter, neben, über, unter, vor*, and *zwischen* (see table that follows).

If the meaning involves location, two-way prepositions take the dative case (e.g., *Meine Katze **liegt auf dem Bett***, "My cat is lying on the bed"; *Die Lampe **steht neben der Couch***, "The lamp is [standing] next to the couch"; *Das Bild **hängt an der Wand***, "The picture is hanging on the wall").

If the meaning involves movement/destination, two-way prepositions take the accusative case (e.g., *Ich **lege** das Buch **auf den Tisch***, "I'm laying the book on the table"; *Ich **stelle** die Lampe **neben die Couch***, "I'm putting the lamp next to the couch"; *Ich **hänge** das Bild **an die Wand***, "I'm hanging the picture on the wall").

The verbs *sein, stehen, liegen, sitzen*, and **hängen* (*instransitive) are typically used together with a two-way preposition in the dative case (e.g., *Ich **sitze auf dem Teppich***, "I'm sitting on the carpet"; *Wir **sind hinter dem Haus***, "We are behind the house"), as well as with the interrogative pronoun *wo* (e.g., *Wo liegt der Hund?*; *Wo steht die Lampe?*; *Wo liegt das Buch?*).

The verbs *gehen*, *stellen*, *legen*, *setzen*, and **hängen* (*transitive) are typically used together with a two-way preposition in the accusative case (e.g., *Ich **setze das Kind in den Stuhl***, "I'm setting the child in the chair"; *Wir **gehen hinter das Haus***, "We are going behind the house"), as well as with the interrogative pronoun ***wohin*** (e.g., ***Wohin** stellst du die Lampe?*; ***Wohin** gehst du?*; ***Wohin** legst du das Buch?*).

GRAMMAR

Two-Way Prepositions

an	at, to	über	over
auf	on, atop, at, in, onto, to	unter	under
in	in	vor	in front of
hinter	behind	zwischen	between
neben	next to		

VOCABULARY

Nouns

-r Bahnhof ¨-e	train station
-r Bastelschrank ¨-e	arts and crafts closet
-r Baum ¨-e	tree
-r Berg -e	mountain
-r Beutel -	bag (i.e., as a container)
-r Boden ¨-	floor (i.e., opposite of ceiling)
-r Flughafen ¨-	airport
-r Fluss ¨-e	river
-r Löffel -	spoon
-r Markt ¨-e	market (i.e., outdoor market)
-r Meilenstein -e	milestone
-r Ofen ¨-	oven
-r Schweinestall ¨-e	pigsty
-r Sessel -	armchair
-r Teller -	plate (i.e., for food)
-r Teppich -e	rug
-r Tisch -e	table (i.e., for eating)
-r Werkzeugschrank ¨-e	tool cabinet/chest
-e Couch -es/-en	couch

-e Einleitung -en	introduction
-e Flasche -n	bottle
-e Gabel -n	fork
-e Insel -n	island
-e Küchentheke -n	kitchen counter
-e Kuckucksuhr -en	cuckoo clock
-e Lötlampe -n	blowtorch
-e Ordentlichkeit	orderliness / neatness
-e Pfanne -n	pan (i.e., for cooking)
-e Sache -n	thing / matter / affair
-e Seite -n	page / side
-e Tafel -n	board (i.e., for writing)
-e Toilette -n	toilet
-e Wand -ë	wall (i.e., inside a house)
-s Bastelmaterial -ien	arts and crafts materials
-s Bastelregal -e	arts and crafts shelf/shelving unit
-s Bild -er	picture
-s Durcheinander	mess / clutter / confusion
-s Fenster -	window
-s Feuerzeug -e	lighter
-s Geschirr	dishes / crockery
-s Klo -s	loo / john
-s Küchenchaos	kitchen disaster
-s Land	country / countryside
-s Meer -e	ocean
-s Messer -	knife
-s Nähzeug	sewing stuff
-s Rathaus ¨-er	courthouse
-s Zeug	stuff
-s Werkzeug -e	tool

Verbs

abwaschen	to wash dishes/wash up
sich beruhigen	to calm down
hängen	to hang (transitive)
hängen (hing, gehangen)	to hang (intransitive)
legen	to lay (transitive)
liegen (lag, gelegen)	to lie (intransitive)
loben	to praise
markieren	to mark
scheuern	to scrub
setzen	to set (transitive)

sitzen (saß, gesessen)	to sit (intransitive)
stehen (stand, gestanden)	to stand (intransitive)
stellen	to put (transitive)
wegräumen	to put away/clear away

Adjectives and Adverbs

chaotisch	chaotic
klebrig	sticky
klug	clever / smart
sauber	clean
schmutzig	dirty
wenigstens	at least
wie immer	as always

Two-Way Prepositions

an	at / to
auf	on / atop / at / in / onto / to
in	in
hinter	behind
neben	next to
über	over
unter	under
vor	in front of
zwischen	between

Phrases

Bist du schon zurück?	Are you back already?
Das war viel Arbeit!	That was a lot of work!
eine Art ...	a sort of/kind of ...
Ich glaub, ich spinn!	I must be losing my mind!
Meinen Sie nicht?	Don't you think?
Raten Sie mal!	Guess!
sich zu Tode lachen	to laugh oneself to death

TEXTS

A. Ralf und Mia diskutieren über die Ordentlichkeit (Teil eins)

MIA: Ich glaub', ich spinn'!

RALF: Mia! Bist du schon zurück?

MIA: Ralf Gruber! Die Küche sieht aus wie ein Schweinestall!

RALF: Die Kinder und ich räumen das noch auf.

MIA: Ist das mein Nähzeug, da vor dem Ofen?

RALF: Nein. Das ist Rahels Bastelmaterial.

MIA: Und warum liegt es auf dem Küchenboden?

RALF: Keine Ahnung. Aber ich sagte ihr, sie soll es zurück ins Bastelregal stellen.

MIA: Und warum ist da so viel Zeug auf der Küchentheke?

RALF: Das sind nur ein paar Sachen.

MIA: „Nur ein *paar* Sachen?" Ich sehe Gabel, Löffel, Messer, Pfannen, Flaschen, Ziplockbeutel und—was ist denn das? Eine Art Feuerzeug?

RALF: Das ist meine Lötlampe.

MIA: Mein Gott! Ralf Gruber, warum steht eine Lötlampe auf meiner Küchentheke!?

RALF: Okay, okay! Beruhige dich. Ich bringe die Lötlampe sofort zurück in die Garage.

MIA: Bravo. Das finde ich klug.

B. Ralf und Mia diskutieren über die Ordentlichkeit (Teil zwei)

MIA: Fertig?

RALF: Ja. Ich habe alles weggeräumt, das schmutzige Geschirr abgewaschen, und ich habe den klebrigen Boden gescheuert. Du hast wieder die sauberste Küche in Augsburg.

MIA: Und die Lötlampe, die auf der Küchentheke gestanden hat?

RALF: Ich habe sie in den Werkzeugschrank gestellt.

MIA: Und das Bastelmaterial, das vor meinem Ofen gelegen hat?

RALF: In Rahels Zimmer.

MIA: Im Bastelschrank?

RALF: Nein ... Sie hat es auf den Boden gelegt.

MIA: Ach nein ... Hat sie schon wieder ein chaotisches Zimmer?

RALF: Ein bisschen.

MIA: Ist es chaotischer als sonst?

RALF: Nein. Es ist so chaotisch wie immer.

MIA: Wenigstens habe ich meine saubere Küche zurück.

GRAMMAR EXERCISES

A. Select the correct verb from the options given in parentheses.

1. Sind das deine Pferde, die neben dem Baum _____?
   (○ setzen, ○ stehen, ○ stellen)

2. Ralf muss das Geschirr zurück in den Schrank _____.
   (○ liegen, ○ sitzen, ○ stellen)

3. Schau mal, was hier in der Zeitung _____: „Prof. Pfrehm will
   nächster amerikanischer Präsident werden." Das ist verrückt!
   (○ liegt, ○ steht, ○ sitzt)

4. Warum _____ diese leeren Bierflaschen auf dem Boden?
   (○ legen, ○ liegen, ○ stellen)

5. Wohin sollen wir die Wanduhr _____?
   (○ hängen, ○ liegen, ○ stehen)

B. Fill in the blank with the correct *ein-* or *der-* word ending.

1. Der Löffel liegt auf d_____ Boden.

2. Bitte, stell den Teller nicht in d_____ Mikrowelle!

3. Seit wie lange steht die Lötlampe hinter d_____ Couch?

4. Ich habe dein_____ Kuckucksuhr an dies_____ Wand gehängt. Ist das ok?

5. Warum hast du mein_____ Nähzeug unter dein_____ Bett gestellt?

6. Welch_____ Bild haben Sie auf d_____ Boden gelegt?

7. Das ist komisch! Ein_____ schwarze Katze sitzt vor jed_____ Tür
   und miaut.

8. Die Möbelträger (*furniture movers*) haben unser_____ Kühlschrank
   zwischen d_____ Ofen und d_____ Mikrowelle gestellt.

VOCABULARY EXERCISES

A. Which word doesn't fit in the sequence?

1. ○ Küchenchaos, ○ Ordentlichkeit, ○ Durcheinander

2. ○ Löffel, ○ Fenster, ○ Messer

3. ○ Sessel, ○ Teppich, ○ Meer

4. ○ schmutzig, ○ klebrig, ○ sauber

5. ○ loben, ○ scheuern, ○ abwaschen

B. Fill in the blank with the appropriate vocabulary word.

1. Unser Sohn ist sehr _____. Er spielt fünf Instrumente und spricht fünf Sprachen.

2. Der Präsident _____ die Soldaten für ihren Mut (*courage*).

3. Ich brauche ein _____, um meine kubanische Zigarre anzuzünden.

4. Manches Eichhörnchen wohnt im _____ und nicht unter der Erde.

5. Ach! Es gibt so viel Zeug auf dem Boden! Das ist ein großes _____!

6. Wohin soll ich den neuen Teppich _____?

7. Warum _____ der Sessel in der Ecke? Wir sollen ihn neben die Couch _____.

8. Aruba ist eine schöne _____ in der Südkaribik.

TRANSLATIONS

A. Translate from German into English.

1. Warum liegt so viel Zeug auf meiner Küchentheke?

   _____.

2. Die Küche sieht aus wie ein Schweinestall!

   _____.

3. Ich habe alles weggeräumt, das schmutzige Geschirr abgewaschen, und den klebrigen Boden gescheuert.

   _____
   _____.

4. Ich bringe die Lötlampe sofort zurück in die Garage.

   _____.

5. Hast du den Hammer, der auf der Küchentheke gelegen hat, zurück in den Werkzeugschrank gestellt?

   _____.
   _____.

B. Translate from English into German.

1. The answer is on page twenty-six in the book.

   _____.

2. I hung the cuckoo clock next to the picture that's hanging above the window.

   _____
   _____.

3. Guess who has to wash the dishes and scrub the floor because there's a mess in the kitchen?

   _____.
   _____.

4. She laid the fork on the table between the knife and the spoon.

   _____
   _____.

5. We'll clean up this stuff before we drive to the countryside.

   _____
   _____.

Answers on page 260

COMPARATIVE/ SUPERLATIVE AND ADJECTIVE ENDINGS

SUMMARY

The use of adjectives and adverbs to compare two nouns or actions (i.e., the **comparative**) works similarly in English and German: You add an -*er* **suffix** to the adjective or adverb (e.g., *Ich möchte schneller fahren*; *Du bist kleiner*; *Er ist braver*).

German uses the word *als* to express "than" when comparing two nouns or actions (e.g., *Ich laufe schneller als du*; *Du bist kleiner als ich*; *Er ist braver als sie*).

German does not use the adverb *mehr*—as English uses "more" with some adjectives and adverbs—**in the comparative. German uses only the -*er* suffix** (e.g., *Meine Frau ist intelligenter als ich*; *Deutsch ist interessanter als Englisch*).

When comparing more than two nouns or actions, speakers often put the adjective or adverb into the **superlative** form (e.g., *Ich bin kleiner als mein Vater, aber mein Bruder ist am kleinsten*; *Meine Frau ist intelligenter als ich, aber meine Schwiegemutter ist am intelligentesten*).

When the adjective or adverb comes after the noun (i.e., the adjective of the predicate), you form **the superlative** in German by adding an -*sten* or an -*esten* **suffix** to the adjective or adverb and putting the contraction *am* in front of the adjective or adverb (e.g., *Ich laufe am schnellsten*; *Du bist am bravsten*; *Wir sind am nettesten*).

Often, the adjective's or adverb's main vowel gets umlauted in its comparative and superlative forms (e.g., *Ich bin größer als mein Bruder, aber unser Vater ist am größten*; *Ich bin jünger als meine Freundin, aber meine Schwester ist am jüngsten*; *Die Königin ist älter als die Prinzessin, aber der König ist am ältesten*).

Several adjectives and adverbs take an irregular form in the comparative and/or superlative (e.g., *gut → besser → am besten*; *viel → mehr → am meisten*; *bald → eher → am ehesten*; *hoch → höher → am höchsten*; *nah → näher → am nächsten*; *gern → lieber → am liebsten*; *teuer → teurer → am teuersten*).

GRAMMAR

Set One Endings: Adjective Preceded by an ein-Word

Case	Singular			Plural
	Masc.	Fem.	Neut.	
Nominative (subject)	-er	-e	-es	-en
Accusative (direct object)	-en	-e	-es	-en
Dative (indirect object)	-en	-en	-en	-en

Set Two Endings: Adjective Preceded by an der-Word

Case	Singular			Plural
	Masc.	Fem.	Neut.	
Nominative (subject)	-e	-e	-e	-en
Accusative (direct object)	-en	-e	-e	-en
Dative (indirect object)	-en	-en	-en	-en

Set Three Endings: Unprecedented Adjectives

Case	Singular			Plural
	Masc.	Fem.	Neut.	
Nominative (subject)	-er	-e	-es	-e
Accusative (direct object)	-en	-e	-es	-e
Dative (indirect object)	-em	-er	-em	-en

VOCABULARY

Nouns

-r Ausgangspunkt -e	starting point / springboard
-r Herzog -ë	count
-r Keks -e	cookie
-r Liebesfilm -e	favorite film
-r Schauspieler -	actor
-r Stoff -e	material (i.e., for clothes)
-r Thunfisch -e	tuna fish
-r Untertitel -n	subtitle
-r Witz -e	joke
-e Auster -n	oyster
-e Herzogin -nen	duchess
-e Schauspielerin -nen	actress
-e Schlange -n	snake / line (i.e., to stand in)
-e Spieldauer	playing time / length (i.e., of a film or play)
-e Wanze -n	bug
-e Wüste -n	desert
-e Zuschauerzahl -en	number of spectators / audience number
-s Erscheinungsjahr -e	year of release / year of publication
-s Wortspiel -e	play on words

Verbs

spendieren	to treat
verarschen	to tease/take someone for a ride

Adjectives and Adverbs (and Comparatives and Superlatives)

albern	silly
alt (älter, am ältesten)	old
bald (eher, am ehesten)	soon
berühmt	famous
dumm (dümmer, am dümmsten)	dumb
dunkel (dunkler, am dunkelsten)	dark
ernst	serious
gering	slight / small / scant / slim
gern (lieber, am liebsten)	like to (prefer to, most prefer to)
gesund (gesünder, am gesündesten)	healthy
groß (größer, am größten)	big / large / tall (i.e., person)
gut (besser, am besten)	good

hoch (höher, am höchsten)	high / tall (i.e., building or structure)
jung (jünger, am jüngsten)	young
kalt (kälter, am kältesten)	cold
klein (kleiner, am kleinsten)	small
klug (klüger, am klügsten)	smart
kurz (kürzer, am kürzesten)	short
lang (länger, am längsten)	long
mild	lenient / mild
nah (näher, am nächsten)	near
rührend	touching / poignant / stirring
sehenswert	worth seeing
spannend	suspenseful / gripping (i.e., book, film, or story)
stark (stärker, am stärksten)	strong
stolz	proud
teuer (teurer, am teuersten)	expensive
viel (mehr, am meisten)	a lot
warm (wärmer, am wärmsten)	warm
wirksam	effective

TEXT

A. Ralf und Mia sprechen über Filme

RALF: Sag mal, wie heißt denn wieder dieser neue Film?

MIA: Er heißt *In die blaue Tiefe hinein.*

RALF: *In die blaue Tiefe hinein* ... Na ja. Das klingt spannend.

RALF: Das ist ein Liebesfilm.

RALF: Ach. Schon wieder ein Liebesfilm?

MIA: Was hast du gegen Liebesfilme?

RALF: Die letzten drei Filme, die wir im Kino gesehen haben, waren Liebesfilme.

MIA: Das ist nicht wahr.

RALF: Doch. Wir haben jeden romantischen Film in der ganzen Stadt gesehen.

MIA: Dieser Film soll sehr gut sein.

RALF: Und welche Schauspieler gibt es in diesem romantischen Film?

MIA: Die bekanntesten Schauspieler in ganz Deutschland.

RALF: Jetzt verarschst du mich.

MIA: Psst ... Der Film fängt an.

GRAMMAR EXERCISES

A. Select the appropriate adjective from those given in parentheses and then construct a sentence with the comparative and superlative to express the relationship among the nouns listed.

1. Der Fuji: 3776 m; Mt. Jefferson: 3199 m; Kilimandscharo: 5858 m (hoch, lang, nah)

   _____

   _____.

   _____.

2. Schach spielen: ausgezeichnet; Karten spielen: gut; Monopoly spielen: sehr gut (teuer, gern, bald)

   _____.

   _____.

3. Prof. Pfrehm: 29; Arnold Schwarzenegger: 71; Angela Merkel: 64 (gut, interessant, jung)

   _____.

   _____.

4. Seattle: 1200 km entfernt; Moskau: 4300 km entfernt; Wien: 900 km entfernt (nah, gesund, bald)

   _____

   _____.

5. Shaquille O'Neal: 216 cm; David Hasselhoff: 193 cm; Justin Bieber: 175 cm (groß, hoch, alt)

   _____

   _____.

6. der Käfer: €8.499; die Mercedes S-Klasse: €91.899; der BMW M4: €69.100 (schnell, teuer, bald)

   _____

   _____.

7. der Amazonas: 6400 km; der Jangtse: 6380 km; der Nil: 6650 km (tief, lang, viel)

   _____

   _____.

8. Gummibärchen schmecken ausgezeichnet; Milchschokolade schmeckt sehr gut; Lakritze schmeckt gut (gut, viel, bald)

   _____

   _____.

VOCABULARY EXERCISES

A. Fill in the blank with the appropriate vocabulary word.

1. Unser Professor ist meistens _____. Er lächelt selten und seine Krawatten sind nie _____.

2. Der Film war sehr _____. Ich habe sogar geweint.

3. Essen Sie lieber _____ oder Muscheln?

4. Ich habe einen Witz für dich! Er lautet so: „Was macht man in der _____, wenn man eine große _____ sieht?"

5. Aus welchem _____ ist diese Jacke: Baumwolle oder Polyester?

6. Das letzte Mal habt ihr gezahlt. Diesmal möchte ich euch einen Drink _____.

TRANSLATIONS

A. Translate from German into English.

1. Die letzten drei Filme, die wir im Kino gesehen haben, waren Liebesfilme.

   _____

   _____.

2. Wir haben jeden romantischen Film in der ganzen Stadt gesehen.

   _____.

3. Trägst du wirklich alberne Krawatten lieber als bunte Hüte?

    _____

    _____?

4. Wer ist am stolzesten?

    _____?

5. Sie kann nicht jünger als ich sein, denn ich bin am jüngsten.

    _____.

B. Translate from English into German.

1. My daughter is taller than me, but my son is the tallest.

    _____.

2. Your (formal, singular) dog looks old, but my dog is actually the oldest.

    _____

    _____.

3. We thought the desert was more interesting than the ocean.

    _____.

4. This actress earns the most because she is also the most intelligent.

    _____

    _____.

5. This film seems the most gripping to me, although its running time is longer than ninety minutes.

    _____

    _____.

Answers on page 260

THE GENITIVE CASE AND THE PASSIVE VOICE

SUMMARY

Whereas the nominative case expresses the subject, the accusative case the direct object, and the dative case the indirect object of a sentence, **the genitive case expresses a relationship of possession between two or more nouns** (e.g., *der Name dieses Buches*, "the name of the book / the book's name"; *die Adresse **meiner** Firma*, "the address of my company / my company's address"; *die Spieldauer **des Films***, "the playing time of the film / the film's playing time").

The genitive is primarily used in more formal styles of speech and in writing. In informal spoken German, speakers use the dative preposition *von* to express a relationship of possession (e.g., *Der Name **vom** Buch, Die Adresse **von meiner** Firma, usw.*).

Proper nouns take an *-s* suffix in the genitive (e.g., *Professor Pfrehms Hobbys, Mias Kinder, Boeings neues Flugzeug, usw.*), but if the proper noun ends in an *s* or *z*, there is no *-s* suffix. However, you add an apostrophe in writing (e.g., **Hans'** Bruder, **Fritz'** Schwester).

In addition to accusative, dative, and two-way prepositions, there are several **genitive prepositions** in German. Among the most commonly used are *während*, "during"; *(an)statt*, "instead of"; *trotz*, "despite/in spite of"; *laut*, "according to"; *wegen*, "because of"; *innerhalb*, "inside of/within"; and *außerhalb*, "outside of" (e.g., *Wir gehen **trotz des Regens** angeln*, "We're going fishing in spite of the rain"; ***Statt einer Mercedes S-Klasse** kaufe ich einen BMW M4*, "Instead of a Mercedes S-Class, I'm going to buy/I'm buying a BMW M4").

In informal speech, speakers tend to use the genitive prepositions *wegen*, *laut*, and *trotz* with the dative case (e.g., ***Wegen dem Regen*** *bleiben wir zu Hause*, "Because of the rain, we're going to stay/we're staying home"; ***Laut dem Polizeibericht*** *hast du nichts gesehen*, "According to the police report, you didn't see anything").

There are **two grammatical voices in German**: the **active** and the **passive**.

The **active voice** is a grammatical perspective for **describing states, actions, and events with a subject that's actively doing something—** which is expressed by conjugating a verb with a subject (e.g., ***Die Kinder waschen*** *den Hund*, "The kids are washing the dog").

The **passive voice** is a grammatical perspective for **describing that something is being done to someone or something** (e.g., ***Der Hund wird von den Kindern gewaschen***, "The dog is being washed by the kids").

The steps to constructing the passive in German include

making the object in the active voice the subject in the passive and **conjugating it with the helping verb** *werden*; and

deriving the past participle form of the main verb and **placing it at the end of the sentence:**

(dir. obj.)
Die Kinder waschen den Hund. (active voice)

Der Hund wird von den Kindern gewaschen. (passive voice)
subject

To express the agent in the passive voice, you use either the dative preposition *von* (for an **animate, initiator agent**):

Mein jüngerer Bruder renoviert dieses Haus.

Dieses Haus wird von meinem jüngeren Bruder renoviert.
[This house is getting / being renovated by my younger brother.]

Or the accusative preposition *durch* (for an **inanimate, instrument agent**):

Die Dorfbewohner werden jede Nacht
durch den heulenden Wind geweckt.
[The villagers get woke up every night by the howling wind.]

> Die Dorfbewohner werden jede Nacht
> **vom Bürgermeister** geweckt.
> [The villagers get woke up every night by the mayor.]

To express the passive with a modal verb, you conjugate the subject with the modal verb and then place a passive infinitive (i.e., the past participle of the main verb, followed by the helping verb *werden* in its infinitive form) at the end of the sentence:

1 subject	2 modal verb	3 time/manner/agent/place	4 passive infinitive
Dieser Rasen	muss	heute	gemäht werden.
This lawn	must	today	mowed become.

[This lawn should be mowed today.]

1 subject	2 modal verb	3 time/manner/agent/place	4 passive infinitive
Dieses Haus	kann	von meinem jüngeren Bruder	renoviert werden.
This house	can	by my younger brother	renovated become

[This can can be renovated by my younger brother.]

GRAMMAR

Definite Articles

Case	Singular			Plural
	Masc.	**Fem.**	**Neut.**	
Nominative (subject)	der	die	das	die
Accusative (direct object)	den	die	das	die
Dative (indirect object)	dem	der	dem	den +n
Genitive (possessive)	**des + (e)s**	**der**	**des + (e)s**	**der**

VOCABULARY

Nouns

-r Affe -n	ape / monkey
-r Brand ¨-e	fire
-r Briefträger -	postman
-r Dorfbewohner -	villager
-r Freundeskreis -e	circle of friends
-r Fuchs -es	fox

-r Hinweisschild -er	information sign
-r Kajak (*also* -s Kajak) -s	kayak
-r Kommentar -e	commentary / comment
-r Mitreisende -n	fellow traveler
-r Tintenfisch -e	octopus
-r Versuch -e	attempt / try
-e Bevölkerung -en	population
-e Briefträgerin -nen	postwoman
-e Kajaktour -en	kayak tour
-e Mahlzeit -en	meal
-e Schildkröte -n	turtle
-e Verfilmung -en	filming
-e Weltpolitik	world politics
-s Geschäft -e	store (i.e., place to buy things)
-s Gesetz -e	law
-s Sondermenü -s	specialty menu
-s Treffen -	meeting
-s Wasserfahrzeug -e	watercraft

Verbs

sich (hinten) anstellen	to get in line / queue up (i.e., at the back)
auftauchen	to emerge/appear/arise/surface
sich begnügen mit	to make do with
fressen	to eat (i.e., for animals)
heulen	to cry/howl
treffen (traf, getroffen)	to meet/hit (i.e., a target)
renovieren	to renovate
schleudern	to fling/toss/hurl
stattfinden	to take place
wecken	to wake

Adjectives and Adverbs

alles	everything
auf einmal	all of a sudden
furchtbar	terrible / horrible
heulend	crying / howling
heutig	today's / of today / contemporary
multikulturell	multicultural

Phrases

Fischsuppe norddeutscher Art	north-German-style fish soup
mitten ins/im Gesicht	in the middle of the face

A. Tintenfisch ins Gesicht

Als ein Tourist seine Kajaktour der neuseelischen Inseln genoss, bekam er die Überraschung seines Lebens. Auf einmal tauchte aus dem Wasser neben ihm eine Robbe mit einem Tintenfisch auf. Die Robbe schleuderte den Tintenfisch gegen das Wasserfahrzeug und traf den Kapitän des Kajaks mitten ins Gesicht.

B. Keine Wurst für Washington

Heute Nachmittag fand das erste offizielle Treffen zwischen der deutschen Bundeskanzlerin und dem amerikanischen Präsidenten statt. Während der Mahlzeit sprach die Kanzlerin über die Weltpolitik. Trumps Kommentare dazu waren: „Gibt es denn keine Wurst?" Leider gab es keine Wurst auf dem Sondermenü. Der US-Präsident musste sich mit Fischsuppe norddeutscher Art begnügen.

GRAMMAR EXERCISES

A. Fill in the blanks with the appropriate ending for the *der-* or *ein-* word.

1. Der Chef wusste die Telefonnummern sein_____ Angestellten nicht.

2. Ich habe alle Kontinente dies_____ Welt besucht.

3. Hast du schon den Namen d_____ Geschäft_____ vergessen?

4. Wann findet das Treffen unser_____ Eltern statt?

5. Das Auto d_____ Briefträger_____ ist kaputt.

B. Determine which of the genitive prepositions given in parentheses fits best in the blank and then fill in the ending for the *der-* or *ein-* word.

1. _____ d_____ Mahlzeit sehen uns die Affen mit gierigen Augen an. (während, statt, wegen)

2. Die Schildkröte kann _____ ihr_____ kurzen Beine schnell schwimmen. (statt, laut, trotz)

3. Der Bürgermeister wird _____ sein_____ Kommentar_____ über die Weltpolitik kritisiert. (wegen, außerhalb, laut)

4. Die Briefträgerin brachte ein großes Paket _____ ein_____ Umschlag_____. (laut, statt, wegen)

5. Wir müssen _____ dies_____ Kreis_____ bleiben. (laut, trotz, innerhalb)

C. Rewrite the following sentences in the passive voice.

1. Die Robbe trifft den Kajakfahrer mitten ins Gesicht.

   _____.

2. Sonntags schließt der Bürgermeister alle Geschäfte des Dorfes.

   _____

   _____.

3. Der Brand zerstört den ganzen Wald.

   _____.

4. Die klugen Füchse fressen die Hühner außerhalb des Zauns.

   _____

   _____.

5. Die Beamten besprechen die Weltpolitik.

   _____.

6. Unser Freundeskreis schließt ihn wegen seiner Meinungen aus.

   _____

   _____.

VOCABULARY EXERCISES

A. Which vocabulary word does each of the following sequences of words indicate?

1. zusammenkommen, sprechen, ein Wiedersehen _____

2. der Schauspieler, der Regisseur, die Kamera _____

3. der Mord, der Krieg, die Krankheit _____

4. mitkommen, der Begleiter, der Gefährte _____

5. der/das Kajak, das Boot, der Schoner _____

B. Fill in the blank with the appropriate vocabulary word. (Note: Don't forget to conjugate verbs and inflect adjectives.)

1. In der _____ Welt soll man wenigstens eine Fremdsprache lernen.

2. Laut dem _____ wird diese Gegend durch Video überwacht.

3. Wie bitte? Es gibt kein Fleisch! Tja …
   Dann muss ich mich mit Gemüse _____.

4. Wann _____ das nächste offizielle Treffen der Weltpolitiker _____?

5. Der Tintenfisch wird von der Robbe _____.

6. Wir wissen nicht, wo wir uns _____ sollen, denn wir sehen keine Schlange.

TRANSLATIONS

A. Translate from German into English.

1. Als ein Tourist seine Kajaktour der neuseelischen Inseln genoss, bekam er die Überraschung seines Lebens.

   _____
   _____.

2. Auf einmal tauchte aus dem Wasser neben ihm eine Robbe mit einem Tintenfisch auf.

   _____
   _____.

3. Die Robbe schleuderte den Tintenfisch gegen das Wasserfahrzeug—und traf den Kapitän des Kajaks mitten ins Gesicht.

   _____
   _____.

4. Heute Nachmittag fand das erste offizielle Treffen zwischen der deutschen Bundeskanzlerin und dem amerikanischen Präsidenten statt.

   _____
   _____.

5. Während der Mahlzeit sprach die Kanzlerin über die Weltpolitik.

   _____

   _____.

6. Trumps Kommentare dazu waren: „Gibt es denn keine Wurst?"

   _____

   _____?"

7. Leider gab es keine Wurst auf dem Sondermenü.

   _____

   _____.

8. Der US-Präsident musste sich mit Fischsuppe norddeutscher Art begnügen.

   _____

   _____.

B. Translate from English into German.

1. The wind was howling when they woke up.

   _____.

2. Our laws have to be written by an honest (male) politician.

   _____

   _____.

3. Your (formal) house is getting renovated by friendly fellow travelers.

   _____

   _____.

4. All of a sudden, the monkey gets hit in the middle of the face by a turtle.

   _____

   _____.

5. Everything can be destroyed by fire if the flames (*Flammen*) burn hot enough.

   _____

   _____.

Answers on page 261

THE SUBJUNCTIVE MOOD

SUMMARY

To express the passive voice in the past tense, you simply put the helping verb *werden* into its simple past form, *wurden* (e.g., *Der Hund **wurde** von den Kindern gewaschen*, "The dog **was/got/was being** washed by the kids"; *Die mutmaßlichen Diebe **wurden** von der Polizei verhört*, "The suspected thieves **were/got/were being** interrogated by the police").

In addition to the indicative and imperative moods, German has a third grammatical mood: the **subjunctive**.

Whereas the **indicative expresses reality and facts** (e.g., *Ich muss mein Zimmer aufräumen, wenn es unordentlich ist*, "I have to clean up my room whenever it's messy") and the imperative expresses commands (e.g., *Räum dein Zimmer auf, wenn es unordentlich ist!*, "Clean up your room if it's messy!"), you use the **subjunctive to express wishful thinking or information that's contrary to fact or hypothetical** (e.g., *Ich müsste Zimmer aufräumen, wenn es unordentlich wäre*, "I would have to clean up my room if it were messy").

Two common expressions with which speakers use the subjunctive are ***Wenn nur ...!*** exclamations (e.g., ***Wenn ich nur** eine Million Dollar **hätte!*** "If I only had a million dollars!") and ***An Ihrer/deiner/seiner/ihrer Stelle ...*** (e.g., *An Ihrer Stelle würde ich einen neuen Job suchen*, "In your place, I would look for a new job").

The verbs ***haben**, **sein**, **geben**, **wissen**,* and ***brauchen**,* as well as **the modal verbs, are commonly expressed in the subjunctive with a single-verb subjunctive form** (e.g., *Wenn es Frieden **gäbe**, **wären** wir glücklich*, "If there were peace, we would be happy"; *Ich **bräuchte** kein Geld, wenn ich Gold **hätte***, "I wouldn't need any money if I had gold"; *Du **wärest** froh, wenn du deinen Job kündigen **dürftest***, "You would be happy if you were allowed to quit your job").

You can express the subjunctive of all verbs with the **würden** + **infinitive** construction, which works similarly to modal verb constructions: You conjugate *würden* with the subject, leave the main verb in its infinitive form, and move it to the end of the sentence (e.g., *Ich **würde** öfter nach Österreich **reisen**, wenn ich genug Zeit und Geld hätte*, "I would travel to Austria more often if I had the time and money").

GRAMMAR

Conjugational Endings for Single-Verb Subjunctives

ich	**-e**	wir	**-en**
du	**-est**	ihr	**-et**
Sie	**-en**	Sie	**-en**
er/sie/es	**-e**	sie	**-en**

wären stem: wär-

ich wär**e**	wir wär**en**
du wär**est**	ihr wär**et**
Sie wär**en**	Sie wär**en**
er/sie/es wär**e**	sie wär**en**

gäben stem: gäb-

ich gäb**e**	wir gäb**en**
du gäb**est**	ihr gäb**et**
Sie gäb**en**	Sie gäb**en**
er / sie / es gäb**e**	sie gäb**en**

INDICATIVE	SUBJUNCTIVE
Wenn du willst… [If you want…]	Wenn du wolltest… [If you would want/wanted…]
Wenn du darfst… [If you are allowed …]	Wenn du dürftest… [If you would be allowed/were to be allowed…]
Wenn du kannst… [If you are able to/can…]	Wenn du könntest… [If you were able to/could…]

Wenn du magst... [If you like to...]	Wenn du möchtest... [If you would like to...]
Wenn du sollst... [If you are supposed to...]	Wenn du solltest... [If you were supposed to/ought to/ should]
Wenn du musst... [If you have to/must...]	Wenn du müsstest... [If you had to...]

VOCABULARY

Nouns

-r Bildschirm -e	screen (i.e., on a computer)
-r Dieb -e	thief
-r IT-Bereich -e	IT field/area
-r Klingelton ¨-e	ringtone
-r Laserkopierer -	laser copier
-r Lautsprecher -	(loud)speaker (i.e., for a stereo)
-r Link -s	link (i.e., on a website)
-r Plan ¨-e	plan
-r Polizist -en	police officer (m.)
-r Schreibtisch -e	desk
-r Zufall ¨-e	coincidence
-e Angst ¨-e	fear
-e Anwendung -en	application (i.e., for a computer)
-e Festplatte -n	hard drive
-e Freisprechanlage -n	hands-free device
-e Internetverbindung -en	internet connection
-e Polizistin -nen	police officer (f.)
-s Benutzerhandbuch ¨-er	user manual
-s Gerät -e	device
-s Smartphone -s	smartphone
-s Teil -e	thing / piece / part (i.e., general part)
-s WLAN -s	Wi-Fi

Verbs

aufgeben (gab ... auf, aufgegeben)	to give up
anklicken	to click (on) (i.e., an internet link)
festlegen	to set/schedule/determine
hochladen (lud ... hoch, hochgeladen)	to upload

kichern	to chuckle/giggle
leisten	to achieve/accomplish/perform
nachschauen	to look up (i.e., a word, figure, or fact)
prahlen	boast, brag
runterladen (lud ... runter, runtergeladen)	to download
speichern	to save (i.e., a file or document)
verpassen	to miss (i.e., a train or target)
vorkommen (kam ... vor, ist vorgekommen)	to happen/seem/appear
verhören	to interrogate

Adjectives and Adverbs

derjenige/diejenige/diejenigen	the one (m.)/the one (f.)/the ones
drahtlos	wireless
dramatisch	dramatic
eigentlich	actually
einfach	simple / simply
endlich	finally
heutzutage	these days
hochmodern	ultramodern / state of the art
jetzig	present / current
mutmaßlich	suspected / alleged
noch	still / yet
sogenannt	so-called
wasserdicht	waterproof / sealed tight
witzig	funny / humorous
ziemlich	considerable / considerably

Phrases

Angst haben	to be afraid/have fear
Da liegst du/liegen Sie falsch!	You're wrong!
Ich kann es kaum fassen!	I can barely believe it!
(Haben Sie) Keine Angst.	Don't be afraid.
Komm schon!	Come on!
Kommen wir zur Sache.	Let's get to the point.
Kommt das Ihnen bekannt vor?	Does this/that seem familiar to you?
selektives Hören	selective listening
So ein Zufall!	What a coincidence!
so was	something like this/that
Wenn nur ...!	If only ...!
Wie schade!	What a pity! / What a bummer!

A. Ralf's New Smartphone

RALF: Ach ... Komm schon! So schwer kann es doch nicht sein ...

MIA: Na? Wie geht's mit dem neuen, hochmodernen Smartphone?

RALF: Wenn ich nur so smart wäre wie dieses Gerät!

MIA: Was ist los?

RALF: Ich versuche, den Klingelton festzulegen.

MIA: Hast du im Benutzerhandbuch nachgeschaut?

RALF: Ach. Wer liest denn noch heutzutage das Benutzerhandbuch?

MIA: Na ja. Diejenigen, die ihr neues Smartphone eigentlich benutzen wollten ...

RALF: Ach. Mist! Ich geb's auf ... Was ist denn so witzig?

MIA: Nichts.

RALF: Doch. Sonst würdest du nicht kichern.

MIA: Ich finde nur, es wäre schön, wenn du das teure Teil auch benutzen könntest.

RALF: Wenn es ein Easyphone gäbe, würde ich *das* viel lieber als ein sogenanntes Smartphone nehmen.

MIA: Tja. So was gibt es leider nicht.

RALF: Darum sage ich das im Konjunktiv: Wenn es ein Easyphone gäbe ...

MIA: Aber Ralf. Wenn du ein Easyphone hättest, dürftest du nicht mehr prahlen.

RALF: Wenigstens müsste ich kein Benutzerhandbuch lesen.

MIA: Ja. Wenn wir alle nur so smart wären wie Ralf Gruber ...

B. Examples of the Subjunctive Mood

Ich würde ein neues Notebook kaufen, wenn es nicht so viel kosten würde.

Wenn die IT-Leute endlich kommen und meine kaputte Festplatte reparieren würden, würde ich die neue Anwendung testen, speichern, und hochladen.

Wenn die neuen Manager wirklich wollten, dass wir mehr leisten, sollten sie endlich mal einen neuen Laserkopierer kaufen. Dann könnten wir Dokus schneller kopieren und müssten nicht alle zwei Tage die IT-Leute anrufen, um das jetzige Gerät zu reparieren.

GRAMMAR EXERCISES

A. Rewrite the following passive sentences in the past tense.

1. Mein Wagen wird von meinem Schwager kostenlos repariert.

   _____.

2. Ganze Städte werden durch den Sandsturm vergraben.

   _____.

3. Warum wirst du von der Polizei verhört?

   _____?

4. Innerhalb einer halben Stunde wird die Datei hochgeladen.

   _____
   _____.

5. Um wie viel Uhr werdet ihr am Flughafen vom Limousinenfahrer abgeholt?

   _____
   _____?

Rudi Ziegelstein has received some emails from fans seeking his advice in certain
matters of their lives. Read the following emails and
1) identify all the subjunctive forms,
2) give the corresponding indicative infinitive of each single-verb subjunctive form,
3) and determine which advice would be most appropriate for Rudi to respond
with. (Note: You will need to use a dictionary to look up unfamiliar words.)

i. Email: Genervt in der Arbeit

Lieber Rudi,

Ich arbeite als Anwaltsgehilfin in einer großen Kanzlei. Über den Gehalt und die
Arbeitsstunden würde ich mich nie beschweren. Aber seit einiger Zeit verärgert
mich eines insbesondere, und zwar: jemand klaut meine Sachen! Zuerst war es
das Ladegerät für mein Handy. Letzten Monat wurden meine USB-Kabel und
Stromkabel power gestohlen. Neulich verschwand sogar mein Mittagsessen aus
dem Büro-Kühlschrank!

Ich habe keine Ahnung, wer es sein könnte, denn es gibt so viele Mitarbeiter.

Wenn es dieses Problem nicht gäbe, wäre das die perfekte Arbeit. Deshalb
frage ich Sie: Was würden Sie tun, wenn Sie an meiner Stelle wären? Würden
Sie schweigen? Würden Sie mit Ihrem Vorgesetztem reden? Wollten Sie einen
Privatdetektiv engagieren? Ich bitte um Ihren Rat.

—Genervt in der Arbeit

1. The subjunctive forms:

_____ , _____ , _____

_____ , _____ , _____

_____ , _____ , _____

2. Indicative infinitive of single-verb subjunctive forms:

_____ , _____ , _____

_____ , _____ , _____

_____ , _____ , _____

3. Most appropriate advice:

_____

_____ .

ii. **Email: Gestalkt von eigenen Eltern**

Lieber Rudi,

Ich bin zwanzig Jahre alt und studiere Sanskrit und altindische Dichtung. Ich wohne noch bei meinen Eltern, und im Grunde genommen finde ich diese Lebenssituation ganz günstig. Ich zahle keine Miete und im Kühlschrank gibt es immer etwas zum Knabbern.

Mein Problem ist meine Eltern. Sie sind besessen davon, wo ich bin und was ich mache. Meine Mutter kontrolliert mein Facebook mehrmals am Tag, und mein Vater hat die neuste Überwachungssoftware auf meinem Handy installiert. Damit kann er mich jede Zeit orten.

Es kommt mir vor, als hätte ich zwei Stalker. Ich bin ein erwachsener Mann und brauche meine Privatsphäre! Mit anderen Worten: ich benötige dringend Ihren Rat. Was würden Sie an meiner Stelle tun?

—Gestalkt von eigenen Eltern

1. The subjunctive forms:

_____ , _____ , _____

_____ , _____ , _____

_____ , _____ , _____

2. Indicative infinitive of single-verb subjunctive forms:

_____ , _____ , _____

_____ , _____ , _____

_____ , _____ , _____

3. Most appropriate advice:

_____

_____.

B. Rewrite the following sentences in the subjunctive mood using either the single-verb subjunctive forms or the *würde* + infinitive construction.

1. Wenn du die Antworten weißt, musst du sie mir sagen.

_____

_____.

2. Der Polizist verhört den mutmaßlichen Verbrecher, wenn er genug Beweisstücke hat.

_____

_____.

3. Sie können im IT-Bereich arbeiten, wenn Sie etwas von Computern verstehen.

_____

_____.

4. An eurer Stelle lerne ich Deutsch.

_____.

5. Das ist großartig, wenn es ein Benutzerhandbuch gibt.

_____

_____.

VOCABULARY EXERCISES

A. Determine which word does not fit in with the other words in each sequence.

1. ◯ der IT-Bereich, ◯ hochmodern, ◯ ziemlich

2. ◯ kichern, ◯ witzig, ◯ verhören

3. ◯ die Angst, ◯ einfach, ◯ gefährlich

4. ◯ der Dieb, ◯ die Anwendung, ◯ die Festplatte

5. ◯ leisten, ◯ die Arbeit, ◯ das Gerät

B. Fill in the blank with the appropriate vocabulary word.

1. A: Das ist unsere letzte Lektion.
   B: Mensch! _____!

2. Doch! Deutsch ist nicht schwer. Es ist ganz _____.

3. Ihr neuer Computer steht dort auf Ihrem _____.

4. Ach Mist! Ich bin zehn Minuten zu spät gekommen. Ich habe den
   Zug _____.

5. Ich habe eine neue _____ für meinen
   Computer runtergeladen.

6. Man soll immer eine_____ benutzen, wenn man Auto
   fährt und telefonieren will.

TRANSLATIONS

A. Translate from German into English.

1. Wer liest denn noch heutzutage das Benutzerhandbuch?

   _____?

2. Diejenigen, die ihr neues Smartphone eigentlich benutzen wollten.

   _____

   _____.

3. Ich finde nur, es wäre schön, wenn du das teure Teil auch benutzen könntest.

   _____

   _____.

4. Wenn du ein Easyphone hättest, dürftest du nicht mehr prahlen.

   _____

   _____.

5. Wenigstens müsste ich kein Benutzerhandbuch lesen.

   _____.

6. Wenn es ein Easyphone gäbe, würde ich DAS viel lieber als ein sogenanntes Smartphone nehmen.

_____

_____.

B. Translate from English into German.

1. If your (informal, singular) smartphone were waterproof, I would throw it into the ocean.

_____

_____.

2. Our child would be afraid if there were (male) police.

_____.

3. In her place, I would actually move to Germany if I wanted to learn German.

_____

_____.

4. We would be allowed to buy an expensive, new hard drive if we had enough money.

_____

_____.

5. How many applications would you guys (informal) have to download if the (female) boss got you guys new devices?

_____

_____?

Answers on page 261

EINE REISE NACH WITTENBERG UND BERLIN

SUMMARY

The subjunctive mood is also used to give an added degree of politeness to commands or requests (e.g., *Würden Sie mir den Salz reichen?*, "Would you pass me the salt"?; *Dürfte ich um Ihre Meinung bitten?*, "Might I be allowed to ask your opinion?"; *Könntest du mir einen Gefallen tun?*, "Could you do me a favor?").

To express the subjunctive mood in the past tense, you use the subjunctive forms of the helping verb *hätten* or *wären*, conjugate it with the subject, put the main verb in its past participle form, and move it to the end of the sentence. In other words, you construct the sentence just like you would for the present perfect tense, only you use *hätten* or *wären* as the auxiliary verb (e.g., *Wir wären mit euch nach Berlin geflogen, wenn wir genug Geld gehabt hätten*, "We would have flown to Berlin with you guys if we had had enough money"; *Ich hätte dich angerufen, wenn ich deine Nummer gewusst hätte*, "I would have called you if I had known your number").

Although you can express the future tense using the present tense and an adverb (e.g., *Kommenden Sommer fahre ich nach Berlin*, "This coming summer I'm flying to Berlin"; *Sie hat gesagt, dass sie mich morgen anruft*, "She said that she's going to/she'll call me tomorrow"), **speakers also express the future tense and the probability that an event will happen by using *werden* as an auxiliary verb** (e.g., *Wir werden schon da sein, wenn du ankommst*, "We will already be there when you arrive"; *In zwanzig Jahren wird er Präsident der Vereigneten Staaten sein*, "In twenty years he will be president of the United States").

VOCABULARY

Nouns

-r Bezirk -e	district / area (i.e., of a city)
-r Experte -n	expert (m.)
-r Lebensgefährte -n	life partner (m.)
-r Priester -	priest
-r Salami (*also* die)	salami
-r Schinken -	ham
-r Staatssicherheitsdienst	state security service of East Germany
-r Vorschlag ¨-e	suggestion
-r Vorwurf ¨-e	reproach / accusation
-e Bootsfahrt -en	boat ride
-e Bundesautobahn -en (BAB)	German autobahn
-e Expertin -en	expert (f.)
-e Geschwindigkeitsbegrenzung -en	speed limit
-e Höchstgeschwindigkeit -en	maximum speed limit
-e Höflichkeit	politeness
-e Glaskuppel -n	glass dome
-e Kirche -n	church
-e Kirchentür -en	church door
-e Landeshauptstadt ¨-e	nation capital
-e Lebensgefährtin -nen	life partner (f.)
-e Putenbrust ¨-e	turkey breast
-e Richtgeschwindigkeit -en	recommended speed limit
-e Schiffstour -en	boat tour
-e Spreefahrt -en	boat ride on the Spree River
-e Treppe -m	step
-e Überstunde -n (often only in the plural)	overtime (i.e., work)
-e Verkehrspolizei	traffic police
-s Blaulicht -er	police (literally "blue light")
-s Brandenburger Tor	Brandenburg Gate
-s Holocaust-Mahnmal	Holocaust memorial
-s Reiseziel -e	travel destination
-s Tempolimit -s	speed limit
-s Erlebnis -se	experience
-s Verkehrszeichen -s	traffic sign

Verbs

anschlagen (schlug ... an, angeschlagen)	to post/put up (i.e., on a wall, board, etc.)
bemerken	to notice
besichtigen	to view/survey/inspect/visit
besteigen (bestieg, bestiegen)	to climb/scale
bereuen	to regret
dauern	to take/last (i.e., time)
empfehlen (empfahl, empfohlen)	to recommend
enthalten (enthielt, enthalten)	to contain/hold
ermorden	to murder
reichen	to hand/reach
zerstören	to destroy

Adjectives and Adverbs

ähnlich (wie)	similar (to)
berühmt	famous
darüber hinaus	moreover / what's more
dort drüben	over there
ermordet	murdered
gefährlich	dangerous
geteilt	separated
gewöhnlich	normal
herrlich	beautiful
höchstens	at (the) most
öffentlich	public(ly)
praktisch	practical(ly)
schwierig	difficult
toll	great / awesome
übermorgen	the day after tomorrow
unbeschreiblich	indescribable
unglaublich	unbelievable
ursprünglich	original
unvergesslich	unforgettable
vielschichtig	multilayered / multifaceted
vorletzt-	next to last
wahrscheinlich	probably
weiter	further
zulässig	permissible / acceptable / allowed

Phrases

Auf keinen Fall!	No way!
beim nächsten Besuch	on the next visit
-e Bundesrepublik Deutschlands (BRD)	the German Federal Republic
Da vorne links	up there on the left
das geteilte Deutschland	Divided Germany
-e Deutsche Demokratische Republik (DDR)	the German Democratic Republic
Es ist kaum zu glauben.	It's hard to believe.
den Mund halten	to keep your mouth shut
(sich) Vorwürfe machen	to reproach (oneself)
Wie die Zeit verfliegt!	How (the) time flies!

TEXTS

A. Ralf and Mia discuss their travel plans to northern Germany

MIA: Ich finde es toll, dass wir endlich eine Reise in den Osten machen.

RALF: Ja, ich wollte schon immer mal die Stadt Wittenberg sehen.

MIA: Martin Luther hat dort gewohnt, oder?

RALF: Richtig. Der offizielle Name der Stadt ist eigentlich „Lutherstadt Wittenberg."

MIA: Gut. Wir fahren nach Wittenberg. Aber, dürfte ich einen Vorschlag machen?

RALF: Natürlich.

MIA: Wir fahren mit dem Auto.

RALF: Auf der Autobahn?

MIA: Ja. Wir nehmen die A9. Es geht praktisch geradeaus von Ingolstadt nach Wittenberg.

RALF: Stimmt. Das wird höchstens fünf oder fünfeinhalb Stunden brauchen ... Ja, ich finde das eine gute Idee.

MIA: Und Berlin ist nur eine Stunde weiter ...

RALF: Echt? Na ja ...

MIA: Ralf, würdest du mich auch nach Berlin fahren?

RALF: Für meine Prinzessin: alles. Also dann. Die Reise ist geplant: zuerst nach Wittenberg, und dann nach Berlin.

MIA: Toll! Du wirst es nicht bereuen. Das wird eine unvergessliche Reise werden.

B. Ralf and Mia in Wittenberg

MIA: Ist das die Schlosskirche?

RALF: Ja. Hier hat Martin Luther seine Thesen angeschlagen.

MIA: Und wo ist die berühmte Kirchentür?

RALF: Ich glaube, sie ist dort drüben. Komm. Wir schauen sie uns an … Das ist sie: die berühmte „Thesentür."

MIA: Schön. Sie ist aus Bronze.

RALF: Richtig. Und sie enthält den ganzen Text von Luthers Thesen.

MIA: Diese ist nicht die originale Kirchentür, oder?

RALF: Nein. Die ursprüngliche Tür war aus Holz und wurde in einem Brand zerstört.

MIA: Schade. Und wie viele Thesen waren es?

RALF: Fünfundneunzig.

MIA: Na ja. Er hatte bestimmt viel zu sagen.

RALF: Ja. Und damals war es gefährlich, öffentlich gegen die katholische Kirche zu sprechen.

MIA: Was hättest du gemacht, wenn du damals Priester gewesen wärest?

RALF: Ich? Na ja … Ganz ehrlich: Ich hätte wahrscheinlich keine fünfundneunzig Thesen geschrieben.

MIA: Echt? Du hättest einfach den Mund gehalten?

RALF: (Seufzt) Leider … Ich hätte zu viel Angst gehabt.

MIA: Mach dir keine Vorwürfe. Ich weiß selber nicht, was ich gemacht hätte.

C. Ralf and Mia in Berlin

MIA: Ist das nicht wunderschön? Diese Schifftour war eine tolle Idee.

RALF: Stimmt. Das Wetter ist herrlich.

MIA: Schau mal. Da vorne links. Das ist der Berliner Dom.

RALF: Sehr schön. Ist er alt?

MIA: Eigentlich nicht. Ich glaube, der ist aus dem zwanzigsten Jahrhundert.

RALF: Echt? Das ist nicht so alt.

MIA: Und siehst du das große Gebäude mit der Glaskuppel?

RALF: Ja.

MIA: Du weißt, was das ist, oder?

RALF: Natürlich. Das ist unser Reichstagsgebäude. Ich würde gern die Glaskuppel besichtigen.

MIA: Es gibt sogar Treppen, und man kann die Kuppel besteigen.

RALF: Toll!

MIA: Das werden wir beim nächsten Besuch tun.

GRAMMAR EXERCISES

A. Use the subjunctive mood to express the following utterances in a more polite manner.

1. Bestell mir ein Weißbier mit Rotkohl.

   _____

2. Wollen Sie mitkommen?

   _____

3. Dürfen wir diesen Sommer bei euch wohnen?

   _____

4. Kannst du das wiederholen?

   _____

5. Hören Sie damit auf!

   _____

6. Seien Sie leiser!

   _____

B. Rewrite the following sentences in the past tense of the subjunctive.

1. Wenn wir klug wären, würden wir Deutsch lernen.

   _____.

2. Ihr hättet mehr Geld, wenn ihr öfter Überstunden (*overtime*) machen würdet.

   _____

   _____.

3. Wenn ich nur die Glaskuppel besteigen würde!

   _____!

4. Wenn mein Mann langsamer fahren würde, würde er das Verkehrszeichen bemerken (*to notice*).

   _____

   _____.

5. Würdest du die Putenbrust probieren, wenn ich sie empfehlen würde?

   _____

   _____?

C. Rewrite the following sentences in the future tense.

1. Wo wohnst du im Jahr 2030?

   _____?

2. Beim nächsten Besuch besichtigen wir das Brandenburg Tor.

   _____

   _____.

3. Wann unternehmt ihr eine Reise durch die deutsche Sprache?

   _____

   _____?

4. Übermorgen (*the day after tomorrow*) kommt sie mit dem Zug von Berlin an.

   _____

   _____.

5. Eines Tages bereuen Sie diese Entscheidung.

   _____.

VOCABULARY EXERCISES

A. Determine which vocabulary word the following antonyms are describing.

1. leicht, problemlos, unkompliziert   _____

2. kreieren, bauen, schaffen   _____

3. Befehl, Anordnung, Kommando   _____

4. kopiert, imitiert, nachgebildet   _____

5. geheim, diskret, hinter verschlossenen Türen _____

6. anders, abweichend, verschieden   _____

7. einfach, komplexlos   _____

8. ignorieren, übersehen, nicht beachten   _____

B. Fill in the blank with the appropriate vocabulary word.

1. In meinem Geschichtekurs haben wir über _____
    gelernt; also, als es noch die DDR und BRD gab.

2. Nein. Ich rufe dich nicht morgen an, sondern _____;
    also, in zwei Tagen.

3. Das ist leider nicht _____ . Das heißt, Sie dürfen das
    nicht machen.

4. Mein Schwager ist Muslim und darf keinen _____
    essen.

5. Die Schlosskirche in Wittenberg _____ den
    ursprünglichen Text der fünfundneunzig Thesen, die Martin Luther geschrieben
    und angeschlagen hat.

6. David Hasselhoff ist in Deutschland ziemlich _____;
    das heißt, fast alle Leute kennen seine Musik.

TRANSLATIONS

A. Translate from German into English.

1. Ich wollte schon immer mal die Stadt Wittenberg sehen.

   _____.

2. Du wirst es nicht bereuen, weil das eine unvergessliche Reise sein wird.

   _____
   _____.

3. Die ursprüngliche Tür war aus Holz und wurde in einem Brand zerstört.

   _____
   _____.

4. Damals war es gefährlich, öffentlich gegen die Katholische Kirche zu sprechen.

   _____
   _____.

5. Mach dir keine Vorwürfe. Ich weiß selber nicht, was ich gemacht hätte, wenn ich im sechszehnten Jahrhundert Priester gewesen wäre.

   _____
   _____.

6. Darüber hinaus möchte ich einen Vorschlag machen: Würdet ihr mich heute Abend mit eurem Auto abholen?

   _____
   _____?

B. Translate from English into German.

1. I would have viewed the glass dome of the Reichstag building if I would have traveled to Berlin.

   _____
   _____.

2. The trip to Munich will only take six hours if we can book a flight without a stopover.

   _____
   _____.

3. My wife would have gotten up this morning at six if I hadn't snored (*schnarchen*) so loudly.

   _____

   _____.

4. What is your (informal, singular) daughter going to be (i.e., professionally) in ten years?

   _____

   _____?

5. No way! The traffic police would have never caught (*erwischen*) us if we would have driven too fast.

   _____

   _____.

Answers on page 263

OUR JOURNEY: THE END OR JUST THE BEGINNING?

SUMMARY

Does *die dreißigste Lektion in Ihrer Reise durch die deutsche Sprache* mark the end or just the beginning of your journey to learn German?

Although your journey through this course concludes here, the real journey is what comes next: going back over the material covered in this course; practicing the words, sounds, and grammatical structures you've learned; and expanding—through your own studies—your vocabulary, listening comprehension, and speaking skills.

The five dialogues in this final lesson showcase many of the language skills that you've learned in this course—namely, how to

- express actions in three different grammatical tenses (i.e., present, past, and future) with a variety of verbs (i.e., main, modal, stem-vowel-changing, and separable-prefix verbs);
- express actions in three different grammatical moods (i.e., indicative, imperative, and subjunctive);
- express actions in two different grammatical voices (i.e., active and passive);
- express grammatical relations among subjects and objects using all four of German's grammatical cases (i.e., nominative, accusative, dative, and genitive); and
- construct open- and closed-ended questions as well as a variety of clauses (i.e., main, relative, and subordinate clauses and indirect questions).

VOCABULARY

Nouns

-r Aufzug ¨-e	elevator
-r Bräutigam -e	groom
-r Finanzberater -	financial adviser (m.)
-r Jude -n	Jewish male
-r Kurs -e	course (i.e., in school)
-r Nachbar -n	neighbor (m.)
-r Vorfahre -n	ancestor (m.)
-r Weg -e	way (i.e., direction)
-e Braut ¨-e	bride
-e Familiengeschichte -n	family history
-e -r Finanzberaterin -nen	financial adviser (f.)
-e Freizeit	free time
-e Geschichte -n	story / history
-e Hochzeitsfeier -n	wedding celebration/reception
-e Informatik	computer science
-e Jüdin -nen	Jewish female
-e Nachbarin -en	neighbor (f.)
-e Studentenstadt ¨-e	city with a lot of university students
-e Vorfahrin -nen	ancestor (f.)
-s Endziel -e	ultimate/final goal
-s Gespräch -e	conversation
-s Internat -e	boarding school
-s Schloss ¨-er	castle / lock
-s Sprachtalent -e	talent for languages
-s Thema (die Themen)	topic / theme (the topics / themes)
-s Wohnheim -e	residential home / dorm

Verbs

aufschreiben (schrieb ... auf, ist aufgeschrieben)	to write down/out
aussteigen (stieg ... aus, ist ausgestiegen)	to get out (i.e., of a traveling vehicle)
sich bemühen	to try/endeavor
einbiegen (bog ... ein, ist eingebogen)	to turn (i.e., onto a street)
einsteigen (stieg ... ein, ist eingestiegen)	to get on (i.e., a traveling vehicle)
eintippen	to put/type into (i.e., a device)
sich auf etwas freuen	to look forward to something

gestehen (gestand, gestanden)	to admit/confess
heiraten	to marry
hochfahren (fuhr ... hoch, ist hochgefahren)	to travel up(ward)
hochsteigen (stieg ... hoch, ist hochgestiegen)	to climb up(ward)
sich interessieren für	to be interested in
programmieren	to program (i.e., a computer)
rechnen	to calculate/do math
sich schämen	to feel ashamed/embarrassed
schicken	to send
sterben (starb, ist gestorben)	to die
unterbrechen (unterbrach, unterbrochen)	to interrupt
verpflegen	to feed/supply with food
zeigen	to show
ziehen (zog, ist gezogen)	to move (i.e., from one place to another)

Adjectives and Adverbs

allergisch (gegen)	allergic
andersrum	the other way around / vice versa
behilflich	helpful
Das ist erst der Anfang!	That/This is just the beginning!
derselbe/dieselbe/dasselbe/dieselben	the same (m./f./n./pl.)
einmal	once
irisch	Irish
komisch	strange / weird
lebensverändernd	life-changing
mütterlicherseits	on the mother's side
polnisch	Polish
sogar	even (e.g., "Even I went.")
schottisch	Scottish
stundenlang	for hours
väterlicherseits	on the father's side

Phrases

Das ist keine schlechte Idee.	That's not a bad idea.
Das tut mir sehr leid.	I'm very sorry to hear that.
Das waren schwere Zeiten.	Those were hard times.
ein Kind bekommen	to have a child
Es ist alles wieder bestens.	Everything is just fine again.
etwas typisch Norddeutsches	something typically north German

Gern geschehen.	My pleasure. / You're welcome.
Her mit ...! / Her damit!	Come on ...! / Bring it on!
Nichts zu danken.	Don't mention it.
Schön wär's!	As if! / If only! / I wish!
Verzeihung.	Pardon.
Wir sind endlich angekommen!	We have finally arrived.

TEXTS

A. Professor Pfrehm and Colin at the Wedding (Part One)

PROF. P:	Woher in Deutschland kommen Sie?
COLIN:	Ach so. Sie sprechen Deutsch.
PROF. P:	Ja, ich lerne es in meiner Freizeit.
COLIN:	Seit wie lange lernen Sie Deutsch?
PROF. P:	Seit einem Jahr.
COLIN:	Meine Güte! Sie sind ein Sprachtalent!
PROF. P:	Ich mache einen Videokurs.
COLIN:	Welchen Videokurs machen Sie?
PROF. P:	Er ist von The Great Courses. Er heißt: *Learning German*.
COLIN:	Schön. Meine Freundin möchte Französisch lernen. Gibt es auch Videokurse dafür?
PROF. P:	Ja. Du sollst ihr einen Videokurs zum nächsten Geburtstag schenken.
COLIN:	Gute Idee.
PROF. P:	Sagen Sie mal, können wir „du" sagen?
COLIN:	Gerne. Ich heiße Colin.
PROF. P:	Ich heiße James.
COLIN:	Schön, dich kennenzulernen, James.
PROF. P:	Kommst du aus Nord- oder Süddeutschland?
COLIN:	Aus Norddeutschland.
PROF. P:	Ich will nächstes Jahr nach Deutschland reisen.
COLIN:	Echt? Dann sollst du nach Hannover fahren. Du kannst meine Eltern besuchen.
PROF. P:	Wirklich?

COLIN: Natürlich. Isst du gern?

PROF. P: Oh ja. Ich esse sehr gern.

COLIN: Perfekt. Meine Mutter kocht dir etwas typisch Norddeutsches.

PROF. P: Super!

COLIN: Und du? Woher kommst du?

PROF. P: Ich komme aus Oregon, aber ich wohne jetzt in New York.

COLIN: Fährst du oft nach Oregon?

PROF. P: Ich fliege nur einmal im Jahr nach Hause. Ich kann mir nur die eine Reise leisten.

COLIN: Du sprichst wirklich gut Deutsch!

PROF. P: Danke. Ich bemühe mich sehr.

B. Professor Pfrehm and Colin at the Wedding (Part Two)

PROF. P: Sag mal, kennst du die Braut oder den Bräutigam?

COLIN: Den Bräutigam. Und du?

PROF. P: Ich kenne ihn auch.

COLIN: Ach so.

PROF. P: Wir haben in derselben Straße gewohnt, als wir klein waren.

COLIN: Schön. Ihr wart Nachbarn?

PROF. P: Ja. Wir sind auch in die gleichen Schulen gegangen. Und wo hast du ihn kennengelernt?

COLIN: Ich habe ihn erst an der Uni kennengelernt. Wir hatten viele Kurse zusammen.

PROF. P: Hast du auch Informatik studiert?

COLIN: Ja.

PROF. P: Und arbeitest du jetzt im Technologiebereich?

COLIN: Nein. Ich bin Finanzberater.

PROF. P: Ach so! Das ist interessant. Warum bist du Finanzberater geworden?

COLIN: Es war so. Ich mochte Mathe und konnte immer gut rechnen. Aber ich wollte nicht stundenlang vor dem Computer sitzen und programmieren.

PROF. P: Na ja. Das kann ich verstehen.

C. Professor Pfrehm and a Woman in Marburg

PROF. P: Entschuldigung. Könnten Sie mir den Weg zum Schloss zeigen?

WOMAN: Klar. Gehen Sie hier geradeaus, bis Sie zum Aufzug kommen. Fahren Sie mit dem Aufzug hoch, und dann gehen Sie rechts in die Reitgasse—

PROF. P: Verzeihung. Dürfte ich kurz unterbrechen?

WOMAN: Bitte.

PROF. P: Haben Sie "Aufzug" gesagt?

WOMAN: Ja. Der Oberstadt-Aufzug.

PROF. P: Ach so. Ich könnte auch zu Fuß gehen.

WOMAN: Ja, aber es wäre am schnellsten, wenn Sie mit dem Aufzug fahren würden.

PROF. P: Ich verstehe.

WOMAN: Nehmen Sie also den Oberstadt-Aufzug. Und wenn Sie oben aussteigen, gehen Sie nach rechts in die Reitgasse. Dann biegen Sie links in den Schloßsteig ein.

PROF. P: Also, das wäre links, dann rechts ...

WOMAN: Andersrum. Zuerst rechts in die Reitgasse, und dann links in den Schloßsteig.

PROF. P: Alles klar.

WOMAN: Der Schloßsteig bringt Sie zur Schloßtreppe. Steigen Sie die Treppen hoch und dann kommen Sie in die Landgraf-Phillip-Straße. Bleiben Sie in der Landgraf Phillip-Straße und in ein paar hundert Metern kommen Sie direkt zum Schloss.

PROF. P: Würden Sie das bitte aufschreiben?

WOMAN: Gerne. Hätten Sie etwas zum Schreiben?

PROF. P: Nein. Hmm ...

WOMAN: Hätten Sie ein Handy? Ich könnte es da eintippen.

PROF. P: Ja. Bitte schön. Und vielen Dank!

WOMAN: Nichts zu danken.

D. Professor Pfrehm and Ralf Discuss Family History

PROF. P: Guten Tag, Herr Gruber!

RALF: Hallo, Professor Pfrehm.

PROF. P: Ich freue mich, dass wir heute über unsere Familien sprechen.

RALF: Sehr gerne.

PROF. P: Also dann. Was können Sie mir über Ihre Familiengeschichte erzählen?

RALF: Also. Meine Großeltern väterlicherseits waren aus Augsburg. Mein Großvater hat als Architekt gearbeitet und meine Großmutter war Hausfrau. Mein Vater wurde schon mit sechs ins Internat nach München geschickt.

PROF. P: Was ist ein Internat?

RALF: Das ist eine Schule, die auch Wohnheime hat. Die Kinder wohnen dort und werden von der Schule verpflegt.

PROF. P: Ach so. Auf Englisch sagen wir „boarding school."

RALF: Und Ihre Familie?

PROF. P: Also, meine Großmutter mütterlicherseits hatte schottische und irische Vorfahren.

RALF: Und Ihr Großvater?

PROF. P: Nun, das ist eine schwierige Geschichte.

RALF: Ich würde sie gern hören, wenn Sie nichts dagegen haben.

PROF. P: Nein. Ich habe nichts dagegen. Also, mein Großvater mütterlicherseits, er war polnischer Jude. Im Jahr 1929 hat er seine Kusine geheiratet, und sie haben eine Tochter bekommen. Sie hat Irene geheißen.

RALF: Und das war Ihre Mutter?

PROF. P: Eigentlich nicht. 1942 wurden Irene und ihre Mutter nach Treblinka gebracht. Dort sind sie gestorben.

RALF: Das tut mir sehr leid.

PROF. P: Ja. Das waren sehr schwere Zeiten.

RALF: Und, wann hat Ihr Großvater dann Ihre Großmutter kennengelernt?

PROF. P:	Erst nach dem Krieg, in Amerika. Sie haben geheiratet und sind nach Kalifornien gezogen. Dort haben sie 1948 meine Mutter bekommen.
RALF:	Mensch. Das ist eine turbulente Familiengeschichte.
PROF. P:	Ja, das ist sie. Also dann. Ich danke Ihnen für das Gespräch, Herr Gruber.
RALF:	Bitte sehr, Professor Pfrehm. Auf Wiedersehen!
PROF. P:	Wiedersehen!

E. Professor Pfrehm and Mia Discuss Learning a Foreign Language

PROF. P:	Grüß Gott, Frau Gruber.
MIA:	Hallo, Professor Pfrehm. Ich habe mich sehr auf unser Gespräch gefreut.
PROF. P:	Das freut mich.
MIA:	Wir wollten über das Thema Fremdsprachenlernen reden, oder?
PROF. P:	Genau. Für welche Fremdsprachen interessieren Sie sich?
MIA:	Also, seit ich ein Teenager war, versuche ich es mit Französisch.
PROF. P:	Na ja. Da kann ich Ihnen behilflich sein. Kaufen Sie den Great Courses Videokurs *Learning French: A Rendezvous with French-Speaking Cultures*.
MIA:	Hmm … Das ist keine schlechte Idee …
PROF. P:	Sie können sogar den Kurs zusammen mit Ralf machen.
MIA:	Na ja … Schön wär's.
PROF. P:	Warum?
MIA:	Er sagt immer: "Ich bin allergisch gegen Fremdsprachen."
PROF. P:	Wirklich? Das ist aber komisch.
MIA:	Einmal hat er mir sogar gesagt: „Mia, Ich muss dir was gestehen. Ich habe Angst vor Fremdsprachen."
PROF. P:	Na so was … An Ihrer Stelle würde ich nicht auf ihn warten. Downloaden Sie den Kurs und fangen Sie damit an.
MIA:	Mache ich. Ich danke Ihnen für die Kurs-Empfehlung.
PROF. P:	Gern geschehen. Auf Wiedersehen.
MIA:	Auf Wiedersehen.

VOCABULARY EXERCISES

A. Determine which word does not fit in the sequence.

1. ○ Gern geschehen, ○ Schön wär's!, ○ Nichts zu danken

2. ○ komisch, ○ gefährlich, ○ Das waren schwere Zeiten

3. ○ schicken, ○ heiraten, ○ der Bräutigam

4. ○ das Wohnheim, ○ das Internat, ○ die Freizeit

5. ○ sich bemühen, ○ der Aufzug, ○ hochfahren

B. Fill in the blank with the appropriate vocabulary word.

1. Ach so! Das ist Ihr zweites Kind! Und wann haben Sie Ihr erstes
Kind _____?

2. Man sollte nicht _____, während andere Leute reden. Das
ist unhöflich.

3. Das ist unsere letzte Lektion! Das heißt, Sie haben Ihr _____
erreicht!

4. Ich habe einmal auf einer _____ gesungen, aber meine
Stimme hat der Braut und dem Bräutigam nicht gefallen.

5. A: Möchtest du meine Katze halten?
B: Nein, danke. Ich bin _____ gegen Katzen.

6. Interviewer: Frau Bundeskanzlerin, ich danke Ihnen für
das _____.
Kanzlerin: Gern geschehen.

7. A: Ich habe eine Stelle bei einer europäischen Firma bekommen.
B: Schön! Und wohin _____ du?
A: Nach Amsterdam.

8. A: Guten Tag. Wie kann ich Ihnen _____ sein?
B: Ja. Morgen gehe ich auf eine Hochzeit, und ich brauche einen neuen Anzug.
A: Anzüge finden Sie in der Herrenabteilung.

A. Translate from German into English.

1. Du sollst ihr einen Videokurs zum nächsten Geburtstag schenken.

   _____.

2. Ich fliege nur einmal im Jahr nach Hause. Ich kann mir nur die eine Reise leisten.

   _____

   _____..

3. Wir sind in die gleichen Schulen gegangen, als wir Kinder waren.

   _____

   _____.

4. Ich bin Finanzberater geworden, weil ich in der Schule Mathe mochte, und weil ich immer gut rechnen konnte.

   _____

   _____.

5. Echt? Dann sollst du nach Hannover fahren. Du kannst meine Eltern besuchen.

   _____

   _____.

6. Sie könnten zu Fuß gehen, aber es wäre am schnellsten, wenn Sie mit dem Aufzug fahren würden.

   _____

   _____.

7. Ich freue mich, dass wir heute über unsere Familien sprechen. Also dann, was können Sie mir über Ihre Familiengeschichte erzählen?

   _____

   _____.

8. Meine Großeltern väterlicherseits kamen ursprünglich aus Augsburg, aber mein Vater wurde ins Internat nach München geschickt, als er sechs Jahre alt war.

   _____

   _____.

   _____.

9. Neunzehnhundertzweiundvierzig wurden Irene und ihre Mutter nach Treblinka gebracht, wo sie auch gestorben sind.

_____

_____ .

10. Wir wollten über das Thema Fremdsprachenlernen reden, oder?

_____

_____ .

B. Translate from English into German.

1. The (male) student confessed that he gave them the answers.

_____

_____ .

2. Don't mention it. I know that you guys (informal) would help me if I needed it.

_____

_____ .

3. You (as in "one") really have to make an effort if you want to learn a foreign language, but it can be life-changing.

_____

_____ .

4. Would you (formal, singular) show me the way to the elevator, please?

_____

_____ .

5. My (female) Scottish ancestors on my mother's side were supplied with food by the American government when they arrived in New York City in the nineteenth century.

_____

_____

_____ .

Answers on page 264

ADDITIONAL RESOURCES FOR KEEPING UP WITH YOUR GERMAN

First, simply google "**German language podcasts**" and explore what you find. An excellent resource for learning German is ***Slow German: Der Podcast zum Deutschlernen mit Annik Rubens***, which is regularly updated with new content for varying levels of German—and it has a great website, too. A few other recommendable podcasts for keeping up with your German are Deutsche Welle's ***Wieso nicht? Learning German*** and ***Langsam gesprochene Nachrichten***, the Goethe Institut's ***Radio D***, and Radio Lingua's ***Coffee Break German***.

Also, one of the more popular **language exchange sites** is **The Mixxer**. It's an entirely free, nonprofit website hosted by Dickinson College that has thousands of native German speakers registered with the site and waiting for you to contact them. A few other language exchange resources you might check out are the website **www.MyLanguageExchange.com**, which requires a minimal fee for its gold membership options, and the free apps **HelloTalk** and **Tandem Language Exchange**, which you can download onto your smartphone.

Next, there are countless **online resources**, such as Duden.de and Langenscheidt.com (both great German-language dictionary sites), and newspaper and magazine sites, such as *Die Zeit*, *Der Spiegel*, and *Frankfurter Allgemeine*.

Finally, explore some of the **German-language television stations** that are available for streaming on the internet (such as ARD, ZDF, ORF1, and ORF2), as well as the **various streaming services**, such as Netflix and YouTube, which carry a lot of German-language content and for which you can turn on the subtitles—in German or English!

ANSWERS

Vocabulary

A. 1. Hallo; 2. Gute Nacht; 3. Keine Panik; 4. Grüß Gott; 5. Das ist richtig; 6. Auf Wiedersehen; 7. Los geht's; 8. Guten Morgen

B. 1. Ich lebe in; 2. Mein Name ist; 3. schön / großartig / wunderbar; 4. Handschuh; 5. die Aussprache; 6. (das) Bier; 7. Herzlich Willkommen; 8. Das Brot

Translations

A. 1. Ladies and gentlemen! 2. A journey through the German language. 3. Welcome! 4. I live in New York. 5. It's wonderful that you are here.

B. 1. Mein Name ist ... / Ich heiße ... 2. Das ist großartig! 3. Vielen Dank! 4. Ich komme aus den USA. 5. Bitte schön.

LESSON 2 • ANSWERS

Grammar

A. 1. der; 2. das; 3. die; 4. die; 5. die; 6. die; 7. das; 8. die; 9. der; 10. die

B. 1. die; 2. die; 3. die; 4. das; 5. der; 6. das; 7. das; 8. die

Vocabulary

A. 1. Nördlich von; 2. Jawohl; 3. Achtung; 4. Bis gleich; 5. Westlich von; 6. Wiederholen Sie, bitte

B. 1. maskulin / männlich; 2. Sehr; 3. Das Land; 4. Die Hauptstadt; 5. neutral / sächlich; 6. auf Deutsch; 7. Die Milch; 8. Der Computer; 9. Das Bier; 10. ausgezeichnet

Translations

A. 1. It is summer and I am in Germany. 2. I am sixteen years old. 3. The weather here is not so good. 4. I am very happy. 5. Hopefully I will come to Germany again in the summer.

B. 1. Das ist ausgezeichnet! 2. Deutschland liegt nördlich von Italien. 3. Die Schweiz liegt westlich von Österreich. 4. Hören Sie zu und wiederholen Sie! 5. Sind Sie bereit?

LESSON 3 · ANSWERS

Grammar

A. 1. sie; 2. wir; 3. sie; 4. er; 5. es

B. 1. sind; 2. ist; 3. ist; 4. sind; 5. sind; 6. seid; 7. sind; 8. bist; 9. bist; 10. ist; 11. sind; 12. Bin

C. 1. Töchter; 2. Landschaften; 3. Messer; 4. Gebäude; 5. Babys; 6. Kinder; 7. Jungen; 8. Wände; 9. Mädchen; 10. Meinungen

Vocabulary

A. 1. der Sohn; 2. die Tochter; 3. die Eltern; 4. der Zungenbrecher; 5. der Neffe / der Enkel; 6. das Baby; 7. die Großmutter / die Oma; 8. der Onkel / der Sohn; 9. der Großvater / der Opa; 10. der Bruder / der Sohn, die Schwester / die Tochter

Translations

A. 1. I am the sister-in-law. 2. We are the grandparents of Westin. 3. He is the nephew of Mia. 4. The girl is the granddaughter of Sabina. 5. They are the children of Ralf and Mia.

B. 1. Das ist meine Familie. 2. Sie sind der Onkel von Mia. 3. Ihr seid die Eltern von Westin. 4. Der Zungenbrecher ist ausgezeichnet. 5. Sie sind sehr brav.

LESSON 4 · ANSWERS

Grammar

A. 1. -et; 2. -en; 3. -est; 4. -et; 5. -et; 6. -e; 7. -et; 8. -t; 9. -t; 10. -en

B. 1. -e; 2. -en; 3. -e; 4. -et; 5. -en; 6. -en; 7. -t; 8. -t; 9. -t; 10. -e; 11. -t; 12. -est; 13. -e; 14. -t

Vocabulary

A. 1. mähen; 2. Wie geht es Ihnen?; 3. reise; 4. südlich von; 5. Französin; 6. arbeitest; 7. zu Fuß; 8. Wo findet man; 9. Schlecht; 10. toll / ausgezeichnet

A. 1. The (male) Danes mow/are mowing the grass. 2. You travel to Europe often. 3.The woman comes from Spain. 4. The Frenchman sings well. 5. The Irishwoman lives in France.

B. 1. Sie arbeiten in München. 2. Er heißt Ralf. 3. Wir gehen zu Fuß. 4. Ihr wohnt in Spanien. 5. Er raucht.

LESSON 5 • ANSWERS

Grammar

A. 1. eine; 2. ein; 3. eine; 4. ein; 5. eine; 6. ein; 7. ein; 8. eine; 9. ein; 10. ein / eine

Vocabulary

A. 1. der Kellner / die Kellnerin; 2. zählen; 3. teuer; 4. bestellen; 5. Was darf es sein? 6. die Kneipe; 7. Zahlen; 8. glaube; 9. Sonst noch was? 10. Backwaren

B. 1. zwölf; 2. fünfundzwanzig; 3. einunddreißig; 4. dreiundachtzig; 5. vierzig; 6. zweiundsiebzig

Translations

A. 1. We are thirsty. 2. The beer is also reasonable. 3. My gosh! That is expensive! 4. I'll order a bottle of carbonated mineral water. 5. The waitress is coming.

B. 1. Ich hätte gern ein stilles Wasser / Ich möchte ein stilles Wasser. 2. Ein Glas Weißwein ist teuer. 3. Ich glaube, ein Dunkelweizen ist günstig. 4. Probieren wir es! 5. Übung macht den Meister!

LESSON 6 • ANSWERS

Grammar

A. 1. Die Grubers reisen gern. 2. Ich trinke gern Kaffeegetränke. / Ich trinke Kaffeegetränke gern. 3. Maria geht gern in Kaffeehäuser. 4. Ich lese gern Liebesromane. / Ich lese Liebesromane gern. 5. Wir sprechen gern Deutsch. / Wir sprechen Deutsch gern.

B. 1. Wir reisen nicht nach Italien. / Wir reisen nach Italien nicht. 2. Ihr sprecht nicht gern Englisch. 3. Mozarts Geburtshaus steht nicht in der Lerchenfelder Straße. / Mozarts Geburtshaus steht in der Lerchenfelder Straße nicht. 4. Ich backe nicht. 5. Ich singe nicht in der Dusche. / Ich singe in der Dusche nicht.

Vocabulary

A. 1. steht; 2. überqueren; 3. du hast Recht; 4. Liebesromane; 5. ein bisschen; 6. bleiben; 7. Smoking; 8. Kaffegetränke; 9. Richtung; 10. schmeckt

Translations

A. 1. First, we go south along the *Buchfeldergasse*. 2. Café Landtmann is located to the left, on the other side of the street. 3. That surely tastes good! 4. We cross the *Griesgasse*, and we go along the *Rathausplatz* as far as the *Getreidegasse*. 5. The Viennese like to drink coffee.

B. 1. Der Fiaker schmeckt gut. Das habe ich gern. 2. Wir überbrücken die Hauptbrücke und gehen Richtung Bahnhofstraße. 3. Zuerst gehen wir nach links. 4. Dann gehen wir drei Straßen bis zur Buchfeldergasse. 5. Ich trinke gern Wasser! / Ich trinke Wasser gern!

LESSON 7 · ANSWERS

Grammar

A. 1. Kommst du aus Österreich? 2. Lernen wir Deutsch? 3. Seid ihr brav? 4. Ist das Wetter schön? 5. Sprechen Sie gern Deutsch?

B. 1. Wann beginnt die Oper? 2. Warum lernst du Deutsch? 3. Wie viel kostet eine Flasche Rotwein aus Italien? 4. Wohin reisen wir nächste Woche? 5. Wo wohnen Sie in Deutschland?

C. 1. Wo; 2. Woher; 3. Wo; 4. Wohin; 5. Wohin

Vocabulary

A. 1. Washington DC; 2. London; 3. Honolulu; 4. Toronto

B. 1. (ein)tausendvierhundertvierzig; 2. (ein)hundertachtundsechzig; 3. dreitausendsechshundertvierzig; 4. zweitausendvierhundert; 5. sechzigtausend; 6. dreihundertvierundachtzigtausendvierhundert; 7. hundert Million sechshunderttausend; 8. vier Milliarde vierhundertfünfundneunzig Million

A. 1. In Vienna, the sun is shining and it is pleasant. 2. Translating is fun!
3. It is storming and it is not at all nice. 4. It is snowing and the sky is gray.
5. Grammar is gratifying!

B. 1. Es ist regnerisch und neblig. 2. Deutsch Sprechen macht Spaß. 3. Es
donnert und regnet. 4. Es ist Hundewetter! 5. Wie viel Grad ist es in Berlin?
/ Was zeigt das Thermometer in Berlin?

LESSON 8 • ANSWERS

Grammar

A. 1. Die; 2. den; 3. die; 4. der; 5. das

B. 1. ein; 2. eine; 3. ein; 4. einen; 5. Ein

C. 1. sie; 2. sie; 3. ihn; 4. es; 5. euch; 6. Sie; 7. dich; 8. mich

D. 1. keinen; 2. keine; 3. keinen; 4. keine; 5. kein

Vocabulary

A. 1. der Keller; 2. das Fenster; 3. die Hängeleuchte; 4. die Spüle; 5. die
Garage; 6. die Heizung; 7. der Ofen; 8. der Spiegel

Translations

A. 1. The children find the dog sweet. / The children think the dog is cute.
2. There are no wall clocks. 3. Does the living room have a hanging light
and a bookshelf? 4. We like the bathroom. 5. We need you guys!

B. 1. Es gibt keine Spiegel. 2. Das Einfamilienhaus hat einen Keller, aber
keine Garage. 3. Sie finden ihn intelligent. 4. Das Badezimmer hat sechs
Fenster. 5. Ich kenne sie nicht.

LESSON 9 • ANSWERS

Grammar

A. 1. Ihr; 2. mein; 3. unser; 4. eure; 5. seine; 6. ihren

B. 1. Heute Nachmittag besuchen wir ein Museum. 2. Morgen fliege ich
nach Deutschland. 3. Heute in der Früh macht er ein Kreuzworträtsel.
4. Morgens trinkt ihr Kaffee mit Milch. 5. Abends lesen wir gern im Bett.

A. 1. Schmetterlinge, Ameisen, Spinnen; 2. fährt der Zug; 3. jetzt; 4. Maschinenbau; 5. Frühstück; 6. schlafe

B. 1. zwölf Uhr einundfünfzig; 2. fünf nach elf / elf Uhr fünf; 3. zehn vor dreiundzwanzig Uhr / dreiundzwanzig Uhr fünfzig; 4. halb sieben / sechs Uhr dreißig; 5. Viertel nach fünfzehn / fünfzehn Uhr fünfzehn

Translations

A. 1. Do you think my hobbies are strange? 2. We are going to take a hike in the forest now, and then we will eat breakfast. 3. This afternoon we are going to practice our German from four until six. 4. The train arrives/will be arriving at half past eight. 5. Is our transfer time an hour, a half hour, or only a quarter hour?

B. 1. Haben wir genug Zeit? 2. Morgens schwimmt sie drei Stunden. / Sie schwimmt morgens drei Stunden. 3. Warum schlafen Sie nachmittags von vier bis acht? / Warum schlafen Sie von sechzehn bis achtzehn Uhr? 4. Abends singen wir gern. / Wir singen gern abends. 5. Sie reparieren unseren Computer nicht gern.

LESSON 10 · ANSWERS

Grammar

A. 1. Ich bestelle keinen Kaffee, sondern ich möchte einen Tee. 2. Wir üben Grammatik, denn es macht Spaß. 3. Alle Kellner im Kaffeehaus tragen keinen Smoking und ich finde das toll. 4. Der Gedankenleser weiß meinen Namen nicht, aber er weiß viel über mich. 5. Sind Sie Richter von Beruf oder arbeiten Sie als Beamter?

B. 1. -e; 2. -e; 3. -en; 4. -es; 5. -e

C. 1. Mein Onkel arbeitet als Bankgestellter in Salzburg. 2. Wir sammeln gern solche Spinnen. / Wir sammeln solche Spinnen gern. 3. Welchen Beruf findet ihr langweilig? 4. Heute bekommen meine Kinder einen Hund. 5. Morgens repariert manche Informatikerin einen Computer zu Hause.

Vocabulary

A. 1. Ich hab's! 2. Was Sind Sie von Beruf? 3. Einverstanden! 4. Entschuldingung ... 5. Ich finde ...

B. 1. brauche; 2. Arzt; 3. Strafe; 4. verstehe; 5. bekommt

A. 1. My niece is a computer scientist by trade. 2. The judge plays chess alone at home in the evenings. 3. Every (male) nurse is friendly. 4. Many people like to speak German. 5. Which dog is this girl getting for her birthday?

B. 1. Ihr Vater ist Verkäufer von Beruf. 2. Dieser Advokat ist unehrlich und braucht eine Strafe. 3. Alle Beamtinnen arbeiten gern in Washington DC. 4. Jedes Kind bekommt ein Handy. 5. Jetzt verstehen wir euch.

LESSON 11 · ANSWERS

Grammar

A. 1. will; 2. muss; 3. wollt, könnt; 4. darfst; 5. sollen

B. 1. um die Ecke; 2. bis diesen Sommer; 3. gegen ihn; 4. ohne ihren Hund; 5. für dein Kind

C. 1. Die Eltern müssen ihren Sohn jetzt bestrafen. 2. Diesen Winter sollst du eine Heizung besorgen. 3. Jeden Sommer darf ich im Meer schwimmen. 4. Können Sie mich nächsten Sommer in Berlin besuchen? 5. Jeden Freitag möchte er einen Smoking in der Arbeit tragen.

Vocabulary

A. 1.witzig; 2.lösen; 3.Frühling; 4.Eis; 5.Geschenke; 6.Vorurteile; 7.Zweck; 8.Spaziergang; 9.Tage; 10.Das Wochenende

Translations

A. 1. Where are you guys driving/going (by vehicle) next weekend? 2. She has to get tissues and clothes for the trip. 3. My jokes can sometimes be mundane. 4. He can solve all math problems without problems. 5. Why would you like to hike through the forest?

B. 1. Unsere Lieblingsjahreszeit ist Herbst. 2. Unsere Mutter muss den ganzen Tag arbeiten. 3. Sie dürfen heute Abend angeln, oder? / Heute Abend dürfen Sie angeln, oder? 4. Ich soll Shampoo und Seife für diese Reise besorgen. 5. Sie bleiben diesen Winter einen ganzen Monat in Wien. / Diesen Winter bleiben sie einen ganzen Monat in Wien.

LESSON 12 · ANSWERS

Grammar

A. 1. weiß; 2. weißt; 3. kennen; 4. weiß; 5. kennen

B. 1. fährst; 2. läuft; 3. stiehlt; 4. sieht; 5. geschieht; 6. wächst; 7. helft; 8. säuft; 9. isst; 10. lest

Vocabulary

A. 1. nass; 2. Fleisch, Gemüse; 3. Wasser, Hopfen, Gerste (Malz); 4. lieber; 5. Wissenschaft; 6. probieren

B. 1. Wie bitte? 2. Prost! / Zum Wohl! 3. Ich bin der Meinung ... / Das können Sie mir glauben! 4. Wie schön! 5. Ich hätte gern eine Maß. / Ich nehme eine Maß. / Für mich eine Maß, bitte.

Translations

A. 1. Are you guys hungry? 2. The city wall and the stairs are not dangerous because there are railings. 3. Should we go by foot, or do you want to rent bikes? 4. The beer tent has no roof, but I think it's comfortable. 5. Why is the patron throwing the mustard and the red cabbage?

B. 1. Sie isst beides Fleisch und Gemüse. 2. Dein Neffe spricht gern Deutsch. 3. Jeden tag trägt er gern Smoking. / Er trägt gern Smoking jeden Tag. / Er trägt Smoking gern jeden Tag. 4. Diese Kneipe ist empfehlenswert, denn sie hat einen Innenhof, und eine Maß ist günstig. 5. Manchmal liest unser Gast die ganze Nacht und schläft den ganzen Tag. / Unser Gast liest manchmal die ganze Nacht und schläft den ganzen Tag.

LESSON 13 · ANSWERS

Grammar

A. 1. Wohin; 2. dafür; 3. dadurch; 4. Für wen; 5. wogegen

B. 1. Der Junge hat Schmetterlinge gesammelt. 2. Jeden Tag haben wir unser Deutsch geübt. 3. Meine Mutter hat den Kühlschrank repariert. 4. Sein Vater hat viele Jahre bei Boeing gearbeitet. 5. Hast du schon dein neues Handy aktualisiert? 6. Die Chefin hat heute Morgen stundenlang über das neue Geschäftsmodell geredet.

A. 1. Etappe; 2. Darum; 3. Hier steht's; 4. höflich, respektvoll; 5. die Zeitung; 6. werden

Translations

A. 1. What's new in the world? (literally "What is there new in the world?") 2. Why did you buy four newspapers this morning in the bakery? 3. As a child I juggled for hours alone in my room. 4. Yesterday evening we had a nice conversation. 5. The federal chancellor went on a big international trip. (literally "made a trip")

B. 1. Gestern habe ich meinen Namen gegoogelt. / Ich habe meinen Namen gestern gegoogelt. 2. Heute haben wir eine Vergangenheitsform gelernt. 3. Für wen stimmen Sie dieses Jahr? 4. Was hat dein Chef gestern gesagt? 5. Habt ihr etwas dagegen?

LESSON 14 · ANSWERS

Grammar

A. 1. siehst, sieht, gesehen; 2. fährst, fährt, gefahren; 3. darfst, darf, gedürft; 4. kennst, kennt, gekannt; 5. trinkst, trinkt, getrunken; 6. treibst, treibt, getrieben; 7. ziehst, zieht, gezogen; 8. schneidest, schneidet, geschnitten; 9. bindest, bindet, gebunden; 10. willst, will, gewollt; 11. vergisst, vergisst, vergessen; 12. verlierst, verliert, verloren; 13. triffst, trifft, getroffen; 14. bringst, bringt, gebracht; 15. musst, musst, gemüsst

B. 1. Das Kind hat den Ball über das Dach geworfen. 2. Warum hast du kein Gemüse gegessen? 3. Unsere Mannschaft hat jedes Spiel gewonnen. 4. Hast du deinen Bruder gebissen? 5. Wie habt ihr euer Kind genannt?

Vocabulary

A. 1. Nicht vergessen; 2. hinreißend; 3. renne; 4. Vorspeise; 5. Entscheidung; 6. binden; 7. eigenständig; 8. ziehen; 9. lächelt; 10. Verändert

Translations

A. 1. Helmut stood there alone, but he didn't have a drink. 2. Gisela wore a pretty summer dress and I thought she was ravishing. 3. I studied education sciences. My parents didn't want that, but that's what I did. 4. The summer of 1910 changed my life. 5. Gisela dreamed of an around-the-world trip. But she was allowed (to do that) because she still lived with her parents.

B. 1. Als Universitätsstudent(in) habe ich Deutsch und Erziehungswissenschaft studiert. 2. Der Hund hat die Katze gerochen. 3. Die Katze hat das nicht gemocht. / Das hat die Katze nicht gemocht. 4. Unsere Baseballmannschaft hat das Spiel verloren und wir haben geschrien. 5. Hoppla! Wir haben nur Getränke gebracht, aber ihr habt Weißwurst und Senf gewollt.

LESSON 15 · ANSWERS

Grammar

A. 1. Im Sommer sind wir nach Deutschland geflogen. 2. Im Jahr 1975 seid ihr erst acht Jahre alt gewesen. 3. Wann bist du nach Berlin umgezogen? 4. Das Baby ist immer im Auto eingeschlafen. 5. Warum habe ich im Restaurant nicht rauchen dürfen? 6. Unser Chef ist diesen Winter auf Hawaii schnorcheln gegangen. 7. Gisela hat in dem Sommerkleid hinreißend ausgesehen.

B. 1. Mein Mann ruft seine Mutter heute Abend an. 2. Willst du morgen in der Stadt etwas essen gehen? 3. Ich probiere diesen Anzug schnell in der Umkleidungskabine an. 4. Der Zug kommt um zehn vor zehn in Zürich an. 5. Wann geht die Sonne morgen auf? 6. Zuerst sollst du an der Rezeption einchecken.

Vocabulary

A. 1. sehe, fern; 2. kompostierbar, umweltbewusst/umweltfreundlich; 3. leer; 4. aufgestanden; 5. Gürtel; 6. Werbung; 7. Tonne; 8. Krawatte; 9. eingeladen; 10. Studentenwohnheim

Translations

A. 1. Of course I wanted to correctly dispose of the empty package. 2. The people in Germany were very environmentally friendly. 3. On the way home, I drank a chocolate milk. 4. Yesterday we watched TV in the dorms all day. 5. What time did you check in at the hotel?

B. 1. Unser Sohn ist gestern Abend um viertel nach acht eingeschlafen. 2. Sie haben schnell einloggen können. 3. Ihr Bruder sieht konfus aus. 4. Im Sommer gebt ihr viel Geld aus. / Ihr gebt viel Geld im Sommer aus. 5. Wir sind spazieren gegangen, und dann haben wir unsere Konservendosen richtig entsorgt.

LESSON 16 • ANSWERS

Grammar

A. 1. Die Chefin ist heute nicht im Büro, weil sie heute Morgen ein Meeting in München hat. 2. Weißt du, wo die Kinder Deutsch gelernt haben? 3. Ich habe nicht gewusst, dass du so schnell einschlafen kannst. 4. Ich habe keine Ahnung, wer die Kinder heute von der Schule abholt. 5. Ihr sollt es aufschreiben, wenn ihr meine Telefonnummer immer vergesst.

B. 1. Ich habe keine Zeit, im Sommer nach Deutschland zu fliegen. 2. Es ist wichtig, heutzutage eine Fremdsprache zu lernen. 3. Ich habe keine Lust, Meinen Chef heute Abend anzurufen. 4. Hast du vor, einen Spaziergang im Wald zu machen? 5. Ich versuche, mein Haus ohne einen Immobilienmakler zu verkaufen.

Vocabulary

A. 1. Was ist los; 2. halb wach; 3. hast ... vor; 4. Überraschung; 5. versucht

Translations

A. 1. The boss came into my office this morning because he had a surprise for me. 2. Do you know where Annemarie is giving her concert? 3. We are trying to convince our parents. 4. Crap! Why didn't you tell me that you don't like country music? 5. You guys have to call me if you want to find out when my party starts.

B. 1. Wir haben keine Lust, nur Obst und Gemüse zu essen. 2. Soll ich versuchen, dieses Auto zu reparieren, oder soll ich es einfach verkaufen ...? Was tun? 3. Mist! Sie weiß, dass ich eine Überraschung für sie habe. 4. Ralf kann nicht ins Konzert gehen, weil er keine Karten gekauft hat. 5. Er hat keine Zeit, jeden Anzug anzuprobieren.

LESSON 17 • ANSWERS

Grammar

A. 1. Das Kind ist eingeschlafen, ohne zu weinen. 2. Man muss arbeiten, um Geld zu verdienen. 3. Ich erzähle eine Geschichte, statt dir ein Weihnachtslied beizubringen. 4 Ihr braucht einen Plan, um das Spiel zu gewinnen. 5. Dieses Jahr schenken wir den Kindern Bücher, statt ihnen Spielzeuge zu besorgen.

B. 1. der Professor, Kenntnisse, uns; 2. Sankt Nikolaus, ein Weihnachtslied, den Studenten; 3. die Eltern, diese Geschenke, ihren Kindern; 4. der Chef, einen Glühwein, seiner Frau; 5. wir, alles Gute, Ihnen

C. 1. -em; 2. -er; 3. -e; 4. -en; 5. -es, -em

D. 1. euch; 2. ihm; 3. ihnen; 4. uns; 5. Ihr

Vocabulary

A. 1. Oje / Das ist schlimm; 2. Viel Erfolg; 3. zuverlässig; 4. aufregend; 5. Meine Zeit ist um.

Translations

A. 1. After all, we still have to get the kids presents. 2. Professor Pfrehm invited me to the seventeenth lesson to celebrate the Sixth of December with you. 3. Do you feel like a Glühwein? I'll fetch/get you one if you want. 4. Why did you give them money without telling me? 5. You have to practice often and have a lot of patience to learn a foreign language.

B. 1. Wir haben unserer Großmutter einen Wagen/ein Auto zu Weihnachten gekauft. 2. Hast du mir Rasierschaum und Rasierklingen besorgt? 3. Wie viele Jahre haben Sie studieren müssen, um Professor/in zu werden? 4. Dieser Hund ist zuverlässig. Jeden Morgen bringt er uns die Zeitung. / Er bringt uns die Zeitung jeden Morgen. / Er bringt uns jeden Morgen die Zeitung. 5. Oje. Leider gibt es keine Zeit, Ihnen ein Weihnachtslied beizubringen.

LESSON 18 • ANSWERS

Grammar

A. 1. -en; 2. -em, -e; 3. -em, -en; 4. -en, -n, -; 5. -em, -en; 6. -em, -

B. 1. Dieses Jahr finanzieren wir unserem Sohn eine Reise nach Berlin. 2. Ich schenke es ihr zum Geburtstag. 3. Dieses Jahr zu Weihnachten darf er ihnen keine iPads kaufen. 4. Gestern hat der Chef dem Angestellten eine Lohnerhöhung angeboten. 5. Heute Abend bringen wir sie euch.

Vocabulary

A. 1. eben; 2. bietet; 3. Eingangshalle; 4. Machen Sie sich bereit!; 5. rund; 6. Kantone; 7. beindruckend; 8. tief durchatmen

A. 1. I offer my princess only the best. 2. I would like to give this man a big kiss, because chocolate makes me happy. 3. You just said that they built them alpine cabins. 4. Should I buy him this dark chocolate or this milk chocolate bar? 5. The prince promised the princess a big adventure.

B. 1. Müssen wir unserer Kusine Geld zum Geburtstag schenken? 2. Wann haben sie Ihnen mehr Geld angeboten? 3. Warum habt ihr euren Eltern keine Schokolade in Zürich gekauft? 4. Das ist ihr Klavier, aber eines Tages will sie es mir vererben. / Das ist ihr Klavier, aber sie will es mir eines Tages vererben. 5. Welchem Kind soll ich mein Fahrrad verkaufen?

LESSON 19 · ANSWERS

Grammar

A. 1. uns; 2. euch; 3. sich; 4. mich; 5. sich; 6. sich; 7. sich; 8. dich

B. 1. Die Kinder duschen sich gern morgens. 2. Darf ich mich setzen? 3. Heute ruht sich meine Frau zu Hause aus. 4. Unsere Großeltern entspannen sich am Wochenende in ihrer Alphütte. 5. Der Professor meldet sich sofort auf der Konferenz an.

Vocabulary

A. 1. Fußknöchel; 2. sich umziehen; 3. sich beeilen; 4. das Auge; 5. sofort

B. 1. Glatze; 2. erinnern; 3. heiser; 4. beeilen; 5. vorstellen; 6. hört, an

Translations

A. 1. I have a headache and my back hurts. 2. I am happy that you're able to recuperate. 3. I've been feeling lousy for a week. 4. We looked around in the department store, but we didn't buy anything. 5. Our son has to rest at home for a few days because he's caught a cold.

B. 1. Entspannt ihr euch dieses Wochenende? 2. Sie fühlen sich mies, weil sie sich gestern nicht ausgeruht haben. 3. Wir wollen uns eine Stunde hinlegen, aber das ist nicht möglich. 4. Ich habe mich schnell umgezogen. 5. Morgens rasiert er sich gern, aber er duscht sich nicht gern.

LESSON 20 · ANSWERS

Grammar

A. 1. sich; 2. sich; 3. mir; 4. euch; 5. dir

B. 1. Ich lerne meinen Wortschatz für Deutsch, während ich Frühstück esse. 2. Wir haben neue iPhones gekauft, obwohl wir kein Geld gehabt haben. 3. Du musst mich anrufen, sobald du in Berlin ankommst. 4. Sie lernt Deutsch, damit sie eine Stelle bei Deutsche Bank bekommen kann. 5. Der Arzt hat uns seine Nummer gegeben, falls/wenn wir uns nächste Woche plötzlich mies fühlen.

C. 1. -em, -er; 2. -en; 3. -er; 4. -en; 5. -er

Vocabulary

A. 1. gratulieren; 2. verzeihen; 3. gefällt; 4. schmeckt, schmeckt; 5. geantwortet

B. 1. bei; 2. nach; 3. mit; 4. aus; 5. außer

C. 1. sich waschen; 2. sich putzen; 3. sich leisten; 4. sich vorstellen; 5. sich leihen; 6. sich anhören; 7. sich kochen; 8. sich brechen

Translations

A. 1. It's very pleasant at our house in the evenings. 2. Ralf likes to sing pop music while he showers, and I have to listen to this noise for ten minutes. 3. We chat a little before the kids get up. 4. I like crime novels the best. 5. I read in bed, as long as it doesn't bother Ralf.

B. 1. Deutsch lernen gefällt ihr. 2. Sie waschen sich gern die Hände, solang es genug Seife gibt. 3. Dieses Auto gehört Ihnen, falls Sie vergessen haben. 4. Er geht gern zum Zahnarzt, obwohl er sich selten die Zähne putzt. 5. Nach ihrem Geburtstag entspannt sich zu Hause. / Sie entspannt sich nach ihrem Geburtstag zu Hause.

LESSON 21 · ANSWERS

Grammar

A. 1. Der Junge war redefreudig und konnte nicht schweigsam sein. 2. Es gab oft Ärger, weil ich frech war. 3. Dürftet ihr ins Kino gehen, wenn ihr Geld hattet? 4. Sie waren schüchtern und wollten nicht reden. 5. Du hattest Durst, aber du wolltest kein Bier trinken, denn du mochtest es nicht.

B. 1. wann; 2. Als; 3. als; 4. wann; 5. als

A. 1. Ich mache reinen Tisch; 2. aufräumen; 3. Kugelschreiber / Kuli, Hausaufgaben; 4. Mikro; 5. schwören, Wahrheit, schwöre

B. 1. artig / gut erzogen; 2. frech; 3. schweigsam / introvertiert; 4. der Zivildienstleistende / der Zivi; 5. extrovertiert; 6. der Professionelle / der Profi; 7. schwierig; 8. das Deodorant / das Deo

Translations

A. 1. She had to clean up her room every weekend. 2. When we were young, we were supposed to be good and polite. 3. Instead of going into the army, he wanted to be a conscientious objector doing civil service. 4. When I was a child, I was not allowed to be cheeky. 5. There was a little trouble because you guys were always hungry.

B. 1. Sie war oft schüchtern, als sie Kind war. 2. Wir mussten jeden Tag bei uns die Küche aufräumen. / Jeden Tag mussten wir bei uns die Küche aufräumen. 3. Ich wollte dem Profi gratulieren, weil er Erfolg hatte. 4. Unsere Freundin konnte keinen Kuli finden, da es nur Bleistifte gab. 5. Solltest du jeden Tag deine Hausaufgaben machen, als du letzte Woche zu Hause geblieben bist?

LESSON 22 · ANSWERS

Grammar

A. 1. biss; 2. zog; 3. half; 4. schwammen; 5. vergrub

B. 1. Bärbel blieb wochenlang verzweifelt, aber sie betrieb den Bauernhof weiterhin. 2. Bärbel lief zum Graben von ihrem Mann und rief seinen Namen. 3. Bärbel nahm die Axt und schnitt sich einen Finger ab. 4. Der Bauer hob die Schaufel und griff nach der Mistgabel. 5. Die Zwerge schliefen im Gebüsch, trugen alte Lappen, und rochen muffig.

Vocabulary

A. 1. Was fehlt dir/Ihnen; 2. verzweifelt; 3. der Krieg; 4. verheiratet; 5. muffig; 6. Gesellschaft

B. 1. Scheune; 2. Geräusch; 3. hoffnungsvoll; 4. Wiese; 5. ahnen

A. 1. On the one hand, she didn't want to cut off her arm; on the other hand, she wished a new husband for herself. She raised the axe and closed her eyes. 2. One day it came to pass/happened that war broke out. 3. Now Bärbel suspected that something wasn't right. But she was very lonely and despaired. 4. The sun shone on the dewy grass, the birds sang, and not a single animal was startled. 5. I swung an axe and dug in the ground all day, and in the evening, I fell into bed exhausted and slept for hours.

B. 1. Bärbel vergrub ihre Finger in der Wiese und lief zum Graben von ihrem Mann. 2. Gewannst du das Spiel Samstagabend? 3. Was geschah gestern Abend und warum trugen Sie eine Axt? 4. Der Zwerg hatte zwei Brüder, rauchte eine Pfeife, und sah sehr alt aus. 5. Du liebe Zeit! Gestern trank mein Mann zwei Liter Bier (zwei Maß), aß fünf Weißwurst, und fuhr zehn Kilometer mit dem Rad.

LESSON 23 · ANSWERS

Grammar

A.

Tier-Chaos in der Großstadt
Heute morgen **entkamen (entkommen, ist entkommen)** drei Zebra aus einem Brüsseler Tiergarten. Die Polizei **konnte (konnte, gekonnt)** die Tiere, die mehr als eine Stunde durch die Straßen von Brüssels **liefen (laufen, ist gelaufen)**, nach mehreren Versuchen einfangen. Bisher ist nicht bekannt, ob die Tiere von alleine **entkamen (entkommen, ist entkommen)**, oder ob jemand sie absichtlich **befreite (befreien, befreit)**.

Schmutziges Geld
Als eine Bankangestellte gestern in einer Bank in Genf auf die Toilette **ging (gehen, ist gegangen)**, **entdeckte (entdecken, entdeckt)** sie zwanzig Fünfhunderteuroscheine im Toilettenbecken. Die Banknoten, die man aus dem Wasser **holte (holen, geholt)** und **reinigte (reinigen, gereinigt)**, **waren (sein, ist gewesen)** unbeschädigt. Wann und warum das Geld ins Klobecken **kam (kommen, ist gekommen)**, ist bisher nicht bekannt. Die aufrechte Angestellte, die die Scheine sofort **meldete (melden, gemeldet)**, **durfte (dürfen, gedurft)** das Geld nicht behalten.

Gewagter Sprung
Es **war (sein, ist gewesen)** vorgestern in San Francisco kein gewöhnlicher Besuch beim Stadtaquarium. Als ein dreißigjähriger Mann zum berühmten Haifischbecken **kam (kommen, ist gekommen)**, **zog (ziehen, gezogen)** er sich plötzlich aus und **sprang (springen, ist gesprungen)** ins Wasser. Der Mann, dem die Polizei eine Strafzettel **aushändigte (aushändigen,**

ausgehändigt), **verbrachte (verbringen, verbracht)** mehrere Minuten nackt im Wasser mit den Haifischen. Als die Polizei ihn hinterher **fragte (fragen, gefragt)**, was er mit seiner riskanten Aktion erreichen **wollte (wollen, gewollt)**, **sagte (sagen, gesagt)** er: „Haifische sind sensible Wesen, genau wie wir Menschen. Sie gehören ins Meer, nicht in ein künstliches Gefängnis. Das ist doch Tierquälerei! Und wenn ich sehe, dass Haifische eingeschlossen sind, muss ich etwas dagegen unternehmen.“

B. 1. Das Kind **kannte** das Märchen, **das** Professor Pfrehm **schrieb**. 2. Die Leute, **die** Deutsch **lernten**, **sahen** intelligent aus. 3. Wo **war** der Pfeil, **den** der Jäger für seine Armbrust **brauchte**? 4. Ich **wollte** die Altenpflegerin kennen lernen, **die** älteren Menschen **hilft**. 5. Das **war** die Richterin, **der** du danken **solltest**. 6. Wir **wollten** den Auftrag, **den** die andere Firma nicht **bekam**. 7. Ich **rief** die Immobilienmaklerin an, **die** dir am besten **gefiel**. 8. Wir **entdeckten** die Unterlagen, **die** sie **versteckten**. 9. Ich **wünschte** mir einen Arbeitsplatz, **der** freundliche Mitarbeiter **hatte**. 10. Der Jäger **erschoss** die Zwerge, **die** Bärbel **betrogen**. 11. Die Studenten, **denen** die Lehrerin schlechte Noten **gab**, **wurden** wütend. 12. Die Klempner, **den** wir **fanden**, **erschienen** sofort.

Vocabulary

A. 1. der Tischler / die Tischlerin; 2. bald; 3. das Gehirn; 4. wütend; 5. betrügen

B. 1. Unterlagen; 2. der Klempner / die Klempnerin; 3. erscheinen; 4. anvertraut; 5. Grabstein

Translations

A. 1. Shortly thereafter, Bärbel and the hunter married. 2. Bärbel immediately dropped the axe that she was holding/held in her hand. 3. She told about the dwarves that betrayed her, and the hunter got/became angry. 4. The upstanding female employee who reported the bills immediately was not allowed to keep the money. 5. The man that the police gave the ticket to spent ten minutes naked in the water with the sharks.

B. 1. Kennt ihr die Lieferanten, die das Bier gebracht haben/brachten? 2. Sie betrogen den Jäger, der ihnen half. / Sie haben den Jäger betrogen, der ihnen geholfen hat. 3. Wo ist der Bauarbeiter, der gestern wütend geworden ist/wurde? 4. Das ist der Tisch, den die Tischlerin gebaut hat/baute. 5. Ich kenne die Altenpflegerin, der Sie diese Blumen gekauft haben/kauften.

Grammar

A. 1. Seien Sie bitte leiser. 2. Bitte scannt diese Unterlagen ein. 3. Sei brav. 4. Sieh gleich nach, bitte. 5. Bitte probieren Sie die Krabben. 6. Bitte hört mit dem Schreien auf. 7. Bitte lad meine Freunde zur Party am Freitagabend ein. 8. Bitte fahr morgen allein nach Hause.

B. 1. Wo sind die Leute, mit denen ich aufgewachsen bin? 2. Wir kennen den Wald, durch den ihr wandert. 3. Das ist die Frau, von der ich erzählen muss. 4. Sie sind mit dem Mann verheiratet, bei dem ich früher gewohnt habe. 5. Ist das die Chefin, für die mein Bruder arbeitet? 6. Dort drüben steht das Haus, aus dem der Hund herausgerannt ist.

Vocabulary

A. 1. Halt/Haltet die Augen offen; 2. Reihe 3. die Wahrheit; 4. beschlossen / vorgeschlagen; 5. ausdrucken; 6. das Stück; 7. Zwischenlandung; 8. überheblich; 9. eintippen; 10. Firma / Fluggesellschaft

Translations

A. 1. Ralf and Mia decide to undertake a trip to northern Germany. 2. I suggest that we fly to Hamburg. After that, we'll go by train to the North Sea. 3. The arrogant guy that was sitting in the row in front of us really angered/bothered me. 4. Do you remember our last theater evening in Munich? 5. He scolded me several times: "Be quiet!" "Stop coughing!" "Don't kick against my chair!" 6. Stay patient and go see when the next train departs to Berlin.

B. 1. Das Stück hat anderthalb Stunden gedauert, aber wir haben es genossen. / Das Stück dauerte anderthalb Stunden, aber wir genossen es. 2. Wir müssen den Zug erwischen, der morgen um fünf Uhr in der Früh ankommt. 3. Wollen Sie den Chef beschimpfen, von dem Sie mir erzählt haben/erzählten? 4. Seid vorsichtig! Ich habe nicht übertrieben, als ich euch gesagt/erzählt habe, dass die Robben sehr wütend sind. 5. Ralf, bleib hier und hilf mir mit den Flugtickets. Das ist die Fluggesellschaft, mit der wir fliegen sollen.

LESSON 25 • ANSWERS

A. 1. stehen; 2. stellen; 3. steht; 4. liegen; 5. hängen

B. 1. dem; 2. die; 3. der; 4. -e, -e; 5. -, -; 6. -es, den; 7. -e, -er;
8. -en, -en, -e

Vocabulary

A. 1. Ordentlichkeit; 2. Fenster; 3. Meer; 4. sauber; 5. loben

B. 1. klug; 2. lobt; 3. Feuerzeug; 4. Baum; 5. Durcheinander; 6. legen;
7. steht, stellen; 8. Insel

Translations

A. 1. Why is there so much stuff lying on my kitchen counter? 2. The kitchen looks like a pigsty! 3. I cleared everything away, washed the dirty dishes, and scrubbed the sticky floor. 4. I'll bring the blowtorch back into the garage right way. 5. Did you put the hammer that was lying on the kitchen table back in the tool chest?

B. 1. Die Antwort steht auf Seite sechsundzwanzig im Buch. 2. Ich habe die Kuckucksuhr neben das Bild gehängt, das über dem Fenster hängt. 3. Raten Sie mal wer das Geschirr waschen und den Boden scheuern muss, weil es ein Durcheinander in der Küche gibt? 4. Sie hat die Gabel auf den Tisch zwischen das Messer und den Löffel gelegt. 5. Wir räumen dieses Zeug auf, bevor wir aufs Land fahren.

LESSON 26 • ANSWERS

Grammar

A. 1. Mt. Jefferson ist höher als Der Fuji, aber Der Kilimandscharo ist am höchsten. 2. Ich spiele lieber Monopoly als Karten, aber ich spiele Schach am liebsten. 3. Angela Merkel ist jünger als Arnold Schwarzenegger, aber Prof. Pfrehm ist am jüngsten. 4. Seattle ist näher als Moskau, aber Wien ist am nächsten. 5. David Hasselhoff ist größer als Justin Bieber, aber Shaquille O'Neal ist am größten. 6. Der BMW M4 ist teurer als der Käfer, aber die Mercedes S-Klasse ist am teuersten. 7. Der Amazonas ist länger als der Jangtse, aber der Nil ist am längsten. 8. Milchschokolade schmeckt besser als Lakritze, aber Gummibärchen schmecken am besten.

A. 1. ernst, albern; 2. rührend; 3. Austern; 4. Wüste, Schlange; 5. Stoff;
6. spendieren

Translations

A. 1. The last three films that we saw in the theater were love films.
2. We've seen every romantic film in the entire city. 3. Do you really prefer
to wear silly ties more than colorful hats? 4. Who's the proudest? 5. She
can't be younger than me because I am the youngest.

B. 1. Meine Tochter ist größer als ich, aber mein Sohn ist am größten. 2. Ihr
Hund sieht alt aus, aber mein Hund ist eigentlich am ältesten. 3. Wir haben
die Wüste interessanter als das Meer gefunden. 4. Diese Schauspielerin
verdient am meisten, weil sie auch am intelligentesten ist. 5. Dieser Film
scheint mir am spannendsten zu sein, obwohl seine Spieldauer länger als
neunzig Minuten ist.

LESSON 27 · ANSWERS

Grammar

A. 1. -er; 2. -er; 3. -es, -s; 4. -er; 5. -es, -s

B. 1. während der Mahlzeit; 2. trotz ihrer kurzen Beine; 3. wegen seines
Kommentars; 4. statt eines Umschlags; 5. innerhalb dieses Kreises

C. 1. Der Kajakfahrer wird von der Robbe mitten ins Gesicht getroffen.
2. Sonntags werden alle Geschäfte von dem Bürgermeister geschlossen.
3. Der ganze Wald wird durch den Brand zerstört. 4. Die Hühner außerhalb
des Zauns werden von den klugen Füchsen gefressen. 5. Die Weltpolitik
wird von den Beamten besprochen. 6. Er wird von unserem Freundeskreis
wegen seiner Meinungen ausgeschlossen.

Vocabulary

A. 1. das Treffen; 2. die Verfilmung; 3. furchtbar; 4. der/die Mitreisende;
5. das Wasserfahrzeug

B. 1. heutigen; 2. Hinweisschild; 3. begnügen; 4. findet, statt; 5. gefressen /
geschleudert; 6. anstellen

A. 1. As a tourist was enjoying his kayak tour of the New Zealand islands, he got the surprise of his life. 2. All of a sudden, a seal with an octopus emerged out of the water next to him. 3. The seal flung the octopus at the watercraft—and hit the kayak's captain in the middle of the face. 4. This afternoon, the first official meeting took place between the German chancellor and the American president. 5. During the meal, the chancellor spoke about global politics. 6. Trump's comments on this were: "Isn't there any sausage?" 7. Unfortunately, there was not any sausage on the specialty menu. 8. The US president had to make do with north-German-style fish soup.

B. 1. Der Wind hat geheult, als sie aufgewacht sind. 2. Unsere Gesetze müssen von einem ehrlichen Politiker geschrieben werden. 3. Ihr Haus wird von freundlichen Mitreisenden renoviert. 4. Auf einmal wird der Affe mitten ins Gesicht von der Schildkröte geschlagen. 5. Alles kann durch Brand zerstört werden, wenn die Flammen heiß genug brennen.

LESSON 28 • ANSWERS

Grammar

A. 1. Mein Wagen wurde von meinem Schwager kostenlos repariert. 2. Ganze Städte wurden durch den Sandsturm vergraben. 3. Warum wurdest du von der Polizei verhört? 4. Innerhalb einer halben Stunde wurde die Datei hochgeladen. 5. Um wie viel Uhr wurdet ihr am Flughafen vom Limousinenfahrer abgeholt?

B. i. würde beschweren; könnte (können); gäbe (geben); wäre (sein); würden tun; wären (sein); würden schweigen; würden reden; wollten (wollen); *most appropriate advice*: 1. An Ihrer Stelle würde ich ein belegtes Brot machen …

ii. hätte (haben); würden tun; *most appropriate advice*: Wenn ich Sie wäre, würde ich einen Teilzeitjob suchen und Geld sparen, damit ich mir eine eigene Wohnung leisten könnte.

C. 1. Wenn du die Antworten wüsstest, müsstest du sie mir sagen. 2. Der Polizist würde den mutmaßlichen Verbrecher verhören, wenn er genug Beweisstücke hätte. 3. Sie könnten im IT-Bereich, wenn Sie etwas von Computern verstehen würden. 4. An eurer Stelle würde ich Deutsch lernen. 5. Das wäre großartig, wenn es ein Benutzerhandbuch gäbe.

Vocabulary

A. 1. ziemlich; 2. verhören; 3. einfach; 4. der Dieb; 5. das Gerät

B. 1. Ich kann es kaum fassen; 2. einfach; 3. Schreibtisch; 4. verpasst; 5. Anwendung; 6. Freisprechanlage

A. 1. Who still reads the user manual these days? 2. The ones who would actually want to use their new smartphone. 3. I just think it would be nice if you could actually use the/that thing. 4. If you had an easyphone, you wouldn't be allowed to brag anymore. 5. At least I wouldn't have to read any user manual. 6. If there were an easyphone, I would much rather take that than a so-called smartphone.

B. 1. Wenn Ihr Smartphone wasserdicht wäre, würde ich es ins Meer werfen. 2. Unser Kind hätte Angst, wenn es Polizisten gäbe. 3. An ihrer Stelle würde ich eigentlich nach Deutschland (um)ziehen, wenn ich Deutsch lernen wollte. 4. Wir dürften eine neue, teure Festplatte kaufen, wenn wir genug Geld hätten. 5. Wie viele Anwendungen müsstet ihr runterladen, wenn die Chefin euch neue Geräte besorgen würde?

LESSON 29 · ANSWERS

Grammar

A. 1. Würdest/Könntest du mir ein Weißbier mit Rotkohl bestellen? 2. Wollten Sie mitkommen? 3. Dürften/Könnten wir diesen Sommer bei euch wohnen? 4. Könntest/Würdest du das bitte wiederholen? 5. Würdest/Könntest du bitte damit aufhören? 6. Könnten/Würden Sie bitte leiser sein?

B. 1. Wenn wir klug gewesen wären, hätten wir Deutsch gelernt. 2. Ihr hättet mehr Geld gehabt, wenn ihr öfter Überstunden gemacht hättet. 3. Wenn ich nur die Glaskuppen bestiegen wäre! 4. Wenn mein Mann langsamer gefahren wäre, hätte er das Verkehrszeichen bemerkt. 5. Hättest du die Putenbrust probiert, wenn ich sie empfohlen hätte?

C. 1. Wo wirst du im Jahr 2030 wohnen? 2. Beim nächsten Besuch werden wir das Brandenburg Tor besichtigen. 3. Wann werdet ihr eine Reise durch die deutsche Sprache unternehmen? 4. Übermorgen wird sie mit dem Zug von Berlin ankommen. 5. Eines Tages werden Sie diese Entscheidung bereuen.

Vocabulary

A. 1. schwierig; 2. zerstören; 3. Vorschlag; 4. ursprünglich; 5. öffentlich; 6. ähnlich; 7. vielschichtig; 8. bemerken

B. 1. das geteilte Deutschland; 2. übermorgen; 3. zulässig; 4. Schinken; 5. enthält; 6. berühmt

A. 1. I've always wanted to see the city of Wittenberg. 2. You won't regret it, because it's going to be an unforgettable trip. 3. The original door was made of wood and was destroyed in a fire. 4. Back then it was dangerous to speak publicly against the Catholic Church. 5. Don't reproach yourself. I don't know myself what I would have done if I would have been a priest in the sixteenth century. 6. What's more, I would like to make a suggestion: Would you guys pick me up tonight with your car?

B. 1. Ich hätte die Glaskuppel des Reichstagsgebäudes besichtigt, wenn ich nach Berlin gereist wäre. 2. Der Flug nach München wird nur sechs Stunden dauern, wenn wir einen Flug ohne Zwischenlandung buchen können. 3. Meine Frau wäre heute Morgen um sechs aufgestanden, wenn ich nicht so laut geschnarcht hätte. 4. Was wird deine Tochter in zehn Jahren von Beruf sein? 5. Auf keinen Fall! Die Verkehrspolizei hätte uns nie erwischt, wenn wir zu schnell gefahren wären.

LESSON 30 • ANSWERS

Vocabulary

A. 1. Schön wär's!; 2. komisch; 3. schicken; 4. die Freizeit; 5. sich bemühen

B. 1. bekommen; 2. unterbrechen; 3. Endziel; 4. Hochzeitsfeier; 5. allergisch; 6. Gespräch; 7. ziehst; 8. behilflich

Translations

A. 1. You should give her a video course for her next birthday. 2. I fly home only once a year. I can only afford the one trip. 3. We went to the same school when we were kids. 4. I became a financial adviser because I liked math in school and because I was always good at calculating/crunching numbers. 5. Really? Then you should travel to Hannover. You can visit my parents. 6. You could go by foot, but it would be faster if you took the elevator/went by elevator. 7. I'm pleased that we're talking/going to talk about our families today. So then, what can you tell me about your family history? 8. My grandparents on my father's side originally came from Augsburg, but my father was sent to boarding school in Munich when he was six years old. 9. In 1942, Irene and her mother were taken to Treblinka, where they also died. 10. We wanted/were wanting to talk about the topic of learning a foreign language, right?

B. 1. Der Student hat gestanden/gestand, dass er ihnen die Antworten gegeben hat/gab. 2. Nichts zu danken. Ich weiß, dass ihr mir helfen würdet, wenn ich es bräuchte. 3. Man muss sich wirklich/echt bemühen, wenn man eine Fremdsprache lernen will, aber es kann lebensverändernd sein. 4. Würden Sie mir den Weg zum Aufzug zeigen, bitte? 5. Meine schottischen Vorfahren mütterlicherseits wurden von der amerikanischen Regierung verpflegt, als sie im neunzehnten Jahrhundert in New York City angekommen sind/ankamen.

RESOURCES

DICTIONARIES

There are innumerous German-to-English and English-to-German dictionaries, but the most user-friendly, up-to-date, and accurate ones are as follows:

Compact Oxford German Dictionary. Oxford University Press, 2017.

Collins German Unabridged Dictionary. 9th ed. HarperCollins Publisher Ltd., 2019.

Oxford German Dictionary. 3rd ed. Oxford University Press, 2008.

Langenscheidt Standard Dictionary German: German-English/English-German. Langenscheidt, 2011.

Merriam-Webster's German-English Dictionary. Merriam Webster Mass Market, 2010.

GERMAN-LANGUAGE REFERENCE APPS

Collins German Dictionary (for iPhone and Android)

dict.cc (for iPhone and Android)

GERMAN CULTURE

Flippo, Hyde. *When in Germany, Do as the Germans Do.* 2nd ed. McGraw-Hill Education, 2018.

Frank, Niklas, and James Cave. *German Men Sit Down to Pee and Other Insights into German Culture.* HJ Publishing, 2016.

Lord, Richard. *CultureShock! Germany: A Survival Guide to Customs and Etiquette.* 3rd ed. Marshall Cavendish Intl., 2008.
Tomalin, Barry. *Culture Smart! Germany: The Essential Guide to Customs & Culture.* Kuperard, 2015.

AUSTRIAN CULTURE

Gieler, Peter. *Culture Smart! Austria: The Essential Guide to Customs & Culture.* 2nd ed. Kuperard, 2017.

Roraff, Susan, and Julie Krejci. *CultureShock! Austria: A Survival Guide to Customs and Etiquette.* 3rd ed. Marshall Cavendish Editions, 2011.

SWISS CULTURE

Hunter, Kendall. *Culture Smart! Switzerland: The Essential Guide to Customs & Culture.* 2nd ed. Kuperard, 2016.

CONTENTS

1 **Listen. Then circle the correct answers.**

1. Right now, Moy is _____ .
   a. working for his uncle
   b. starting his own business
   c. studying at Valley Tech

2. Moy's main goal is _____ .
   a. to talk to Ms. Hall
   b. to start his own business
   c. to save some money

3. The first step in Moy's plan is _____ .
   a. to get a job with his uncle
   b. to pass an exam and get his license
   c. to work hard and save money

4. Last summer, Moy _____ .
   a. worked for his uncle
   b. studied at Valley Tech
   c. passed his exam

5. Ms. Hall says that Moy _____ .
   a. will have to graduate in June
   b. will need to save money
   c. will start his business right away

6. Moy hopes to have his own business _____ .
   a. in about five years
   b. in June
   c. this summer

2 Complete the sentences about Mayra's goal.

Mayra has a degree in nursing from a university in Guatemala. Now she lives in Houston, Texas.

1. Mayra _____wants to get_____ a job in a hospital in Houston, Texas.
   (want / get)

2. First, she _____ her English.
   (need / improve)

3. Second, she _____ more nursing classes at a university.
   (need / take)

4. Then she _____ a U.S. nursing license.
   (need / get)

5. Finally, she _____ for jobs at several hospitals.
   (need / apply)

6. Mayra _____ as a nurse because she likes to help people.
   (want / work)

3 Write sentences. Use the information in the chart.

Name	Want to	Need to
Emile	1. open a men's clothing store	2. find a good location for the store
Farah and Ali	3. study engineering in college	4. take a lot of math classes
Monica	5. pass the GED exam	6. take some special classes
Adrian	7. buy a new car	8. save his money

1. Emile _wants to open a men's clothing store._____

2. He _____

3. Farah and Ali _____

4. _____

5. Monica _____

6. _____

7. Adrian _____

8. _____

4 Complete the sentences. Use the simple present or the present continuous.

1. Miguel ____is____ from Brazil.
   be

2. Right now, he _____ in Newark, New Jersey.
   live

3. He _____ a job at a supermarket.
   have

4. At the moment, he _____ as a stock clerk.
   work

5. Every day, he _____ the food on the shelves and _____ the prices.
   put   check

6. Miguel _____ to get a job as a cashier.
   want

7. He _____ to a cashier's training class every Saturday morning.
   go

8. Right now, he _____ how to operate a cash register.
   learn

5 Write sentences. Use the simple present or the present continuous.

1. at the moment / Miguel / live / with his brother Tony

   At the moment, Miguel is living with his brother Tony.

2. Tony / have / a job / at a computer store

   _____

3. right now / he / work / as a salesperson

   _____

4. he / want / become / a computer technician

   _____

5. Tony / take / English classes / every Thursday evening

   _____

6. Tony and Miguel / study / English together / now

   _____

7. Their teacher / always / give / a lot of homework

   _____

6 **Complete the sentences. Use the simple past or the future.**

1. Michio Tarumi _____*came*_____ to the United States in 2013.
   come

2. At that time, he _____ to become a professional baseball player.
   want

3. He _____ for a team in a small town in Florida for two years.
   play

4. Then he _____ to help some boys in the town form their own baseball team.
   begin

5. After that, Michio _____ to change his career plan.
   decide

6. Next September, Michio _____ a new job at a sports center in the town.
   start

7. Michio _____ working with the boys' baseball team last year.
   like

8. In the future, Michio _____ more young people to play baseball and other sports.
   teach

7 **Read the answers. Complete the questions.**

1. When *did you come to this country* _____?

   I came to this country in 2014.

2. Why _____?

   I came here because I wanted to become a professional baseball player.

3. What team _____?

   I played for a team in a small town in Florida.

4. How long _____?

   I played for them for two years.

5. Why _____?

   I decided to change my career plan because I like working with young people.

6. When _____?

   I'll start my new job with the sports center in September.

7. What _____?

   I'll teach young people to play baseball and other sports.

8. How long _____?

   I'm not sure, but I hope I will stay in this town for a long time.

UNIT 1 PERSONAL INFORMATION

Lesson A Listening

1 **Read and circle the correct answers. Then listen.**

Juliana

Anika

Juliana and Anika are friends. Juliana is quiet and shy. She dislikes going to dance clubs or other noisy places. She often writes emails to her friends, but she doesn't like meeting new people. She likes being alone or meeting with just one or two friends. On the weekend, she likes staying home. She loves reading and watching movies. Last weekend, she read two books and watched three movies.

Anika is very different from Juliana. She is friendly and outgoing. She dislikes being alone at home. She loves meeting new people and talking on her cell phone. On the weekend, she enjoys dancing and going to parties with a group of her friends. Last night, they went to a dance club and danced until midnight.

1. Juliana dislikes _____ .
   a. going out
   b. reading books
   c. writing emails
   d. watching movies

2. Juliana likes _____ .
   a. meeting people
   b. talking
   c. staying home
   d. dance clubs

3. Juliana isn't _____ .
   a. quiet
   b. outgoing
   c. shy
   d. happy

4. Anika dislikes _____ .
   a. dancing
   b. dance clubs
   c. staying home
   d. going to parties

5. Anika likes _____ .
   a. making friends
   b. staying home
   c. being alone
   d. writing emails

6. Anika isn't _____ .
   a. outgoing
   b. friendly
   c. shy
   d. fun

2 **Complete the sentences. Use the information in Exercise 1.**

> alone   dislikes   enjoys   going out   outgoing   shy

1. Anika is an _____ person.

2. Juliana _____ meeting with only one or two people at a time.

3. Anika likes _____ with her friends.

4. Juliana _____ going to parties.

5. Juliana is quiet and _____ .

6. Anika doesn't like being _____ .

3 **Circle the correct word.**

1. Pietro is quiet. He **enjoys** / (**dislikes**) talking.

2. Salma is outgoing. She **enjoys** / **dislikes** meeting new people.

3. Chen is friendly. He **enjoys** / **dislikes** talking to other people.

4. Naomi is shy. She **enjoys** / **dislikes** meeting new people.

5. Enrico likes to stay home. He **enjoys** / **dislikes** going out.

4 **Write the opposites.**

> dislike   outgoing   quiet   stay home

1. shy: _____ *outgoing* _____

2. noisy: _____

3. go out: _____

4. like: _____

5 **Listen. Then check four things that Ruben enjoys doing.**

☐ going to parties   ☐ fixing old cars

☐ reading books   ☐ listening to music

☐ learning new dances   ☐ talking about movies

Lesson B Verbs + gerunds

Study the chart and explanation on page 126.

1 Read the chart. Complete the sentences. Use gerunds.

 Francisco
 Erika
 Chang

	Francisco	Erika	Chang
playing soccer	✓✓	✓	✓
doing homework	✓	X	O
getting up early	O	O	XX

Key   ✓ = like   ✓✓ = love   X = dislike   XX = hate   O = not mind

1. Chang hates _____*getting up early*_____ .

2. Erika dislikes _____ .

3. Chang doesn't mind _____ .

4. Francisco loves _____ .

5. Erika and Chang like _____ .

6. Francisco and Erika don't mind _____ .

2 Circle the correct answers. Use the information in Exercise 1.

1. Does Francisco like doing homework? (Yes, he does.) / No, he doesn't.

2. Does Erika dislike getting up early? Yes, she does. / No, she doesn't.

3. Does Chang dislike doing homework? Yes, he does. / No, he doesn't.

4. Do Erika and Chang like playing soccer? Yes, they do. / No, they don't.

5. Does Chang like getting up early? Yes, he does. / No, he doesn't.

6. Does Francisco mind getting up early? Yes, he does. / No, he doesn't.

3 **Complete the sentences. Use gerunds.**

be   clean   do   go out   listen   play   read   take   use   work

Antonio loves ___*going out*___ with his friends. He hates _____ alone. In
                        1   2

English class, he likes _____ in small groups. He doesn't mind _____
                                3   4

a textbook or _____ to a CD. He dislikes _____ a test or _____
                     5   6   7

homework. On the weekend, Antonio enjoys _____ soccer. He also likes
                                                                    8

_____ social media. He doesn't like _____ his room!
        9   10

4 **Complete the questions. Then write answers.**
Use the information in Exercise 3.

1. **A** Does Antonio like _____*going out*_____ with his friends?
                                            (go out)

   B _____*Yes, he does*_____ .

2. **A** Does he hate _____ alone?
                                    (be)

   B _____ .

3. **A** Does he mind _____ a textbook?
                                    (read)

   B _____ .

4. **A** Does he like _____ homework?
                                    (do)

   B _____ .

5 **Write Yes / No questions. Use gerunds.**

1. you / enjoy / go to the beach

   *Do you enjoy going to the beach* ?

2. you / dislike / stand in line

   _____ ?

3. you / hate / work out

   _____ ?

4. you / like / play / video games

   _____ ?

5. you / mind / take out the garbage

   _____ ?

6. you / avoid / eat vegetables

   _____ ?

Lesson C Comparisons

Study the explanation about comparisons on page 132.

1 Read the paragraph. Then complete the chart.

Angelina likes socializing with her friends as much as playing sports. She likes dancing more than cooking. She likes watching movies less than cooking, but she likes reading less than watching movies.

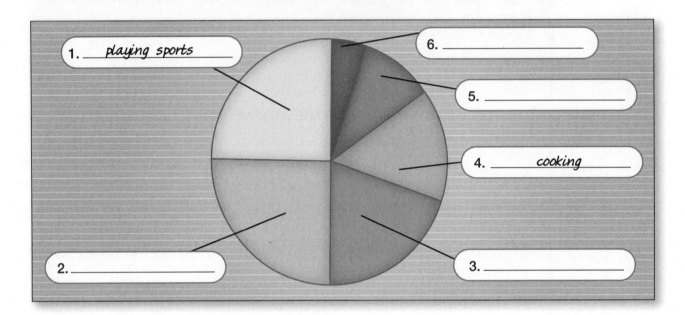

1. _playing sports_

2. _____

3. _____

4. _cooking_

5. _____

6. _____

2 Write sentences about Angelina.

1. cooking / watching movies (less than)
   Angelina likes watching movies less than cooking.

2. watching movies / reading (more than)
   _____

3. dancing / cooking (less than)
   _____

4. dancing / socializing with friends (more than)
   _____

5. playing sports / socializing with friends (as much as)
   _____

3 **Complete the sentences about the people in the pictures. Use *more than*.**

    playing an instrument / painting

    driving a car / riding a bicycle

    reading / washing the dishes

    shopping / going to the movies

1. Ling likes _painting more than playing an instrument_____.

2. Frank enjoys _____.

3. Suzanna enjoys _____.

4. Annie and Steve like _____.

4 **Look at the pictures in Exercise 3. Add the missing word in each sentence.**

1. Annie and Steve like shopping less ~~than~~ watching movies. (than)

2. Ling likes playing an instrument than painting. (less)

3. Suzanna enjoys washing the dishes less reading. (than)

4. Frank enjoys riding a bicycle than driving a car. (more)

Lesson D Reading

1 **Look at the pictures. Predict the job that each ad will describe. Read and write. Then listen.**

1.

Are you creative? Do you like imagining things? Do you love making things? Do you enjoy thinking of new ideas? We are looking for creative people to join our team of architects. Help us design exciting new homes. Your future is with us!

Job: _____*architect*_____

2.

Are you intellectual? Do you enjoy solving difficult problems? Do you like working alone more than working in a group? Yes? Then you are the right person for us! We need computer programmers to help create new computers for the future.

Job: _____

3.

Are you friendly and outgoing? Do you like talking with people and helping others? Do you enjoy meeting people and finding out about them? If your answer is yes, then teaching is the job for you. Come and join our friendly team of teachers. Apply today!

Job: _____

2 **Read the ads in Exercise 1. Write the best job for each person.**

1. Phil is creative. _____*architect*_____

2. Beverley is intellectual. _____

3. Sarah is outgoing. _____

4. Michael likes working alone. _____

5. Elena enjoys meeting new people. _____

6. Julio loves imagining new ideas. _____

3 **Match the jobs with the activities. Use the information from the ads in Exercise 1.**

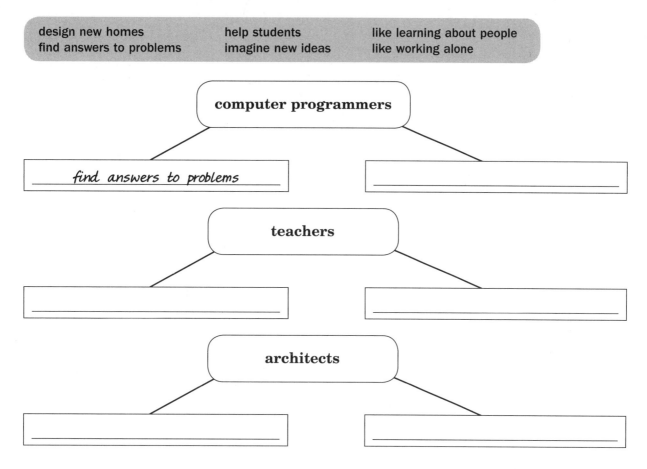

design new homes
find answers to problems

help students
imagine new ideas

like learning about people
like working alone

computer programmers

find answers to problems

teachers

architects

4 **Complete the sentences.**

artist   creative   friendly   intellectual   outgoing   personality   type

1. Your _____ is the way you think, feel, and act.

2. Su-lin likes thinking and finding answers. She is _____.

3. Osman enjoys making things. He is _____.

4. Jenny loves painting and drawing. She wants to be an _____.

5. Ann enjoys meeting people and doing things. She is _____.

6. Jim's personality _____ is intellectual.

7. Albert likes talking to people and socializing. He's very _____.

Lesson E Writing

1 Complete the chart.

architect	drawing	helpful	reliable	talking
creative	finding answers	helping people	scientist	teacher
designer	friendly	outgoing	social worker	using social media

Jobs	Personality adjectives	Activities
architect		

2 Read the paragraph. Then complete the award.

My friend Peter Jones is a social worker at the community center in our town. He is the winner of our town's "Employee of the Month" award. Peter is very friendly and outgoing. He enjoys meeting and helping people who come to the community center. He is also very hardworking. I think Peter has the right job for his personality type.

TOWN EMPLOYEE OF THE MONTH AWARD

Name: Peter Jones

Job: _____

Place of work: _____

Personality: _____

Likes: _____

3 **Read the chart. Then complete the sentences.**

Name:	Rosa Jamulka
Job:	computer programmer
Place of work:	home
Personality:	reliable and intellectual, careful and hardworking
Likes:	using social media, finding answers to problems

Rosa Jamulka has the right job for her personality. She's a

computer programmer . She works at home. Rosa is a very reliable and
     1

_____ person. She is also careful and _____ .
     2   3

She loves using social media, and she enjoys _____ to problems.
                                                      4

Computer programming is a good job for her since it fits her personality.

4 **Read the profile. Write a paragraph about Romano's job and personality type.**

Romano Pereira's Blog Profile

Age: 33
Gender: male
Job: architect at New Designs Company
Place of work: Raleigh, North Carolina

About me
• creative and helpful
• enjoy drawing
• like imagining things that are new and different

Romano Pereira's job fits his personality. _____

_____

_____

_____

Lesson F Another view

1 **Read the questions. Look at the ads. Then fill in the correct answers.**

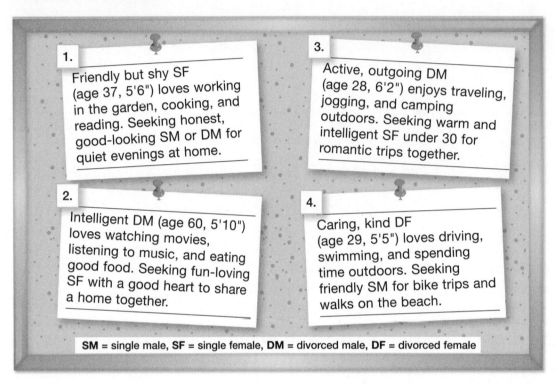

1. _____
Friendly but shy SF (age 37, 5'6") loves working in the garden, cooking, and reading. Seeking honest, good-looking SM or DM for quiet evenings at home.

2. _____
Intelligent DM (age 60, 5'10") loves watching movies, listening to music, and eating good food. Seeking fun-loving SF with a good heart to share a home together.

3. _____
Active, outgoing DM (age 28, 6'2") enjoys traveling, jogging, and camping outdoors. Seeking warm and intelligent SF under 30 for romantic trips together.

4. _____
Caring, kind DF (age 29, 5'5") loves driving, swimming, and spending time outdoors. Seeking friendly SM for bike trips and walks on the beach.

SM = single male, **SF** = single female, **DM** = divorced male, **DF** = divorced female

1. The older man enjoys _____.

   A) traveling

   B) camping

   ● watching movies

   D) going to the beach

2. The younger woman enjoys _____.

   A) swimming

   B) gardening

   C) cooking

   D) staying home

3. What word does NOT describe the younger man?

   A) shy

   B) active

   C) outgoing

   D) divorced

4. Which two people like going out more than staying home?

   A) 1 and 2

   B) 2 and 3

   C) 1 and 4

   D) 3 and 4

5. What does the single female enjoy doing?

   A) traveling

   B) swimming

   C) cooking

   D) driving

6. How tall is the single female?

   A) 5 feet 5 inches

   B) 5 feet 6 inches

   C) 5 feet 10 inches

   D) 6 feet 2 inches

2 **Read the situation. Circle the letter of the best answer. Write a sentence with *must*.**

1. Ruben doesn't like parties. He enjoys quiet evenings at home.
   a. be fun-loving
   b. be very friendly
   (c.) be a little shy
   d. be very outgoing

   _Ruben must be a little shy_____ .

2. Miguel plays guitar in a band. He's also a pretty good singer.
   a. love music
   b. know how to dance
   c. be an honest person
   d. like to be alone

   _____ .

3. Adriana loves math. She's studying computer science. She gets good grades.
   a. be a kind person
   b. be a little shy
   c. be good at sports
   d. be very intelligent

   _____ .

4. In the summer, Hana takes tennis lessons. In the winter, she likes to go skiing.
   a. like sports a lot
   b. like spending weekends at home
   c. be a quiet, shy person
   d. be a good dancer

   _____ .

3 **Complete the sentences. Use words from the box and *must* or *must not*.**

| be a reliable employee | be very creative | like working out |
| be a very good cook | know how to swim | |

1. No one likes Julia's food. Her cakes are terrible, and she can't even make good sandwiches. She _must not be a very good cook_____ .

2. Vincent likes art and music a lot. That's one of his paintings on the wall.
   He _____ .

3. Malcom is often late for work. At work, he spends time talking on his cell phone and using social media. He _____ .

4. Melinda never exercises. She doesn't like going for walks in the park.
   She _____ .

5. In the summer, Abby goes to the beach or to the pool almost every day.
   She _____ .

UNIT 2 AT SCHOOL

Lesson A Listening

1 **Complete the conversation. Then listen.**

concentrate   discouraged   index cards   list   paper   underline

Victor Hi, Frank. How's it going?

Frank Not so good. Can you help me? I have so much homework. I have to write a

_____*paper*_____ for Monday, and I have a test tomorrow!
1

Victor You need to make a _____ of all your homework. Then write the due date
2

of each item on your calendar.

Frank OK, but what about the test?

Victor You should study your textbook and _____ all the main ideas. Write the
3

important words on _____ and study them in your free time. Do you live
4

near a quiet place where you can _____?
5

Frank Well, there's a library a few blocks away.

Victor Good! You should study and write your paper there. Don't feel _____!
6

2 **Circle the correct answers. Use the information in Exercise 1.**

1. Frank needs some _____.
   a. homework
   b. advice
   c. friends
   d. paper

2. Frank has to _____.
   a. study less
   b. help Victor
   c. plan his work
   d. get a calendar

3. Victor is _____.
   a. boring
   b. helpful
   c. discouraged
   d. quiet

4. Victor tells Frank how to _____.
   a. do his homework
   b. concentrate
   c. get to the library
   d. write a paper

3 Match the sentences.

1. Tami can't finish her book. __d__
2. Bernie underlines the main ideas. _____
3. Sue can't remember new words. _____
4. Pam has too much homework. _____
5. Paolo is not happy. _____
6. The book isn't interesting. _____

a. He is an active reader.
b. He is discouraged.
c. It's boring.
d. She needs to concentrate.
e. She needs to make a list of things to do.
f. She needs to write them on index cards.

4 Complete the sentences.

active	concentrate	index cards	paper
boring	discouraged	list	vocabulary

1. I have to make a _____ list _____ of all my homework.

2. I have to finish this _____ by tomorrow morning.

3. It's hard to _____ in this noisy room.

4. I really need to be a more _____ reader.

5. I need to look up the new _____ in the dictionary.

6. I will write the most important information on _____.

7. This book is _____. I can't read it.

8. I feel _____ because I never know all of the answers.

5 Mark an ✗ next to the bad study habits. Put a (✓) next to the good study habits.

☒ doesn't study new words
☐ is late for class
☐ hands in homework late
☐ makes to-do lists

☐ forgets homework
☐ doesn't study for tests
☐ writes new words on index cards
☐ underlines the main ideas

6 Listen. Then check (✓) the statement that is true.

☐ Amelia thinks Mr. Wilson's strategies are crazy.
☐ Mr. Wilson thinks that Amelia is not a very good student.
☐ Mr. Wilson has talked about learning strategies in class.

Lesson B Present perfect

Study the chart and explanation on page 128. For a list of irregular verbs, turn to page 131.

1 Circle *for* or *since*.

1. I have known Elsa (for)/ **since** two years.

2. Tina has taught this class **for** / **since** September.

3. Jasmine has worked in the store **for** / **since** last year.

4. We have lived in Miami **for** / **since** six months.

5. Kelly has had her car **for** / **since** 2015.

6. They have been in the library **for** / **since** 4:00 p.m.

7. I have studied computers **for** / **since** two weeks.

8. They have been in our class **for** / **since** Tuesday.

2 Complete the sentences. Use *have* or *has*.

1. How long _____*have*_____ you had your car?

2. How long _____ I known you?

3. How long _____ she studied Spanish?

4. How long _____ they lived in this city?

5. How long _____ he been in Canada?

6. How long _____ we worked here?

3 Complete the sentences. Use the present perfect.

1. Bianca works in a restaurant. She _____*has worked*_____ there for five years.

2. Federico and Sonya live in Brazil. They _____ there since April.

3. My sister and I study piano. We _____ piano for 15 years.

4. Mei-lin has a motorcycle. She _____ a motorcycle since 2016.

5. Ms. Green teaches English. She _____ English for twelve years.

6. Tom is a student. He _____ a student for three months.

4 **Complete the sentences. Write the answers.**

1.

A (he / be) How long ___has he been___ on the computer?

B For ___four hours___ .

Since ___3:00 p.m.___

2.

A (she / know) How long _____ Dave?

B For _____ .

Since _____ .

3.

A (he / live) How long _____ in the U.S.?

B For _____ .

Since _____ .

5 **Write questions. Use the present perfect.**

1. they / work / in this school

   How long *have they worked in this school* _____?

2. she / have / a driver's license

   How long _____?

3. he / live / in this apartment

   How long _____?

4. you / be / married

   How long _____?

Check your answers. See page 135.

Lesson C Present perfect

Study the chart and explanation on page 128. For a list of irregular verbs, turn to page 131.

1 **Complete the sentences. Use the correct form of the verb.**

1. Have you ever _____*lost*_____ a library book?
   (lose)

2. Has your teacher ever _____ your name?
   (forget)

3. Have you ever _____ the newspaper online?
   (read)

4. Have you ever _____ the bus to school?
   (take)

5. Have you ever _____ the best grade in the class?
   (get)

2 **Read the chart. Complete the sentences.**

	Study skills survey: Do you . . .	Janice	Hiroshi
1.	study English online?	yes	no
2.	talk to a school counselor?	no	no
3.	make to-do lists?	yes	no
4.	write new words in a vocabulary notebook?	yes	yes
5.	do your homework on the computer?	yes	no

1. **A** ____*Has*____ Janice ever ____*studied*____ English online?
   B ____*Yes, she has*____ .

2. **A** _____ Janice and Hiroshi ever _____ to a school counselor?
   B _____ .

3. **A** _____ Janice ever _____ a to-do list?
   B _____ .

4. **A** _____ Janice and Hiroshi ever _____ new words in a vocabulary notebook?
   B _____ .

5. **A** _____ Hiroshi ever _____ his homework on the computer?
   B _____ .

3 **Complete the sentences. Use *ever*.**

1. _____*Have you ever used*_____ the computer in the library?
   (you, use)

2. _____ to you after class?
   (your teacher, talk)

3. _____ with you?
   (your friends, study)

4. _____ an email to your teacher?
   (you, write)

5. _____ the main ideas in your textbook?
   (you, underline)

6. _____ all the questions correct on a test?
   (they, get)

4 **Read the conversations. Write sentences about the people in the conversations.**

1. **Kate**   Have you ever forgotten to study for a test?

   Melissa No, I haven't.

   Kate   Have you ever lost your textbook?

   Melissa Yes, I have. I left it on a bus.

   _*Melissa hasn't ever forgotten to study for a test.*_____

   _*She has lost her textbook.*_____

2. **Luis**   Have you ever had trouble concentrating on your homework?

   Franco   Yes!

   Luis   Have you ever done the wrong homework?

   Franco   No, I don't think so.

   _____

   _____

3. **Maria**   Have you ever read a newspaper in English?

   Rose   Yes, I have.

   Maria   Have you ever tried to speak English with your neighbors?

   Rose   No, I haven't. But I want to!

   _____

   _____

Lesson D Reading

1 Read and answer the questions. Then listen.

Strategies for Learning New Words

Have you ever felt discouraged because there are so many new words to learn in English? Have you tried to set goals for learning new words? Here are some ideas to help you practice and remember vocabulary.

Strategy #1: Keep a vocabulary notebook.
Buy a small notebook. Take it with you everywhere. When you see new words around you in the street, in an advertisement, or in a newspaper, write the new words in your notebook. Use clues to guess the meanings. At the end of the day, use your dictionary to check the meanings. Write an example sentence, or draw a picture to help you remember the new words.

Strategy #2: Make vocabulary cards.
Have you ever felt bored waiting in line or taking the bus? Use the time to practice vocabulary. Choose five words from your English class or from a newspaper or magazine. Write each word on a small card. Write the word on one side of the card. Then write the definition or a translation on the other side. Test yourself on the definitions.

Strategy #3: Use new words in conversations every day.
Choose one new word from your notebook or vocabulary cards every day. Try to use it in a conversation some time during the day with your friends, classmates, family, or with your teacher. Using the words you learn will help you remember them.

1. What is the article about?

   The article is about strategies for learning new words.

2. What are the three strategies described in this article?

   1. _____

   2. _____

   3. _____

3. If you write a new word on one side of a card and write the definition on the other side, what strategy are you using?

   _____

2 Circle the correct answers. Use the information in Exercise 1.

1. The article says you can use *all* of these strategies _____ .
   a. in class
   (b.) every day
   c. on the bus
   d. with pictures

2. The article says these strategies should help you to _____ new words.
   a. draw
   b. write
   c. translate
   d. remember

3. The article says you should use _____ to check definitions.
   a. a dictionary
   b. a notebook
   c. an index card
   d. an advertisement

4. The article says you can practice using new words when _____ .
   a. watching TV
   b. talking to friends
   c. listening to the radio
   d. reading a newspaper

3 Make sentences. Match the sentence parts. Use the information in Exercise 1.

1. You can draw pictures __c__
2. You can use new words _____
3. You can look at vocabulary cards _____
4. You should guess the meaning first _____
5. You should write definitions _____

a. and use a dictionary later.
b. on the back of vocabulary cards.
c. in your vocabulary notebook.
d. when you talk to friends.
e. when you are waiting in line.

4 Look at the bold words. Write a word from the box with a similar meaning.

| clues | gestures | plan | practice | set | strategies |

1. The article suggests some easy **methods** for learning new words. __*strategies*__

2. I need to **decide on** a few goals for learning English. _____

3. Have you made a **decision** to help you reach your goals? _____

4. I need to **use** new words every day to help me remember them. _____

5. Certain **information** in a sentence can help you guess the meaning. _____

6. **Hand movements** can sometimes help to explain the meaning. _____

Lesson E Writing

1 Complete the charts.

> Ask questions in class every day.
> Listen to the radio.
> Look up new words in a dictionary.
> Read newspapers in English.
> Talk to people at work in English.
>
> Underline new words with colored pens.
> Use new words in everyday conversation.
> Watch movies in English.
> Watch the news in English.

Listening strategies	Speaking strategies	Reading strategies
Listen to the radio.		

2 Read Omar's journal. Then answer the questions.

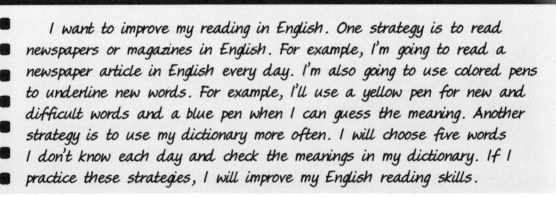

I want to improve my reading in English. One strategy is to read newspapers or magazines in English. For example, I'm going to read a newspaper article in English every day. I'm also going to use colored pens to underline new words. For example, I'll use a yellow pen for new and difficult words and a blue pen when I can guess the meaning. Another strategy is to use my dictionary more often. I will choose five words I don't know each day and check the meanings in my dictionary. If I practice these strategies, I will improve my English reading skills.

1. What is Omar's first strategy for improving his reading? Give an example.

   Omar's first strategy is to read newspapers or magazines in English.

   He is going to read a newspaper article in English every day.

2. What is Omar's second strategy for improving his reading? Give an example.

   _____

   _____

3. What is Omar's third strategy for improving his reading? Give an example.

   _____

   _____

3 **Read the strategies. Write the number of the strategy next to the example.**

Strategy 1: Guess the meaning of new words.

Strategy 2: Use one new word every day.

Strategy 3: Make a vocabulary notebook.

Strategy 4: Review new words after class.

___4___ 1. I'll make vocabulary cards and look at them on the bus.

_____ 2. I'll write the new word in a sentence and send it in an email to my friend.

_____ 3. I'll write three new words in my notebook every day.

_____ 4. I can look at the pictures and sentences around a new word and figure out the meaning.

4 **Write a paragraph about four strategies for learning new words. Give one example for each strategy. Use the strategies and examples in Exercise 3.**

I have learned some useful strategies for learning new words.

_____

_____

_____

_____

_____

_____

_____

_____

_____

_____

_____

Lesson F Another view

1 Complete the sentences.

answer   look   make   read   skim   spend   worry

Test-taking tips

1. _____Read_____ the directions carefully.

2. _____ the whole test before you start.

3. _____ the most difficult questions at the end.

4. Don't _____ too much time on one question.

5. Don't _____ if the other students finish before you.

6. _____ sure you have answered all questions on the test.

7. Don't _____ at other students' tests.

2 Which tips did these students need to follow? Write the number of the tip from Exercise 1.

1. I spent 20 minutes on the first question, and I didn't have time to finish the other questions. Tip __4__

2. Everyone finished before me, and I started to worry. Tip _____

3. I forgot to answer some of the questions. Tip _____

4. I tried to look at another student's test, and I failed the test. Tip _____

5. I didn't know the test had three parts. I only finished two parts. Tip _____

6. I spent too much time on the difficult questions. I wasn't able to answer the easy questions. Tip _____

7. I circled the answers, but the directions said: "Underline the answers." Tip _____

3 **Complete the story. Use the correct words.**

Vicky _____*has been*_____ a student at the City University for
(1. was / has been)

two years. She _____ good grades, but
(2. always got / has always gotten)

since last January, her grades _____ down.
(3. went / have gone)

Why? Well, in January, she _____ a problem.
(4. had / has had)

She _____ more money to pay for school and
(5. needed / has needed)

for rent. So, on January 10th, she _____
(6. started / has started)

a job as a server at a café near the school. She _____ there for two
(7. worked / has worked)

months now. Last week, Vicky _____ to her school counselor about the
(8. talked / has talked)

problem and asked, "How can I work and study at the same time?" In their meeting, the

counselor _____ her some good ideas about organizing her time. Since
(9. gave / has given)

then, her grades _____ , and she's still working.
(10. improved / have improved)

4 **Complete the sentences. Use the present perfect or
the simple past. Use the information in the chart.**

	Naomi	Tran
1. forget to put (his / her) name on a test		on a history test last week
2. watch a TV show in English	the news on TV last night	
3. study geometry	in the first year of high school	in the first year of high school

1. Has Tran ever forgotten to put his name on a test?

   Yes. He _____.

2. _____ Naomi ever _____?

   Yes. _____.

3. _____ Naomi and Tran ever _____?

   Yes. _____.

UNIT 3 FRIENDS AND FAMILY

Lesson A Listening

1 **Read and complete the paragraph. Then listen.**

borrow   broken   came over   complain   favor   noisy

I Owe You One

My neighbor Amy ___*came over*___ yesterday to ask a _____.
¹   ²

Her light was _____, and it was too high for her to reach. She wanted to
³

_____ my ladder. We had a cup of coffee and started to talk about our
⁴

other neighbors. Two weeks ago, they had a party, and Amy told them the music was too

loud. Then, last weekend, they had another party. Amy couldn't sleep because they were too

_____. I said she should _____ to the building manager,
⁵   ⁶

and I gave her the phone number. Then I helped her carry my ladder to her apartment. "Rita,

thanks for your help," she said. "I owe you one!"

---

2 **Circle the correct answers. Use the information in Exercise 1.**

1. Amy asked Rita for a _____.
   a. ladder
   b. new light
   c. phone number
   d. cup of coffee

2. Amy couldn't sleep because _____.
   a. her light was broken
   b. the neighbors had a party
   c. she needed to call the manager
   d. she needed to borrow a ladder

3. Amy _____ Rita's help.
   a. doesn't need
   b. doesn't want
   c. complains about
   d. really appreciates

4. Amy owes Rita a _____.
   a. favor
   b. ladder
   c. phone number
   d. cup of coffee

3 Complete the sentences.

> appreciates   borrow   complained   noise
> battery   come over   favor   owe

1. Mary hasn't read this book. She is going to ___*borrow*___ it from me.

2. I think our smoke alarm needs a new _____.

3. Meg thanked Tina for her help. She always _____ Tina's help.

4. You lent me 10 dollars. Here's a dollar. I now _____ you nine dollars.

5. My neighbors were so noisy last night. I _____ to the apartment manager.

6. Our old dishwasher made a lot of _____. Our new one is quiet.

7. Could you do me a _____ and babysit my children tonight?

8. My daughter wants her friend to _____, but I said no. It's a school night.

4 Circle the correct word.

1. Rita (**lent**) / **borrowed** a ladder to Amy.

2. Amy **lent** / **borrowed** a ladder from Rita.

3. My friend **lent** / **borrowed** a book from me.

4. I **lent** / **borrowed** a book to my friend.

5 Complete the sentences. Use *lend* or *borrow*.

1. Could you ___*lend*___ me some money? I want to buy a cup of coffee.

2. I can't _____ you my cell phone right now. It's broken.

3. Could I _____ your dictionary? I forgot how to spell this word.

4. Do you want to _____ my umbrella? It's raining outside.

6 How is Daniel going to get into his apartment? Listen and check.

☐ His wife is going to come home and open the door.

☐ His neighbor, Edgar, has a copy of his key.

☐ He's going to borrow a key from the building manager.

Lesson B Clauses and phrases with *because*

Study the explanation on page 132.

1 Make sentences. Match the sentence parts.

1. Stan borrowed some money __c__
2. Dan travels a lot _____
3. Alfredo and Maria were late _____
4. Dolores studied for three hours _____
5. Tran called the building manager _____

a. because of his job.
b. because she had a big test.
c. because he wants to buy a car.
d. because his window was broken.
e. because of a flat tire.

2 Circle *because* or *because of*.

1. Ana couldn't sleep (**because**) / **because of** the baby was crying.

2. I couldn't go to work **because** / **because of** my car broke down.

3. We didn't go out **because** / **because of** the bad weather.

4. Tanya needed a ladder **because** / **because of** the broken light.

5. Joseph couldn't take a vacation **because** / **because of** his busy work schedule.

6. Marietta didn't come to class **because** / **because of** she had a bad headache.

3 Rewrite the sentences. Use the words in parentheses.

1. We couldn't sleep *because it was noisy*. (the noise)

   We couldn't sleep because of the noise.

2. We couldn't play soccer *because it was raining*. (the rain)

   _____

3. They were late for the appointment *because there were a lot of cars*. (the traffic)

   _____

4. Reyna stayed at home *because she had the flu*. (the flu)

   _____

5. Sam stayed up late *because he watched the basketball game*. (the basketball game)

   _____

6. Beatriz moved to this country *because her children live here*. (her children)

   _____

4 **Complete the sentences. Use *because* or *because of*.**

1. Teresa couldn't sleep last night _____*because*_____ she had a headache.

2. Keizo couldn't lock his door _____ he lost his keys.

3. We moved to California _____ my husband's job.

4. William couldn't drive his car _____ the broken door.

5. Karen likes her neighborhood _____ it is safe at night.

5 **Complete the sentences. Use *because* or *because of* and words from the box.**

1.

2.

3.

4.

5.

6.

he was sick	it was her son's birthday	the smoke
it was closed	the rain	there were so many people

1. They couldn't go to the supermarket *because it was closed*_____.

2. They couldn't play baseball _____.

3. She made a cake _____.

4. My neighbor called 911 _____.

5. He couldn't go to school _____.

6. We had to wait a long time _____.

Lesson C Adverbs of degree

Study the explanation on page 132.

1 Write the opposites.

| close | hot | small | strong | tall | young |

1. cold   _____*hot*_____
2. short   _____
3. big   _____

4. weak   _____
5. far   _____
6. old   _____

2 Complete the sentences. Use the adjectives in Exercise 1.

1. The water is _____*hot*_____ enough to make coffee.
2. He isn't _____ enough to reach the ceiling.
3. They're not _____ enough to lift the box.
4. The car is too _____ for five people.
5. He is too _____ to get married.
6. The train station isn't _____ enough to walk.

3 Complete the sentences. Use the correct adjective and *too* or *enough*.

1. She's _____*too young*_____ .
2. She's not _*old enough*_ .

3. He's _____ .
4. He's not _____ .

5. It's _____ .
6. It's not _____ .

34 UNIT 3

4 **Complete the sentences. Use *too* or *not . . . enough* with the word in parentheses.**

1. **A** I don't want to live in the city anymore. It's _____ *too noisy* _____ .
   (noisy)

   B I agree. It's _____ *not quiet enough* _____ .
   (quiet)

2. **A** The rent for this apartment is _____ .
   (expensive)

   B You're right. It's _____ .
   (cheap)

3. **A** We need a new house. Our house is _____ .
   (small)

   B That's true. Our house is _____ .
   (big)

4. **A** I don't like this exercise. It's _____ .
   (difficult)

   B I agree. It's _____ .
   (easy)

5. **A** I want to quit my job. It's _____ .
   (boring)

   B You've complained to me before that your job is _____ .
   (interesting)

6. **A** My daughter wants to take a trip by herself. She's _____ .
   (young)

   B I agree. She's _____ .
   (old)

5 **Complete the sentences. Use the correct adjective and *too* or *enough*.**

| big   experienced   high   old   strong   tall   weak   young |

1. I have five children. This house isn't _____ *big enough* _____ for us.

2. James is 6'10". He's _____ to reach the ceiling.

3. My daughter is six months old. She's not _____ to talk.

4. The books are on the top shelf. They're _____ to reach.

5. This box is not very heavy. I'm _____ to carry it.

6. Meredith is 14 years old. She's _____ to drive.

7. My husband hasn't finished his training. He's not _____ to be an engineer.

8. I need some help! I'm _____ to lift this TV.

Lesson D Reading

1 **Read and correct the information in the sentences. Then listen.**

MY NEIGHBORHOOD

People sometimes ask me about my neighborhood. Is it nice? Is it safe? My answer is that I'm very lucky to have nice neighbors. They are very friendly and kind. For example, they help me with shopping when I feel too sick to go out. They look after my house when I am away. Once a month, we get together to talk about any problems.

Last week, my neighbors saw some teenagers near my house. They were painting graffiti on a wall. My neighbors shouted at them, and they ran away. The next day, my neighbors came over with some brushes and some paint. We painted over the graffiti together, and the teens haven't come back. I am so happy that I have such nice neighbors. Because we work together, this neighborhood is a safe place to live.

1. The writer doesn't like to spend time with her neighbors.

   The writer gets together with her neighbors once a month.

2. The writer's neighbors painted graffiti.

   _____

3. The writer's neighbors talked to the teenagers, and they walked away.

   _____

4. The writer's neighborhood is not safe.

   _____

2 **Circle the correct answers. Use the information in Exercise 1.**

1. What is the main idea of the first paragraph?
   a. The writer's neighbors watch her house.
   b. The writer's neighbors talk every month.
   c. The writer's neighbors are friendly.
   d. The writer's neighbors are too noisy.

2. The writer gives examples to show that _____.
   a. her neighbors are nice people
   b. her neighbors talk too much
   c. she has very few neighbors
   d. she has a lot of neighbors

3. What did the neighbors see?
   a. teenagers talking
   b. teenagers painting graffiti
   c. teenagers breaking a window
   d. teenagers breaking into the writer's house

4. What did the neighbors do?
   a. They ran away.
   b. They called the police.
   c. They stayed in their houses.
   d. They shouted at the teenagers.

3 **Complete the sentences.**

| break into | get into | get together | goes off | look after | run away |

1. You can _____ get into _____ my car and wait for me. Here's the key.

2. When do you want to _____ again?

3. My neighbors _____ my dog when I'm on vacation.

4. My smoke alarm sometimes _____ when I am cooking.

5. I close the windows so my cat can't _____ .

6. Someone tried to _____ my car yesterday, so I called the police.

4 **Look at the bold words. Write verbs from Exercise 3 with a similar meaning.**

1. The men tried to **escape** when they saw the police car. _____ run away _____

2. I **take care of** my neighbor's children in the afternoon. _____

3. My friends and I often **meet** at a coffee shop after class. _____

4. My alarm clock **makes a loud noise** at 6:00 every morning. _____

5. My shoes are very dirty. I shouldn't **enter** your car. _____

6. Someone tried to **enter** my home last night, so I called the police. _____

Lesson E Writing

1 **Read the email. Label the parts of the email.**

problem   request   today's date   writer

1. ___today's date___

2. _____

3. _____

4. _____

● ● ●	Reply Forward

To: centurymanagement@netmail.com
From: n_akerjee@gmail.com
Subject: Broken light   July 15, 2018

To Whom It May Concern:

My name is Nazmi Akerjee. I live at 310 Walnut Street in Apartment 5. I am writing because the hallway outside my apartment has a broken light. I tried to fix it, but my ladder is not tall enough to reach it. The hallway is not safe at night because of the broken light.

Could you please come as soon as possible to fix the light? Thank you in advance for your help.

Sincerely,
Nazmi Akerjee

2 **Circle *T* (True) or *F* (False). Use the information in Exercise 1.**

1. Nazmi knows the name of the person to whom she is writing.	T	(F)
2. Nazmi's address is 310 Chestnut Street, Apartment 5.	T	F
3. The broken light is inside Nazmi's apartment.	T	F
4. Nazmi feels that her hallway is not safe at night.	T	F
5. Nazmi wants someone to fix the light.	T	F
6. Nazmi tried to fix the light.	T	F
7. The ladder is tall enough to reach the light.	T	F
8. Nazmi thanks the company for their help before the light is fixed.	T	F

3 **Complete the sentences.**

advance   because   because of   soon   very

1. Could you please send a repair person as _____*soon*_____ as possible?

2. I am writing _____ my window is broken.

3. It is _____ cold and I can't sleep.

4. Thank you in _____ for fixing the problem.

5. My apartment is very cold _____ the broken window.

4 **Write a complaint email about a broken window.**
Use the information in Exercise 3.

● ● ●
                                                            Reply   Forward

To: info@PrestigeApts.com
From: _____
Subject: _____   February 21st, 2018

My name is _____

_____

_____

_____

_____

_____

_____

_____

_____

_____

Sincerely,

_____

Lesson F Another view

1 **Read the questions. Look at the ad. Then fill in the correct answers.**

Hillside Hospital Seeks Four Volunteers
Start immediately!

Hours: 1:00 p.m.–7:00 p.m., three afternoons a week

Job Duties: Greet visitors with a smile, and take them to patients' rooms. Serve tea, coffee, and cold drinks to visitors. Play games with patients, and take books to their rooms.

Requirements: 18 years old or older. Seniors welcome to apply. Must be friendly, helpful, and patient. Teamwork skills a plus.

Send resume and letter of interest to:
Volunteer Division
Hillside Hospital
1200 Hillside Avenue
Los Angeles, CA 90027
No phone calls, please.

1. Volunteers must be —— years old.
   - ● at least 18
   - B over 65
   - C under 18
   - D under 65

2. How many hours do volunteers have to work a day?
   - A one
   - B three
   - C six
   - D seven

3. Which statement is NOT true?
   - A Volunteers should be patient.
   - B Volunteers should be very friendly.
   - C Volunteers should be experienced nurses.
   - D Volunteers should like meeting people.

4. What will a volunteer at the hospital do?
   - A assist nurses
   - B assist visitors
   - C give medicine
   - D serve food

5. What are *teamwork skills*?
   - A the ability to play sports
   - B the ability to work with other people
   - C the ability to communicate with patients
   - D the ability to find people to work with

6. Which statement is true?
   - A Volunteers must prefer to work alone.
   - B Volunteers must like meeting people.
   - C Volunteers must call to apply.
   - D Volunteers must like children.

2 **Complete the sentences. Use the affirmative or negative of *be able to*.**

1. We ___*aren't able to do*___ the laundry today. The washing machine is broken.
   (do)

2. Most people in Quebec _____ two languages — French and English.
   (speak)

3. They're complaining because they _____ a conversation. It's too noisy in here.
   (have)

4. My neighbor has a set of my keys. She _____ my door if I lose my keys.
   (open)

5. The technician _____ my computer now. I have to wait until tomorrow.
   (fix)

6. I'm sorry, but Tom _____ here today. He's too busy.
   (be)

7. They _____ the apartment now because it has a new smoke alarm.
   (rent)

8. I _____ the office at 5:00 today. I have too much work to do.
   (leave)

3 **Write sentences that are true for you. Use *be able to* and the words in parentheses.**

1. (run a mile in 10 minutes)

   ___*I'm able to run a mile in 10 minutes.*___ OR ___*I'm not able to run a mile in 10 minutes*___

2. (lift 10 pounds with one hand)

   _____

3. (speak Japanese)

   _____

4. (play the piano for my classmates)

   _____

5. (fix a computer)

   _____

6. (change a flat tire)

   _____

UNIT 4 HEALTH

Lesson A Listening

1 Read and complete the paragraph. Then listen.

advice   diet   exercise   pressure   tired   weight

Dear Alice,

My husband Alex is an office assistant. He drives to work every day.

He works on the tenth floor, and he always takes the elevator. His ___*diet*___ is
                                                                      1

not very healthy. For example, for lunch, he usually eats pizza or a hamburger and

fries. On the weekend, he often eats a lot of ice cream and cookies. He doesn't

_____ very much. In fact, he usually takes a walk only once a week on
       2

Saturday. He never rides his bike. He is worried because his blood _____

                                                                              3

is high, and he has gained 15 pounds. He knows he has to lose some

_____ . He has also been very _____ lately. What should he do?
       4   5

                                              Worried in Seattle

Dear Worried in Seattle,

Your husband needs to make an appointment to see his doctor so that he can

ask the doctor for some _____ .
                               6

Alice

2 Circle the correct answers. Use the information in Exercise 1.

1. Alex always _____ .
   (a.) takes the elevator
   b. walks up the stairs

2. Alex does not _____ .
   a. take walks
   b. exercise enough

3. Alex is worried because _____ .
   a. he never rides his bike
   b. he has gained weight

4. Alice says Alex needs to _____ .
   a. change his job
   b. talk to his doctor

3 Complete the chart.

> check your weight   eat breakfast   go to bed late
> drink a lot of soda   eat fish   ride a bicycle
> eat a lot of hamburgers   gain 20 pounds

Healthy activities	Unhealthy activities
check your weight	

4 Complete the sentences.

> diet   exercise   healthy   medication   weight

1. **A** Pat eats too many hamburgers. He needs to change his ____*diet*____.

   B I know.

2. **A** Alex has high blood pressure. He needs to take _____.

   B That's too bad.

3. **A** I've gained 20 pounds. I need to lose _____.

   B You should try going to the gym three times a week.

4. **A** Ali sits at work all day.

   B He needs to _____ regularly.

5. **A** I really want to stay _____.

   B Then you need to follow your doctor's advice.

5 Listen. Then write *P* for the things Stan did in the past and *N* for the things he does now.

_*N*_ walk up the stairs		____ eat breakfast
____ eat fast food for lunch		____ go to the gym
____ take the elevator		____ work 12 hours a day
____ have soup for lunch		____ leave work at 5:30

Lesson B Present perfect

Study the chart and explanation on page 128. For a list of irregular verbs, turn to page 131.

1 Complete the paragraph. Use the present perfect.

be   eat   exercise   gain   give   go   start

I __have gained__ weight recently, so I have decided to change my diet and
___1___

get in shape. I _____ up potato chips, and I _____
___2___   ___3___

(not) any pizza recently. I _____ to eat more salad and fruit. I
___4___

_____ at the gym three times this week already. I can see that I
___5___

am losing weight, and I'm sure my blood pressure _____ down. I feel
___6___

healthier, and I _____ (not) tired in a long time.
___7___

2 Write sentences. Use the present perfect.

1. You / not / exercise / this week

   You haven't exercised this week.

2. Paul / gain weight / recently

   _____

3. Ray and Louisa / lose weight / recently

   _____

4. Alicia / be unhappy / lately

   _____

5. My blood pressure / go up / recently

   _____

6. Greg / not / visit a dentist / recently

   _____

7. Sarah / give up / desserts / lately

   _____

3 **Write sentences about Annette. Use the present perfect with *recently*.**

> Annette's Goals for November
>
> 1. Check blood pressure.
> 2. Go to the gym. ✓
> 3. Eat more fruits and vegetables. ✓
> 4. Sleep eight hours a day. ✓
> 5. Take vitamins.

1. Annette hasn't checked her blood pressure recently.

2. _____

3. _____

4. _____

5. _____

4 **Write questions and answers. Use the present perfect.**

1. Bill / lose weight / recently

   A Has Bill lost weight recently _____?

   B No, _____ .

2. Tina and Mario / give up desserts / recently

   A _____?

   B Yes, _____ .

3. you / check your blood pressure / lately

   A _____?

   B No, _____ .

4. Barbara / sleep much / lately

   A _____?

   B Yes, _____ .

5. Lisa / start taking vitamins / recently

   A _____?

   B No, _____ .

Lesson C *Used to*

Study the chart and explanation on page 129.

1 Circle *use* or *used*.

1. Did Angie (use)/ **used** to have high blood pressure?

2. They **use** / **used** to drink a lot of coffee.

3. Tia and Arturo **use** / **used** to go to the gym every weekend.

4. Did Wesley **use** / **used** to drive to work?

5. We **use** / **used** to eat hamburgers and fries.

6. Did you **use** / **used** to feel tired all the time?

2 Complete the sentences. Use *used to* or *use to*.

1. When I was a teenager, I ____*used to*____ play soccer.

2. Did you _____ exercise a lot when you were young?

3. In my country, I _____ eat rice every day.

4. When I was a child, I _____ drink milk every morning.

5. Did you _____ watch TV when you were a child?

6. I _____ get up late every day, but now I get up early.

3 Complete the paragraph. Use *used to* or the simple present tense.

Samantha _____*used to eat*_____ a lot of chocolate and ice cream. Now, she
        1. eat

_____*eats*_____ a lot of fruit and _____ vitamins every day.
   2. eat   3. take

She _____ only once a week, but now she _____
      4. exercise   5. go

to the gym three times a week. She _____ to work, but now she
                                        6. drive

_____ a bike. She _____ a lot of coffee, but now
   7. ride   8. drink

she _____ tea or fruit juice. She _____ tired all the
      9. drink   10. feel

time, but now she _____ a lot of energy. Samantha has changed her
                    11. have

habits and feels much better now.

4 ## Read the chart. Write sentences about Emilia.

	Before	Now
1.	Stay up until 2:00 a.m.	Go to bed at 10:00 p.m.
2.	Eat meat every day	Eat fish twice a week
3.	Go straight home after work	Go to the gym three times a week
4.	Eat a lot of fatty foods	Eat salad and vegetables
5.	Skip breakfast	Eat fruit and yogurt for breakfast

1. *Emilia used to stay up until 2:00 a.m., but now she goes to bed at 10:00 p.m.*

2. _____

3. _____

4. _____

5. _____

5 ## Write questions and answers about what Emilia used to do. Use the information in Exercise 4.

1. Emilia / stay up until 2:00 a.m.

   A *Did Emilia use to stay up until 2:00 a.m.* _____?

   B _____ .

2. she / eat meat every day

   A _____?

   B _____ .

3. she / go to the gym three times a week

   A _____?

   B _____ .

1 **Read and answer the questions. Then listen.**

THREE **BENEFICIAL** HERBS

Many herbal plants are easy to grow. You can use them in cooking and to prevent illness. You can grow thyme, lavender, and mint in a garden or in your home.

Thyme is a small herbal plant. You can use it in cooking and as a medicine. The leaves are gray-green, and the flowers are usually purple, white, or pink. Many people use thyme to cook chicken and fish. You can also dry the leaves and make tea with them. Thyme tea with honey is very good for a cough or a sore throat.

Lavender is a popular garden plant with silver-green leaves and tiny purple flowers. The flowers have a beautiful smell. You can use the dried flowers to keep clothes and sheets fresh. You can use lavender when cooking meat, and you can make tea from the dried flowers for headaches. Using lavender may even keep blood pressure low. Some people use lavender oil in their bath to help them relax.

Mint is a beneficial plant that grows quickly. You can use the leaves in salads and with meat or fish. You can use the fresh or dried leaves to make tea. It helps with indigestion and upset stomachs. Add sugar to iced mint tea for a delicious summer drink.

Use thyme, lavender, and mint to stay healthy and prevent illness.

1. Which of the herbs in the article is good for treating indigestion?

   _____

2. Which of the herbs in the article is good for treating headaches?

   _____

3. Which of the herbs in the article is good for treating stomachaches?

   _____

4. What illnesses in the article can thyme tea help treat?

   _____

2 **Complete the chart. Use the information in Exercise 1.**

Name of plant	Use it to make . . .	Use it to cook . . .	Use it to treat . . .
Thyme	*tea*		
Lavender			
Mint			

3 **Complete the sentences. Use the information in Exercise 1.**

| digest | digestion | herbal | prevent | treat | treatment |

1. I'm having problems with my ___*digestion*___ . I think I'll drink some mint tea.

2. Some people use thyme tea as a _____ for sore throats.

3. Lavender can help _____ high blood pressure.

4. You can use mint to make delicious _____ tea.

5. Mint can help you _____ your food.

6. Some people use lavender tea to _____ headaches.

4 **Write *adjective*, *noun*, or *verb*.**

1. digestive: ___*adjective*___

2. prevention: _____

3. treat: _____

4. herbs: _____

5. digest: _____

6. prevent: _____

7. treatment: _____

Lesson E Writing

1 Read about sage. Then answer the questions.

> Sage is a popular herbal plant used for cooking and medicine. It is easy to grow in your garden. It has green-gray leaves and purple flowers. You can make tea from the leaves to treat sore throats and breathing problems. I also use it to add flavor to meat or vegetables. I sometimes use sage tea as a mouthwash, too.

1. What is sage used for? _cooking and medicine_ _____

2. What does it look like? _____

3. What health problems can you treat with sage? _____

4. How can you use it in cooking? _____

5. How else can you use it? _____

2 Complete the paragraph. Use the information in the chart.

Plant name	rosemary
Grows	in the garden or in your home
Description	sharp, narrow leaves
Treats	headaches
Cooking uses	adds flavor to meat or oil

> _____Rosemary_____ is my favorite herbal plant. It is widely used for
>   1
> cooking and medicine. It is easy to grow in your _____. It has
>   2
> _____. You can use the leaves to treat _____.
>   3   4
> I also use it in cooking to _____.
>   5

3 **Read the chart. Answer the questions.**

Plant name	aloe vera
History	people have used it for 6,000 years
Grows	in hot, dry places
Description	• long, spiky leaves • leaves have juice inside them
Treats	• burns • insect bites • dry skin
Used in	• skin creams and lotions • shampoos • soaps

1. Where does aloe vera grow? _in hot, dry places_

2. What kind of leaves does it have? _____

3. What problems can you treat with aloe vera? _____

4. What products have aloe vera in them? _____

4 **Write a paragraph about aloe vera. Use the information in Exercise 3.**

People have used aloe vera for thousands of years.

_____

_____

_____

_____

_____

_____

_____

_____

_____

_____

_____

Lesson F Another view

1 **Read the questions. Look at the form. Then fill in the correct answers.**

Medical History Form

1. What is the reason for your visit?

Problem | Date problem began
allergies | *3 weeks ago*

2. Have you ever had any of the following?

☑ allergies	☐ back pain	☑ headaches	☑ high blood pressure
☐ arthritis	☐ chest pains	☐ heart attack	☑ high cholesterol
☑ asthma	☐ diabetes	☐ heart disease	☐ tuberculosis

3. Please list all medications, including vitamins and herbal supplements.

Vitamin C, garlic pills, and aspirin

4. List any other major illnesses, injuries, or surgeries you have had in the last year.

The above information is correct to the best of my knowledge.

Signature *Eva Hernandez*　　　Date *August 25, 2018*

1. Eva went to the doctor because of _____.

   Ⓐ arthritis

   ⬤ allergies

   Ⓒ diabetes

   Ⓓ back pain

2. Eva does not take _____.

   Ⓐ aspirin

   Ⓑ garlic pills

   Ⓒ Vitamin C

   Ⓓ Vitamin D

3. In the past, Eva has had _____.

   Ⓐ chest pains

   Ⓑ tuberculosis

   Ⓒ heart disease

   Ⓓ high cholesterol

4. In the past, Eva has not had _____.

   Ⓐ asthma

   Ⓑ headaches

   Ⓒ heart disease

   Ⓓ high blood pressure

2 **Look at the pictures. Complete the indirect commands.**

Don't eat sweets between meals.

Try to get more exercise.

1. Dr. Chang told Harry Johnson
   not to eat sweets between meals .

2. He also _____
   _____ .

Take your vitamins.

Don't stay out late every night.

3. Alec's mother told him
   _____ .

4. His father _____
   _____ .

Don't stay up late studying for the test.

Test tomorrow

Eat a good breakfast in the morning.

5. Ms. Bailey told the class
   _____ .

6. She also _____
   _____ .

Use mint leaves to make iced tea.

Don't put too much sugar in it.

7. Magda told Helen
   _____ .

8. Then she _____
   _____ .

Lesson A Listening

1 **Read the ads. Match the ads with the sentences.**

A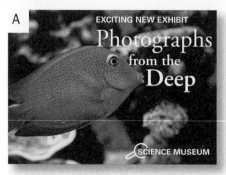

B

C

D

1. Rick and Becky can't afford to spend a lot on entertainment. __*B*__

2. Bill and Margie want to get some exercise and be outside. ____

3. Maria's daughter loves books. ____

4. The weather is bad, so Lin wants to do something interesting indoors. ____

2 **Complete the sentences.**

admission   afford   concerts   events   exhibits   storytelling

1. We usually check the newspaper for community _____*events*_____.

2. I love music. I like going to rock _____.

3. We don't have any money. We can't _____ expensive tickets.

4. The garden tour is free. There is no _____ fee.

5. My children love stories. They love listening to _____ at the library.

6. My wife loves art. She often goes to art _____.

3 **Read and circle the correct answers. Then listen.**

A Yan, do you have any plans for Saturday?

B No, Lin, not yet.

A There's a free concert in the park on Saturday afternoon. Do you want to go?

B That sounds good. What time does it start?

A It starts at 3:00. And there's a new art exhibit at the museum.

B What time does the museum open?

A 10:00. And it's free admission.

B OK. Let's meet at the museum at 11:00. We'll have lunch in the museum café, and then we'll go to the concert.

1. Yan and Lin are _____ .
   a. going shopping
   b. discussing music
   c. choosing a good restaurant
   d. planning their weekend

2. They are going to go to _____ .
   a. a park and a concert
   b. a park and a movie
   c. an art exhibit and a concert
   d. an art exhibit and a movie

3. First, Yan and Lin will _____ .
   a. walk in the park
   b. eat lunch at a café
   c. go to a free concert
   d. meet at an art museum

4. The museum opens at _____ .
   a. 9:00 a.m.
   b. 10:00 a.m.
   c. 11:00 a.m.
   d. 3:00 p.m.

5. Which statement is true?
   a. The concert tickets are not cheap.
   b. There is no admission fee for the concert.
   c. Admission to the museum is not free.
   d. Admission to the museum is expensive.

6. Yan and Lin will spend _____ .
   a. no money at all
   b. no money on food
   c. some money on food
   d. some money on entertainment

4 **What are Leo and Noriko going to do? Listen and check.**

☐ go to a movie   ☐ go out for dinner

☐ go to a museum   ☐ go out for coffee

Lesson B Verbs + infinitives

Study the chart and explanation on page 127.

1 **Complete the sentences. Use the infinitive. Then listen.**

| come home | eat | go | meet | see | take |

A Nina, where have you decided _____*to go*_____ this afternoon?
      1

B I'm going to the art museum with my friend Gabe.

A What do you want _____?
                        2

B There's a new exhibit on American paintings.

A Where have you agreed _____ Gabe?
                          3

B Outside the art museum at 1:00.

A Where do you plan _____?
                       4

B We'll eat lunch at home.

A Can you afford _____ a taxi?
                    5

B No, we'll take the subway.

A What time do you expect _____?
                            6

B I should be home before 6:00.

2 **Complete the sentences. Use the infinitive.**

1. Nina doesn't _____*want to ride*_____ her bike this afternoon.
                 (want / ride)

2. She _____ at home.
       (plan / eat)

3. She _____ Gabe at the museum.
       (intend / meet)

4. She doesn't _____ a taxi.
               (need / take)

5. She _____ home by 6:00.
       (expects / be)

6. She _____ something from the gift shop.
       (would like / buy)

7. She _____ something that is not too expensive.
       (hope / find)

3 Rewrite the sentences. Use the verb in parentheses and an infinitive.

1. Tony will visit his family every year. (promise)

   Tony promises to visit his family every year.

2. Lee will finish work early tonight. (expect)

3. I'll go to Florida this winter. (plan)

4. Shin will buy some concert tickets tomorrow. (intend)

5. We will visit our daughter in California next month. (hope)

6. Paul will not go to the beach this weekend. (refuse)

7. I will meet my friends on my birthday. (want)

8. I will take a trip with my family next year. (would like)

4 Complete the sentences about Chris's goals.

CHRIS'S GOALS

January	February	March	April	May	June
Watch less TV	Go to an art museum	Visit relatives more often	Walk to work every day	Give up desserts	Buy organic vegetables

1. (plan) In January, *Chris plans to watch less TV* .

2. (intend) In February, _____.

3. (want) In March, _____.

4. (plan) In April, _____.

5. (would like) In May, _____.

6. (hope) In June, _____.

Lesson C Present perfect

Study the chart and explanation on page 128. For a list of irregular verbs, turn to page 131.

1 **Complete the sentences. Use the present perfect.**

1. Have Sue and Martin _____seen_____ that movie already?
   (see)

2. Has Tim _____ dinner yet?
   (make)

3. We haven't _____ the newspaper yet.
   (read)

4. Have you _____ the credit card bill already?
   (pay)

5. My brother has already _____ his ticket.
   (buy)

6. Have the children _____ their homework yet?
   (do)

2 **Complete the sentences. Use *already* or *yet*.**

1. It's 8:00 p.m.

   The violin concert ____*hasn't started yet*____ .
   (start)

2. It's 6:30 p.m.

   The coffee shop _____ .
   (close)

3. It's 7:00 p.m.

   The movie _____ .
   (end)

4. It's 9:00 a.m.

   The museum _____ .
   (open)

3 **Max and Maria are planning a birthday party. Complete the sentences and answer the questions.**

> _TO DO_
>
> **Max**
> _bring my CDs_ ✓
> _get a present_
> _buy drinks_ ✓
>
> **Maria**
> _invite friends_ ✓
> _bake a cake_
>
> **Max and Maria**
> _set up tables and chairs_
> _put up decorations_ ✓

1. ____Has____ Max ____brought____ his CDs yet? ____Yes, he has.____

2. _____ Maria _____ their friends yet? _____

3. _____ Max _____ a present yet? _____

4. _____ Maria _____ a cake yet? _____

5. _____ Max _____ drinks yet? _____

6. _____ Max and Maria _____ decorations yet? _____

7. _____ Max and Maria _____ the tables
and chairs yet? _____

4 **Each of the sentences below is missing a word. Write the sentences with the missing word in parentheses.**

1. We haven't gone to the park. (yet)
   We haven't gone to the park yet.

2. Our favorite TV show hasn't yet. (started)
   _____

3. Have bought tickets for the fund-raiser yet? (you)
   _____

4. They eaten lunch yet. (haven't)
   _____

5. Ivan and Alex already been to that restaurant. (have)
   _____

6. Julie visited the art exhibit yet? (has)
   _____

Lesson D Reading

1 Scan the article. Circle *T* (True) or *F* (False). Then listen and read.

1. Four hundred people attended this superb performance. T (F)
2. The show started at 7:00 p.m. with Alvarez's band. T F
3. Alvarez performed four new songs. T F
4. Some people waited in line for 30 minutes to buy a soda. T F
5. There was no food available after 9:00 p.m. T F
6. Alvarez performed until 11:00 p.m. T F
7. Alvarez will perform four more times. T F

RUDY ALVAREZ at the Park Theater

by Mike Clark

A huge crowd gathered to see the rock musician Rudy Alvarez perform at the Park Theater on Saturday night. Over 500 people attended this superb event.

The show started at 7:00 p.m. with a salsa band. The band's music was unremarkable, and the lead singer did not sing well at all. It was irritating, and everyone wanted Alvarez to come on stage. Finally, the salsa band finished, and Alvarez came on stage at 8:30 p.m. The versatile artist performed his most popular songs and five new songs. The audience went wild! Everyone danced and sang along, and children climbed onto the stage and started dancing.

One negative side to the event was that the lines were long for refreshments. The waiting time was really excessive. Some people waited in line for 30 minutes to buy a soda, and there was no food available after 9:00 p.m. I also expected Alvarez to perform until about 11:00 p.m., but the show ended at 10:30 because of a serious problem with the sound system. We didn't get to hear Alvarez sing his most famous song, "Missing You."

Alvarez will give three more performances at the Park Theater and one additional performance at the Grand Theater. If you haven't attended one of his shows yet, don't miss your chance!

2 Circle the correct answers. Use the information in Exercise 1.

1. Why did the concert finish early?
   a. The weather was bad.
   b. The lines were too long.
   c. The audience was too wild.
   (d.) The sound system wasn't working properly.

2. What word did Mike Clark use to describe the salsa band?
   a. popular
   b. versatile
   c. excessive
   d. unremarkable

3. What word did Mike Clark use to describe Alvarez?
   a. superb
   b. versatile
   c. irritating
   d. available

4. Which statement is true?
   a. The audience liked the salsa band.
   b. The audience didn't sing any of the songs.
   c. Alvarez played his least popular songs.
   d. Alvarez played his most popular songs.

5. What was one negative thing about the concert?
   a. Children tried to get on stage.
   b. There wasn't enough food.
   c. Alvarez's music was unremarkable.
   d. Alvarez sang too many new songs.

3 Look at the bold words. Write the sentences. Use words from the box with a similar meaning.

| crowd | excessive | missed | musicians | superb | unremarkable |

1. We **didn't go** to the concert.   _We missed the concert._

2. The concert was **excellent**.   _____

3. There was a **large group of people**.   _____

4. The waiting time was **too long**.   _____

5. There were five **people playing drums**.   _____

6. The stage was **not interesting**.   _____

Lesson E Writing

1 Complete the word maps.

| amazing | fabulous | irritating | superb |
| excessive | incredible | ominous | unremarkable |

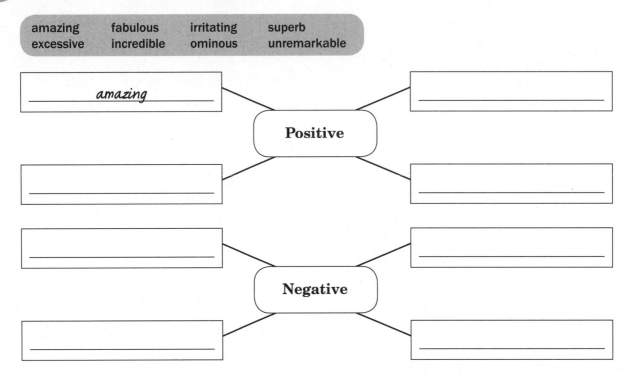

amazing

Positive

Negative

2 Read the postcard. Circle three positive adjectives. Underline three negative adjectives.

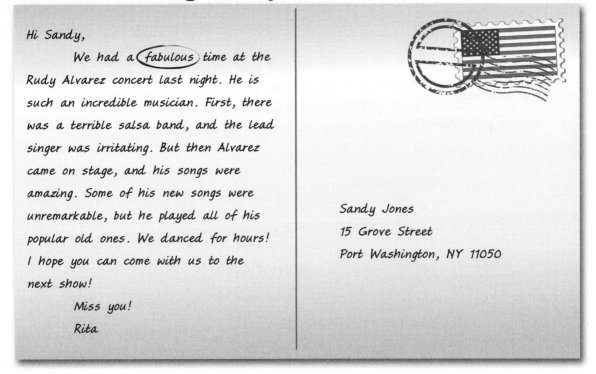

Hi Sandy,

We had a (fabulous) time at the Rudy Alvarez concert last night. He is such an incredible musician. First, there was a terrible salsa band, and the lead singer was irritating. But then Alvarez came on stage, and his songs were amazing. Some of his new songs were unremarkable, but he played all of his popular old ones. We danced for hours! I hope you can come with us to the next show!

Miss you!

Rita

Sandy Jones
15 Grove Street
Port Washington, NY 11050

3 **Match the sentence parts. Write *N* for negative information and *P* for positive information.**

1. _N_ The musicians were irritating because

2. ____ Our seats were in the back, so

3. ____ The weather was bad, and

4. ____ The music was awesome, and

5. ____ The music wasn't loud enough, and

a. we couldn't see very well.

b. they couldn't sing.

c. we danced all night.

d. we couldn't hear anything.

e. we were cold.

4 **Read Bill's notes about a jazz concert. Write an email about the concert. Use positive and negative information.**

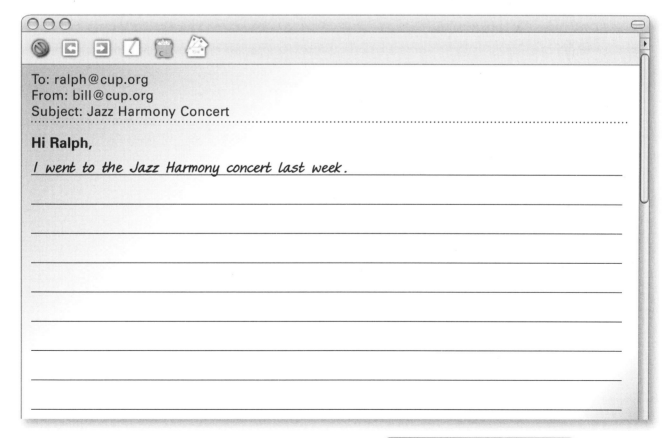

Jazz Harmony Concert

POSITIVE	NEGATIVE
concert started on time	music wasn't loud enough
fabulous seats	concert hall was too big
band played for a long time	tickets too expensive
band played awesome new songs	got home very late

To: ralph@cup.org
From: bill@cup.org
Subject: Jazz Harmony Concert

Hi Ralph,

I went to the Jazz Harmony concert last week.

Lesson F Another view

**1 Read the questions. Look at the announcements.
Then fill in the correct answers.**

International Fair

Food and music from 20 different countries. Sat. 10:00 a.m. to 5:00 p.m., Sun. 10:00 a.m. to 3:00 p.m. at the Community Center. Free admission.

Animal Movies

Educational movies – fun for children and adults. Wednesday, September 19th, at 5:00 p.m. East Riverside Public Library. No admission fee.

Nature Tour

Have you joined the Friends of Mission Park yet? Come for an easy guided walk around the park on Sunday. Meet at the Information Center at noon. Tickets: $3.00 for adults, $2.00 for children.

Community Barbecue

Have you seen your friends and neighbors lately? Then join us for burgers and all the fixin's. This Sunday, 11:00 to 3:00. All you can eat meal tickets: $7.00.

1. At which event can you get some exercise?
   - Nature Tour
   - B Animal Movies
   - C International Fair
   - D Community Barbecue

2. Which event starts at 10:00 a.m. on Sunday?
   - A Nature Tour
   - B Animal Movies
   - C International Fair
   - D Community Barbecue

3. Which event is the most expensive?
   - A Nature Tour
   - B Animal Movies
   - C International Fair
   - D Community Barbecue

4. Which events are free?
   - A International Fair and Nature Tour
   - B Nature Tour and Animal Movies
   - C Animal Movies and International Fair
   - D Community Barbecue and Nature Tour

5. Which event does not take place on a weekend?
   - A Nature Tour
   - B Animal Movies
   - C International Fair
   - D Community Barbecue

6. Which statement is true?
   - A You can take a nature tour on Saturday.
   - B Animal movies are only for children.
   - C The International Fair continues all night.
   - D You can eat food at the Community Barbecue and International Fair.

2 **Complete the sentences with an infinitive or a gerund.**

1. I've already finished ____reading____ the story.
   (read)

2. We've decided _____ on the garden tour.
   (go)

3. Rick intends _____ the tickets.
   (buy)

4. Mayuko dislikes _____ late for concerts.
   (be)

5. Do you enjoy _____ to country music?
   (listen)

6. Alan refused _____ the scary movie.
   (see)

7. We usually avoid _____ in that park at night.
   (walk)

8. They wanted _____ at the library, but it was closed.
   (study)

3 **Write new sentences with an infinitive or a gerund when possible. If not possible, put an ✗ in the box.**

1. Betty prefers to go to crafts fairs, not to the mall.

   ☐ *Betty prefers going to crafts fairs, not to the mall.*

2. The guide suggested going on the historic walking tour.

   ✗ _____

3. The lights went out, but the musicians continued playing.

   ☐ _____

4. I avoided going to the dentist, and now my tooth hurts.

   ☐ _____

5. I started reading the book last night.

   ☐ _____

6. Why do you dislike watching tennis on TV?

   ☐ _____

7. The band plans to give another concert tomorrow.

   ☐ _____

8. Raul hates to drive in the city during rush hour.

   ☐ _____

UNIT 6 TIME

Lesson A Listening

1 **Complete the sentences.**

chores   due   prioritize   tasks
deadline   impatient   procrastinating

1. One of my _____*chores*_____ is to take out the trash.

2. The _____ for my project is tomorrow.

3. I have another project _____ next week.

4. You have to make a to-do list of _____ in order of importance.

5. Do your homework now and stop _____!

6. I have too many things to do this weekend. I need to

   _____ them.

7. Please don't be so _____! Your food will be ready soon.

2 **Read and complete Olivia's journal entry. Then listen.**

chores   due   impatient   prioritize   procrastinating   to-do list

> *I have too many things to do today. My friends are coming over for dinner tonight.*
>
> *I need to make a ____to-do list____ and stop _____.*
>   1   2
> *I have to buy food for dinner. I have some _____ to do around the*
>   3
> *house, and I also have to finish my homework. It's _____ tomorrow.*
>   4
> *Now I need to _____ the tasks on my list. First, I want to do the*
>   5
> *shopping because it is the most important. Next, I'll cook the food. My friends might get*
>
> *_____ if they have to wait for dinner. Then, I'll clean up the house.*
>   6
> *Will I have time to do my homework before they arrive? Probably not.*

3 Circle the correct answers. Use the information in Exercise 2.

1. What is Olivia's problem?
   (a.) She has too many things to do.
   b. She has too much homework.
   c. She doesn't want to prioritize.
   d. She doesn't have enough work to do.

2. Olivia needs to stop _____.
   a. cooking
   b. procrastinating
   c. doing chores
   d. doing her homework

3. When Olivia *prioritizes*, she'll do _____.
   a. some of her tasks
   b. the most difficult tasks later
   c. the most important tasks first
   d. all of the tasks as quickly as possible

4. What will she do before she cooks?
   a. clean up
   b. go shopping
   c. take out the trash
   d. finish her homework

5. When friends are *impatient,* they are not willing to _____.
   a. eat
   b. wait
   c. prioritize
   d. procrastinate

6. When you don't *have time,* you are too _____.
   a. busy
   b. late
   c. upset
   d. tired

4 Match.

1. do   _b_
2. make ____
3. take out ____
4. prioritize ____
5. be ____
6. order ____

a. impatient
b. homework
c. tasks
d. of importance
e. the trash
f. a to-do list

5 Listen. Then check (✓) two true statements.

☐ Thomas makes to-do lists at work.
☐ Alicia has learned to manage her time.
☐ Thomas often procrastinates.
☐ Alicia doesn't have time to go to the gym.

Lesson B Adverb clauses

Study the explanation on page 133.

1 Make sentences. Match the sentence parts.

1. When I need to concentrate, __b__
2. When I feel tired, ____
3. When I have a deadline, ____
4. When I don't understand a grammar question, ____
5. When I don't understand a word, ____
6. When I have many tasks to do, ____

a. I don't procrastinate.
b. I turn off the TV.
c. I use a dictionary.
d. I make a to-do list.
e. I take a break.
f. I ask my teacher.

2 Combine the sentences. Use *when*.

1. Parvana has a lot of homework. She makes a to-do list of her tasks.

   When _____.

2. She wants to concentrate. She goes to the library.

   When _____, _____.

3. She looks at the clock. She starts her work.

   _____ when _____.

4. She finishes a task. She checks it off her to-do list.

   When _____, _____.

5. She takes a short break. She feels tired.

   _____ when _____.

6. She doesn't hand in her homework on time. Her teacher is upset.

   When _____, _____.

7. She eats a snack. She feels hungry.

   _____ when _____.

8. She needs to focus. She doesn't answer the phone.

   When _____, _____.

9. She does the difficult tasks first. She has a lot of work to do.

   _____ when _____.

10. She has a deadline. She doesn't procrastinate.

    When _____, _____.

3 **Read the sentences. Add commas if necessary. Write *no comma* if you do not need a comma.**

1. When I finish my homework I take a break. _____

2. Than procrastinates when he doesn't want to do his homework. _____

3. Suzanna uses a dictionary when she reads the newspaper. _____

4. When we don't hand in our homework our teacher is very upset. _____

5. When I have a deadline I stay up late. _____

6. Sushila doesn't like to work when she is tired. _____

4 **Write questions. Then write the answers.**

I ask my teacher	I procrastinate	I study my notes
I go to the library	I rest	I take a break

1. (do / finish a difficult task)

   A What *do you do when you finish a difficult task* ?

   B *I take a break* .

2. (do / need to concentrate)

   A What _____ ?

   B _____ .

3. (do / don't understand the homework)

   A What _____ ?

   B _____ .

4. (do / have a quiz or test)

   A What _____ ?

   B _____ .

5. (do / feel tired)

   A What _____ ?

   B _____ .

6. (do / don't want to work)

   A What _____ ?

   B _____ .

Lesson C Adverb clauses

Study the explanation on page 133.

1 Complete the sentences. Use *after*.

Mannie's morning schedule

5:30 wake up
5:45 get dressed
6:00 eat breakfast
6:30 work out
7:15 take a shower
8:00 go to work

1. Mannie gets dressed _____ *after he wakes up* _____.

2. Mannie eats breakfast _____.

3. Mannie works out _____.

4. Mannie takes a shower _____.

5. Mannie goes to work _____.

2 Write sentences. Use *before*.

Janet's evening schedule

5:30 get home
6:00 eat dinner
7:00 walk the dog
8:00 watch TV
9:00 read a book
9:30 go to bed

1. get home / eat dinner

   Janet gets home before she eats dinner.

2. eat dinner / walk the dog

   _____

3. walk the dog / watch TV

   _____

4. watch TV / read a book

   _____

3 **Write questions. Then write the answers. Use the information in Exercises 1 and 2.**

1. Mannie / do / before / eat breakfast

   A What *does Mannie do before he eats breakfast* ?

   B *He gets dressed.*

2. Mannie / do / before / work out

   A What _____?

   B _____

3. Mannie / do / before / go to work

   A What _____?

   B _____

4. Janet / do / after / get home

   A What _____?

   B _____

5. Janet / do / after / watch TV

   A What _____?

   B _____

6. Janet / do / after / read a book

   A What _____?

   B _____

4 **Underline the activity that happens first. Circle the activity that happens second.**

1. I watch TV after I have dinner.

2. Before Sandy goes to work, she buys a newspaper.

3. Ivana goes to school after she finishes work.

4. After Simon finishes his homework, he takes a break.

5. They usually go swimming after they go to the park.

6. Before you go out, you need to take out the trash.

7. Melanie puts on makeup after she takes a shower.

8. Alan washes the dishes before he goes to bed.

Check your answers. See page 138.

1 **Read and circle the correct answers. Then listen.**

Feature Story

Personal Rules about Time

Everyone has his or her own personal rules about time. These rules depend on the personality of the person as well as on the culture of the country.

Some individuals – no matter where they are from – have very strict rules about time. They like to keep a schedule. They are always early for meetings. When they catch a train, they arrive at the station 30 minutes before the train leaves. When they go to a party, they are often the first guests to arrive. It is sometimes difficult for these people to understand why their co-workers and friends cannot be on time. They get angry when their friends are late.

Other people are not very strict about time – even in places like the United States, Canada, and England, where punctuality is generally considered to be very important. They don't think keeping a schedule is the most important thing. For example, they are sometimes late for work, they often miss trains and buses, and they arrive at a party one or two hours after the party has started. They don't understand why other people get upset when they are late. On the other hand, these people do not get impatient when their friends are late!

1. This article talks about two different _____ .
   a. ways to keep a schedule
   b. reasons why punctuality is important
   c. ways of thinking about time
   d. types of social and business events

2. When people are strict about time, they _____ .
   a. keep a schedule
   b. come from special countries
   c. are always late for appointments
   d. are good and understanding friends

3. What does the word *punctuality* mean?
   a. always late
   b. being on time
   c. very important
   d. always impatient

4. According to the article, people should _____ .
   a. always be on time
   b. have personal rules about time
   c. understand their friends
   d. understand different rules about time

2 **Complete the sentences.**

impatient   impolite   irresponsible   uncommon   unspoken

1. In Canada, it is ___*impolite*___ to arrive at a dinner party more than 10 minutes late.

2. People who are strict about time get _____ when their friends are late.

3. In England, punctuality is an _____ rule. People expect you to be on time without telling you.

4. It is _____ to be late for a job interview in the United States.

5. In Brazil, it is not _____ for guests to arrive two hours after a social event begins.

3 **Rewrite the sentences. Write the bold words with the prefixes *un-*, *dis-*, *ir-*, or *im-*.**

1. It is **not common** to miss a plane.

    ___*It is uncommon to miss a plane.*___

2. It is **not polite** to be late.

    _____

3. It is **not usual** to be early for a party.

    _____

4. He is **not patient**.

    _____

5. They are **not responsible**.

    _____

6. She is **not organized**.

    _____

4 **Write the opposites.**

1. unlucky   ___*lucky*___   4. unfriendly   _____

2. impossible   _____   5. unkind   _____

3. dishonest   _____   6. irrational   _____

Lesson E Writing

1 Read the paragraph. Then answer the questions.

> ## An Organized Student
>
> Nita is a very organized person. For example, she keeps all of her class notes in one binder with different sections. Each section has a label. She also writes all of her homework assignments and due dates in a special notebook. Before she goes home, she checks her bag carefully. She makes sure she has all the books she needs. After she gets home, she has dinner. Then she plans how much time she will need for each assignment. She makes a list of tasks and crosses them out when she finishes them. When she feels tired, she takes a short break. In summary, Nita is an organized person and a successful student.

1. What is the topic sentence?

   Nita is a very organized person.

2. What is the first example?

   _____

3. What is the second example?

   _____

4. Which words signal the conclusion?

   _____

2 Answer the questions. Use the information in Exercise 1.

1. Why doesn't Nita forget the due dates of her assignments?

   She writes all her homework assignments and the due dates in a special notebook.

2. Where does she keep her notes?

   _____

3. What does she do before she goes home?

   _____

4. What does she plan after dinner?

   _____

5. What does she do when she feels tired?

   _____

3 **Write the sentences in the correct order to make a paragraph.**

An Impatient Boss

She is also not a good listener, and she often interrupts.

For example, she often gets angry when you are three minutes late.

Finally, she is always in a hurry and never has enough time.

My boss Frida is a very impatient person.

In conclusion, Frida is a very impatient person, and it is difficult to work for her.

My boss Frida is a very impatient person.

_____

_____

_____

_____

_____

4 **Write a short paragraph about Paula. Include a topic sentence, examples to support your topic sentence, and a signal before your conclusion.**

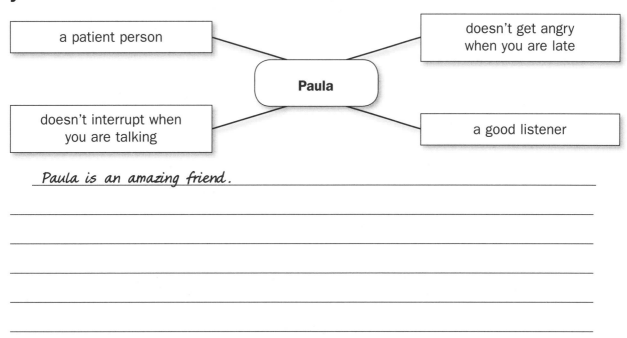

Paula is an amazing friend.

_____

_____

_____

_____

_____

Lesson F Another view

1 **Read the questions. Look at the pie chart. Then fill in the correct answers.**

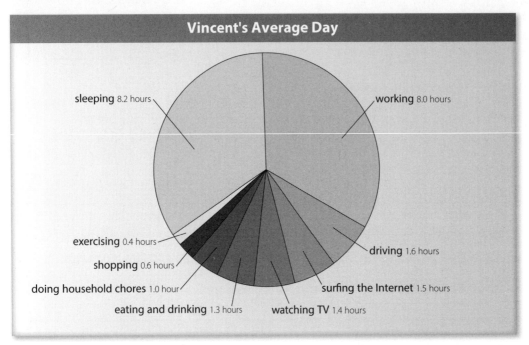

Vincent's Average Day

sleeping 8.2 hours
working 8.0 hours
exercising 0.4 hours
driving 1.6 hours
shopping 0.6 hours
doing household chores 1.0 hour
surfing the Internet 1.5 hours
eating and drinking 1.3 hours
watching TV 1.4 hours

1. Which activity does Vincent spend the most time doing?

   Ⓐ driving

   Ⓑ working

   ⬛ sleeping

   Ⓓ watching TV

2. Which activity does Vincent spend the least time doing?

   Ⓐ eating

   Ⓑ driving

   Ⓒ shopping

   Ⓓ exercising

3. How much time does Vincent spend doing household chores?

   Ⓐ 0.4 hours

   Ⓑ 0.6 hours

   Ⓒ 1.0 hour

   Ⓓ 1.3 hours

4. Vincent spends more time _____.

   Ⓐ working than sleeping

   Ⓑ watching TV than eating and drinking

   Ⓒ shopping than doing household chores

   Ⓓ doing household chores than eating and drinking

5. Vincent spends as much time _____.

   Ⓐ shopping and exercising as doing household chores

   Ⓑ eating and drinking as doing household chores and exercising

   Ⓒ driving as watching TV and exercising

   Ⓓ surfing the Internet as exercising and shopping

2 Circle the correct word.

1. **Before** / **After** I plan a picnic, I check the weather.

2. My boss keeps talking **when** / **before** I ask him a question.

3. **Before** / **When** my aunt visits me, we eat at our favorite restaurant.

4. My husband Jim always reads the newspaper **when** / **after** he cooks breakfast.

5. **When** / **Before** someone interrupts me, I usually stop talking.

6. I make a to-do list **after** / **before** I start my day.

3 Write sentences with the same meaning. Use the word in parentheses.

1. Mary took out the trash after she ate dinner. (before)

   Before she took out the trash, Mary ate dinner.

2. The Walters finished their hike before the rain began. (after)

3. After I brushed my teeth, I went to bed. (before)

4. Before Deidre watched the news, she fed the cat. (after)

5. Eduardo made a to-do list when he arrived at work. (before)

4 Write sentences using the two sentences and the word in parentheses.

1. Sometimes I read the newspaper. I eat breakfast. (when)

   Sometimes I read the newspaper when I eat breakfast.

2. Jane usually checks her email. She goes to bed. (before)

3. Did you buy tickets for the concert? They went on sale. (after)

4. I go to the supermarket to buy food. I make dinner. (before)

Check your answers. See pages 138–139. **UNIT 6** **77**

UNIT 7 SHOPPING

Lesson A Listening

1 **Read and circle the correct answers. Then listen.**

Sofia	Do you use your credit card a lot?
Jackie	Yes. All the time! I have four cards.
Sofia	Really? Isn't it difficult to pay them off? The interest rates are so high!
Jackie	I never charge more than $100 on each card.
Sofia	I'm thinking about buying a new refrigerator, but I can't afford it.
Jackie	Why don't you buy it on credit? You can pay for it later.
Sofia	I don't want to get into debt. We already have to pay off our car loan.
Jackie	Maybe you could look in the newspaper or online and find a used refrigerator.
Sofia	That's a good idea.

1. Sofia wants to buy a refrigerator. What is the problem?
   a. She doesn't have a car.
   b. She doesn't have any credit.
   c. She doesn't have a credit card.
   d. She doesn't have enough money.

2. What does Jackie think Sofia should do?
   a. take out a loan
   b. get a new credit card
   c. pay off her car loan
   d. buy a used refrigerator

3. Which statement is true?
   a. Sofia wants a new credit card.
   b. Sofia never borrows money.
   c. Sofia is worried about getting into debt.
   d. Sofia needs to borrow money for her car loan.

4. Which statement is true?
   a. Jackie never uses a credit card.
   b. Jackie has more than one credit card.
   c. Jackie uses her credit card every day.
   d. Jackie spends too much on her credit card.

2 Complete the sentences.

afford   balance   cash   credit   interest   pay off

1. That car costs $30,000. We can't _____ it.

2. I'll buy the refrigerator on _____. I don't want to use my savings.

3. You should pay _____ for food. Don't use your credit card.

4. The _____ rate for the loan is too high.

5. If we _____ the loan in six months, there's no interest.

6. At the end of the month, the _____ in my bank account is usually low!

3 Solve the problems.

1. Su-lin and Chung-hee have a balance of $28,000.00 in their savings account. They want to buy a new car that costs $30,500.00. If they use all the money in their savings account, how much do they need to borrow to buy the new car? _____

Cost of new car:	$30,500.00
Balance in savings account:	-$28,000.00
Money they need to borrow:	$2,500.00

2. Suzanne and Pete have a balance of $950.00 in their savings account. They want to buy a new refrigerator. It costs $1,200.00. If they use all the money in their savings account, how much do they need to borrow? _____

3. Dora and Julian have saved $1,500.00. They want to buy a television. It costs $1,200.00. They also need a new washing machine. It costs $800.00. If they use all their savings, how much do they need to borrow to buy the TV and the washing machine? _____

4 Listen. Then circle the correct amounts.

1. The price of the first TV with the taxes and installation is about **$2,000** / **$2,500**.

2. The interest rate on the loan for the TV is **24** / **36** percent.

3. The monthly payment on the TV loan would be almost **$36** / **$100**.

4. The smaller TV costs only **$550** / **$1,550**.

Lesson B Modals

Study the chart on page 130.

① Match the problems with the suggestions.

1. I can't afford gas for my car. __b__
2. My credit card bills are too high. _____
3. I need to find a job. _____
4. I can't afford a new computer. _____
5. My rent is too expensive. _____
6. My cell phone bill is too high. _____

a. You could use email instead.
b. You could take the bus.
c. You could find a cheaper apartment.
d. You could look at an online job site.
e. You could talk to a debt counselor.
f. You could use your credit card.

② Circle the correct form of the verb.

1. You should (buy) / buying a new car.
2. How about take / taking out a loan?
3. You could use / using a credit card.
4. Why don't you talk / talking to a debt counselor?
5. You should apply / applying for a scholarship.
6. How about look / looking in the newspaper?

③ Complete the sentences. Use *could* or *should*.

1. **A** I don't have enough money at the end of each month.
   Do you have any advice?

   B You ___*should*___ try to save a little each month.

2. **A** Where do you suggest I buy a new camera?

   B You _____ find one online, or you could go to the mall.

3. **A** I don't know how to apply for college. Can you give me any advice?

   B You _____ talk to a counselor.

4. **A** My tooth hurts. What should I do?

   B You _____ go to the dentist.

5. **A** Can you suggest a good place to go on vacation?

   B You _____ go to Hawaii or maybe Las Vegas.

6. **A** I want to get a good grade on my test. What should I do?

   B You _____ study hard this weekend.

4 **Complete the sentences. Use an expression in the box.**

> buy a new one   looking for a cheaper plan   using your credit card
> buy a used one   open a savings account   walking more often

1. **A** I don't have enough cash to pay for the tickets. What should I do?

 B How about _____*using your credit card*_____?

2. **A** We need a car, but we can't afford to buy a new one.

 B You could _____.

3. **A** This sweater looks old.

 B You should _____.

4. **A** The price of gas is going up to $5.00 a gallon. What am I going to do?

 B You could start _____.

5. **A** I'm spending too much money on cell phone calls. Do you have any suggestions?

 B How about _____?

6. **A** I got a great bonus at work. What should I do with the money?

 B Why don't you _____?

5 **Complete the sentences. Use *should* and the verbs in the box.**

> buy   do   make   tell   wear

1. **A** We don't have plans this weekend. What _____*should we do*_____?

 B I don't know. Maybe we could go to the movies.

2. **A** I didn't finish the homework. What _____ my teacher?

 B You should tell your teacher the truth. You didn't have enough time.

3. **A** I'm going shopping tomorrow. What _____?

 B I think you should get a new pair of pants.

4. **A** I want to make a special dinner tonight. What _____?

 B Well, I like fish.

5. **A** I don't have any nice clothes for the party. What _____?

 B You should borrow my black jacket.

Lesson C Gerunds after prepositions

Study the chart and explanation on page 126.

1 Write the gerund form of each verb.

1. apply ___applying___
2. be _____
3. buy _____
4. find _____
5. get _____
6. lend _____
7. lose _____

8. make _____
9. move _____
10. open _____
11. pay _____
12. spend _____
13. study _____
14. wait _____

2 Complete the sentences. Use words from Exercise 1.

1. He is tired of ____waiting____ .

2. She is happy about _____ a new car.

3. He is interested in _____ for a loan.

4. She is thinking about _____ a savings account.

5. He is excited about _____ auto mechanics.

6. She is afraid of _____ into debt.

3 **Circle the correct preposition.**

1. Martina is worried (about)/ **of** paying her bills.

2. Sam is nervous **about** / **of** starting college next week.

3. Tran is tired **about** / **of** working in a supermarket.

4. Louisa is thinking **about** / **in** going to school next semester.

5. I want to thank you **about** / **for** helping me.

4 **Complete the sentences.**

| about finding a job | for driving me to work | of getting up early |
| about getting a scholarship | in learning about computers | of losing their jobs |

1. I'm worried _about finding a job_ .

2. Thank you _____ .

3. Serena is happy _____ .

4. Chang is tired _____ .

5. Lisa and Theo are afraid _____ .

6. Maurice is interested _____ .

5 **Complete the sentences. Use the information in the chart.**

Name	Feelings	Activity
Ron	excited	go to college
Miguel	afraid	lose his job
Vincent and Anna	happy	pay off their loan
Tim and Betsy	worried	get into debt
Steve	interested	buy a new car

1. Ron _is excited about going to college_ .

2. Miguel _____ .

3. Vincent and Anna _____ .

4. Tim and Betsy _____ .

5. Steve _____ .

Check your answers. See page 139.

1 Read and answer the questions. Then listen.

How many credit cards should you have?

How many credit cards do you have in your wallet? Are you worried about getting into debt? Many Americans carry four or five credit cards, but others have more than ten. Is it a good idea to have so many credit cards?

Some people almost never pay cash. It's easier to use a credit card. They use their credit cards for everything – food, clothes, gas, utility bills, and rent. However, when the bills arrive, people who have too many cards sometimes can't afford the minimum payments. It's also difficult to keep track of so many cards.

It's not uncommon to have store credit cards. Some stores offer a 10–15 percent discount when you use their credit card. They also offer coupons and other discounts. But be careful. The interest rates on these cards can be very high. It's a good idea to use a store credit card at your favorite store if you shop there often. But you should pay off the account balance immediately. That way, you won't pay any interest.

Debt counselors say that it's a good idea to have at least two cards. Use one card for everyday living expenses, and keep the other one for emergencies. They suggest choosing credit cards with low interest rates, keeping your account balance low, always trying to pay more than just the minimum payments, and having no more than six cards.

1. What happens to some people when they have too many credit cards?

   They can't afford the minimum payments.

2. What do some stores offer when you use their credit card?

   _____

3. Why is it important to pay off your account balance immediately?

   _____

4. How many credit cards do debt counselors say you should have?

   _____

2 **Write four tips for using credit cards. Use the information from the article in Exercise 1.**

1. _Choose credit cards with low interest rates._

2. _____

3. _____

4. _____

3 **Match.**

1. minimum __e__   a. card
2. credit ____   b. budget
3. interest ____   c. counselor
4. debt ____   d. rate
5. family ____   e. payment

4 **Complete the sentences. Use words in Exercise 3.**

1. I don't have any _____ _credit_ _____ cards.

2. The _____ rate is very high.

3. We always make a family _____.

4. What is the _____ payment?

5. Why don't you talk to a debt _____?

5 **Complete the sentences. Use words in Exercise 3.**

1. I canceled my credit card because the _____ _interest rate_ _____ was over 25 percent.

2. We made a _____. Now we can save enough every month.

3. When you use a _____, you borrow money and pay it back later.

4. We talked to a _____ to help us solve our financial problems.

5. The smallest payment you can make each month is the _____.

Lesson E Writing

1 Match the money problems with the suggestions.

1. I don't have enough money to buy lunch. _c_
2. I'm worried about being in debt. _____
3. I don't have enough nice clothes for work. _____
4. I'm too tired to cook dinner after work, but take-out meals are unhealthy. _____

a. Why don't you cook meals on the weekends and freeze them?
b. You could go to a thrift store.
c. How about bringing lunch from home?
d. You should see a debt counselor.

2 Read the letters. Answer the questions.

Dear Money Guy,

    I drive to work every day, but gas is very expensive. My car uses a lot of gas, and I can't afford to fill up my car. I also need to see an auto mechanic for repairs. I'm worried about having the car break down on the way to work. What should I do? Can you give me advice?

                          Worried Larry

Dear Worried Larry,

    I have a few suggestions for you. First, ask a co-worker to give you a ride to work, and you can share the cost of gas. Second, you could drive to work three times a week and take the bus twice a week. Finally, you could think about taking the bus for a couple of months and saving money for your car repairs. You might enjoy taking the bus. Then you could sell your car!

                          Money Guy

1. What are Worried Larry's problems?

   a. _Gas is very expensive._

   b. _____

   c. _____

2. What are Money Guy's suggestions?

   a. _____

   b. _____

   c. _____

3 **Read the letter to Money Guy.**

Dear Money Guy,

I spend too much money on clothes. I don't really need new clothes, but when I go to the mall, I always want to buy something new. I use my store credit card. At first, I tried to pay off my bill every month. But now I have reached my spending limit, and the bills are too high. What should I do?

Clothes Crazy

4 **Read the solutions. Write an answer to Clothes Crazy. Use *First*, *Second*, *Third*, and *Finally*.**

Solution 1	Solution 2	Solution 3	Solution 4
Pay all your bills before you go back to the mall.	After you pay your bills, cancel your store credit card. Always pay cash.	Make a list of clothes you really need before you go shopping.	Go shopping with a friend. Ask your friend's advice before you buy anything.

Dear Clothes Crazy,

I have a few suggestions for you. _____

_____

_____

_____

_____

_____

_____

_____

_____

_____

I hope this advice is helpful!

Money Guy

**1 Read the questions. Look at the credit card brochure.
Then fill in the correct answers.**

	City Spender credit card	Super Express credit card
Annual fee	• none	• 1st year free, then $75
Monthly interest rate	• 0% interest rate for the first six months • After six months, the interest rate is 13.4%	• 0% interest rate for the first three months • After three months, the interest rate is 11.49%
Rewards program	• Five points for every $1.00 spent	• One point for every $1.00 spent • 1,000 bonus points with your first purchase and 100 bonus points with your 100th purchase
Minimum monthly payment	• 1% of the account balance	• 2% of the account balance

1. What is the interest rate with a Super Express credit card after two months?

   ● 0%

   Ⓑ 1%

   Ⓒ 2%

   Ⓓ 11.49%

2. What does the City Spender credit card offer?

   Ⓐ bonus points with the first purchase

   Ⓑ one reward point for every $5.00 spent

   Ⓒ 0% interest for the first six months

   Ⓓ 13.4% interest for the first three months

3. What does the Super Express credit card offer?

   Ⓐ 0% interest for the first six months

   Ⓑ one reward point for every dollar spent

   Ⓒ no annual fee in the second year

   Ⓓ none of the above

4. What is the minimum monthly payment with a City Spender credit card?

   Ⓐ 0% of the account balance

   Ⓑ 1% of the account balance

   Ⓒ 2% of the account balance

   Ⓓ 13.4% of the account balance

5. Which is true about both credit cards?

   Ⓐ no annual fees in the first year

   Ⓑ 2% minimum monthly payment

   Ⓒ 0% interest for the first six months

   Ⓓ all of the above

6. Which is true about both credit cards?

   Ⓐ one point for every dollar spent

   Ⓑ 11.49% interest for the first three months

   Ⓒ both a and b

   Ⓓ neither a nor b

2 **Complete the sentences with a form of *get* or *take*.**

1. Last year, we _____*took*_____ our vacation in August.

2. Becky can't understand her bank statement. She always _____ confused when she sees so many numbers.

3. My parents _____ very upset when they saw the balance on my credit card.

4. I like to study with Kenji because he _____ good notes.

5. I'm tired of shopping. Let's _____ a break and have a snack.

6. We should _____ a bus to go downtown. Taxis are too expensive.

7. Many people _____ nervous when they have to speak in front of a big group.

8. I think I'm _____ sick. I have a headache, and I'm really tired.

3 **Write new sentences with a similar meaning. Use an expression from the box.**

get dressed	got fired	take a trip
got divorced	take a nap	take notes

1. You should always <u>write down information</u> during class.

   You should always take notes during class.

2. Milos and Judy were married, but last month they <u>decided to stop being married</u>.

   _____

3. I'm tired. I'm going to <u>sleep for a short time</u>.

   _____

4. Harriet used to work for the phone company, but she <u>lost her job</u> last week.

   _____

5. It takes Lucy an hour to <u>put on her clothes</u>.

   _____

6. I'm going to <u>travel to another place</u> next month.

   _____

UNIT 8 WORK

Lesson A Listening

1 **Read and complete the paragraph. Then listen.**

degree   employed   gets along   personnel   reliable   shift   strengths

> Marina is from Senegal and has been living in the United States for one year.
>
> She has been ___employed___ as a cashier in a pharmacy for about six months.
>   1
>
> She has several _____ as an employee. She is _____ and
>   2   3
>
> friendly. She also _____ well with her co-workers. She is taking business
>   4
>
> courses at night and wants to get a _____ in hotel management.
>   5
>
>   Last week, she applied for a job as a reservations clerk at a big hotel. In the
>
> future, she hopes to get a job as an assistant manager or a manager. Today she
>
> got a call from the _____ manager asking her to come in for an interview.
>   6
>
>   Marina is confident that she can do the job. She speaks English well, and
>
> she speaks French fluently. She knows how to use a computer, a copy machine,
>
> and a fax machine. But she can't work the night _____ because of her
>   7
>
> business classes.

2 **Complete the chart. Use the information about Marina in Exercise 1.**

	Topic	Marina's answers
1.	job she is applying for	*reservations clerk*
2.	native country	
3.	current job	
4.	office machines she can use	
5.	strengths	

3 **Answer the personnel manager's questions. Use the information about Marina in Exercise 1.**

1. **A** Where are you from?

   B *I'm from Senegal.* _____

2. **A** What kind of work do you do?

   B _____

3. **A** What office machines can you use?

   B _____

4. **A** What other job skills do you have?

   B _____

5. **A** Are you taking any classes to improve your job skills?

   B _____

6. **A** What are your personal strengths?

   B _____

4 **Complete the sentences.**

> background   employed   get along   interview   shift   strengths

1. I have many friends at school. I _____*get along*_____ with everybody.

2. I don't have a job now. I am not currently _____.

3. One of my _____ is that I am very reliable.

4. I have a job _____ next week.

5. I can't work during the day. I need to work the night _____.

6. Can you tell me more about your _____? I'd like to know more about you.

5 **Listen. Then circle the correct words.**

1. Geraldo is applying for a job as **a building manager** / **an electrician**.

2. Geraldo is from **Argentina** / **Canada**.

3. At the moment he's working part-time as a **plumber** / **custodian**.

4. Geraldo tells Ms. Lee that he is **hard-working** / **qualified**.

Lesson B Present perfect continuous

Study the chart and explanation on page 129.

1 Complete the chart.

| a long time | morning | September | Tuesday | 2010 | week |
| day | one hour | three months | 2:00 p.m. | two weeks | year |

for	since	all
a long time		

2 Write sentences. Use the present perfect continuous with *for*, *since*, and *all*.

1. Kendra / work / in the library / October

   <u>Kendra has been working in the library since October.</u>

2. Frank and Marta / study computers / two years

   _____

3. Carla / look for a job / January

   _____

4. I / wait for an interview / 1:30 p.m.

   _____

5. You / talk on the phone / two hours

   _____

6. We / use the library computers / morning

   _____

7. Kemal / drive a cab / 20 years

   _____

8. Gloria / cook / day

   _____

3 **Write questions and two answers. Use the present perfect continuous with *for* and *since*.**

1. Alicia and Claire started painting the house at 11:00 a.m. It is now 11:30 a.m.

   A How long *have Alicia and Claire been painting the house* ?

   B Since *11:00 a.m.*

   For *30 minutes.*

2. Inez started cooking at 4:00 p.m. It is now 6:00 p.m.

   A How long _____?

   B Since _____

   For _____

3. Tony and Leon started studying computers on June 1st. Today is July 1st.

   A How long _____?

   B Since _____

   For _____

4. Yoshi started working in the restaurant on Tuesday – five days ago.

   A How long _____?

   B Since _____

   For _____

5. I started using a computer in August. It is now November.

   A How long _____?

   B Since _____

   For _____

6. Lenka started driving this morning at 10:00 a.m. It is now 1:00 p.m.

   A How long _____?

   B Since _____

   For _____

7. Juan started attending this school three weeks ago. It is now February 5th.

   A How long _____?

   B Since _____

   For _____

Lesson C Phrasal verbs

Study the explanation and list of phrasal verbs on page 132.

1 Complete the sentences.

> away   back   down   out   up

1. I'm busy now. Could you please call _____ *back* _____ later?

2. Could you please fill _____ this application?

3. I don't want to listen to music. Could you turn _____ the volume?

4. Could you clean _____ your room, please?

5. Please put _____ your dictionary. You can't use a dictionary during the test.

2 Look at the words in bold. Write the sentences again with *him*, *it*, or *them*.

1. Anton needs to turn down **the music**.

   He *needs to turn it down* _____.

2. Rita is cleaning up **the kitchen**.

   She _____.

3. Martine is throwing away **old newspapers**.

   She _____.

4. The students are putting away **their books**.

   They _____.

5. I need to call back **my father**.

   I _____.

3 Complete the sentences. Use phrasal verbs and *him*, *it*, or *them*.

1. These clothes are clean. Please put _____ *them away* _____.

2. Your room is a mess! Please clean _____.

3. Your husband just called and left a message. Please call _____.

4. The volume on your cell phone is not loud enough. Please turn _____.

5. Here is the job application. Please fill _____.

4 **Add the missing word in each sentence.**

him

1. I don't have time to call back. (him)

2. There's too much trash. Please throw out. (it)

3. We don't need these winter jackets anymore. Please put them. (away)

4. I want to watch TV. Let's turn on. (it)

5. It's too bright in here. Please turn off. (the lamp)

5 **Complete the sentences.**

call back　　clean up　　hand out　　put away

1.

She's _____*putting away*_____ her clothes.

She's _____*putting*_____ her clothes _____*away*_____.

She's _____*putting*_____ them _____*away*_____.

2.

He's _____ the tests.

He's _____ the tests _____.

He's _____ them _____.

3.

She's _____ her kitchen.

She's _____ her kitchen _____.

She's _____ it _____.

4.

He's _____ Doctor Kim.

He's _____ Doctor Kim _____.

He's _____ him _____.

Lesson D Reading

1 **Scan the blog. Answer the questions. Then listen and read.**

1. Who wrote the blog?

   Ivan wrote the blog.

2. What is the blog about?

   _____

3. How long has the writer been writing the blog?

   _____

4. What does the writer ask readers to do?

   _____

Ivan's Blog

Friday **3/06**	It's been a busy week! I've been learning a lot and I'm excited about learning more.
Thursday **3/05**	Today I was really tired. I almost fell asleep on the train coming home. I was too tired to cook dinner and fell asleep in front of the TV. This job is harder than I expected. I feel a bit depressed.
Wednesday **3/04**	Today I went to lunch with two of my co-workers. I think I'm starting to make friends here! They told me it's hard work – I'm worried about that, but I'm not going to give up!
Tuesday **3/03**	I've been trying very hard to talk to everyone here because it's important to network. I'm not very confident yet, but I have been smiling at everyone and introducing myself. Most people are really friendly. But some are too serious, and they don't say much!
Monday **3/02**	The first day in my new job! All morning, I filled out forms for the human resources department. In the afternoon, I met the other people on my team and learned how to use the copier. There's a lot to learn, but I'll try to be patient.

If you have any tips about starting a new job – please share them with me!

2 **Number the events from Ivan's blog in Exercise 1 in the order they happened.**

_____ Ivan almost fell asleep on the train home.

_____ Ivan met the other people on his team.

_____ Ivan had lunch with his co-workers.

__1__ Ivan filled out human resources forms.

_____ Ivan was too tired to cook dinner.

_____ Ivan learned how to use the copier.

3 **Match the days with Ivan's feelings. Use the information in Ivan's blog in Exercise 1.**

1. Monday __d__   a. not confident

2. Tuesday _____   b. depressed

3. Wednesday _____   c. excited

4. Thursday _____   d. trying to be patient

5. Friday _____   e. a little worried

4 **Find the adjectives in Ivan's blog. Underline them. Then circle the definition that best fits the reading.**

1. confident   ⓐ sure of yourself   b. firm

2. serious   a. critical   b. quiet

3. depressed   a. unhappy   b. sick

4. busy   a. filled with people b. working hard

5. excited   a. nervous   b. happy

6. patient   a. not angry   b. able to wait

5 **Complete the chart. Use a dictionary to help you.**

	Adjective	Noun
1.	confident	_confidence_
2.	depressed	
3.	excited	
4.	patient	
5.	serious	

1 **Complete the thank-you email. Use the information in the chart.**

Your name	Sarah Bonarelli
Your email address	sarah.bonarelli3@netmail.com
Today's date	August 18, 2018
Name of interviewer	Ms. Ann Robinson
Interviewer's title	Office Manager
Interviewer's email address	arobinson@cityofficeservices.com
Date of interview	August 17, 2018
Reason for saying thank you	Job interview on Friday, August 17th
Something specific you appreciate	You saw the office and learned about the company.

To: _____   Date: _____

From: _____

Subject: Interview

Dear _____ :

I would like to thank you for the _____ I had with

you on _____ . I appreciate the time you spent with me.

I enjoyed seeing the _____ and learning more about the

_____ .

Thank you again for your time. I hope to hear from you soon.

Sincerely,

_____

2 **Tony Wilson went to a job interview. Write Tony's thank-you email. Use the information from his notes.**

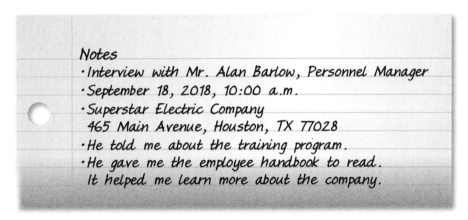

Notes
- Interview with Mr. Alan Barlow, Personnel Manager
- September 18, 2018, 10:00 a.m.
- Superstar Electric Company
  465 Main Avenue, Houston, TX 77028
- He told me about the training program.
- He gave me the employee handbook to read.
  It helped me learn more about the company.

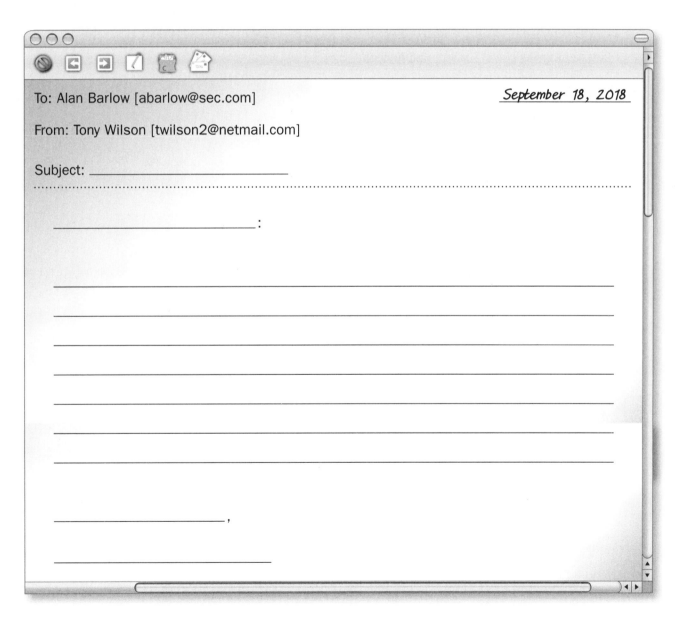

To: Alan Barlow [abarlow@sec.com]   September 18, 2018

From: Tony Wilson [twilson2@netmail.com]

Subject: _____

_____ :

_____

_____

_____

_____

_____

_____

_____ ,

_____

Lesson F Another view

1 **Read the questions. Look at the chart. Then fill in the correct answers.**

Changing Job Market 2014 to 2024				
Occupation	Jobs in 2014	Jobs in 2024	Change	Percent Change
Home health aides	913,500	1,261,900	+348,400	+38%
Registered nurses	2,751,000	3,190,300	+439,300	+16%
Truck drivers	1,797,700	1,896,500	+98,800	+5%
Post office workers	484,600	348,600	−136,000	−28%
Construction laborers	1,386,400	1,566,500	+180,100	+13%
Restaurant cooks	2,290,800	2,387,800	+97,000	+4%

Source: U.S. Bureau of Labor Statistics

1. Which job will increase the most in 10 years?
   - A registered nurse
   - ● home health aide
   - C post office worker
   - D truck driver

2. Which is probably not a good job to plan for in 2024?
   - A truck driver
   - B post office worker
   - C home health aide
   - D construction laborer

3. According to the chart, which is probably the best job area in 2024?
   - A restaurant work
   - B transportation
   - C construction
   - D health care

4. Which job employed the most people in 2014?
   - A home health aide
   - B truck driver
   - C construction laborer
   - D registered nurse

5. Of the jobs that increase, which job increases the least?
   - A construction laborers
   - B registered nurses
   - C truck drivers
   - D restaurant cooks

6. What information is included in this chart?
   - A Salary information about jobs over 10 years
   - B The changing demand for jobs over 10 years
   - C A comparison of the most popular jobs
   - D The most important jobs of 2014

2 **Complete the sentences. Use the present continuous and the present perfect continuous.**

1. Eliza / read a mystery story

   Eliza's reading a mystery story now.

   She's been reading it for

   the last three hours.

2. The Jensens / live in Miami

   _____ now.

   _____ there

   for three years.

3. I / study Russian

   _____ in the

   language lab now.

   _____ since

   last year.

4. Esteban / look for a job

   _____ now.

   _____ for

   six months.

5. Jun / organize his papers

   _____ now.

   _____ them

   since this morning.

6. Julie / write her blog

   _____ at

   home now.

   _____ since

   last January.

3 **Complete the story. Use the present continuous or the present perfect continuous.**

Megan _has been working_ as an office assistant in a big
          1. work
computer company for about five years. Lately, she

_____ bored with her job. It's the same routine
    2. feel
every day. Recently, she _____ for some different
         3. look
career ideas. Last week, she saw an article about a job in a safari

park in Botswana, a country in Africa. So now she _____ to apply
         4. plan
for a job there. At the moment, she _____ a letter to the safari
         5. write
park, and she _____ a lot of books about Botswana. She says, "For
    6. read
the last five years, I _____ to work at the same place every day. Now I
         7. go
_____ the first step toward an exciting change in my life."
    8. make

UNIT 9 DAILY LIVING

Lesson A Listening

1 Complete the conversation. Then listen.

broke into   crime   robbed   robber   stole

Anton Did you hear that someone ____*broke into*____ Arthur's car last night
1

and _____ his computer?
2

Fred That's terrible!

Anton Arthur's really upset. He uses that computer for work, and it has the names and
addresses of his customers in it.

Fred What's he going to do?

Anton Well, the computer has a secret code in it. If the _____ tries to use it,
3
an alarm will go off and tell the police where it is.

Fred That's smart! By the way, did you hear that someone _____ the bank
4
on South Street last week?

Anton There is so much _____ in this neighborhood now!
5

2 Circle the correct answers. Use the information in Exercise 1.

1. What happened to Arthur?
   a. Someone stole his car.
   b. Someone stole his computer.
   c. Someone broke into his house.
   d. Someone broke his computer.

2. Why is Arthur upset?
   a. His car is broken.
   b. His car is expensive.
   c. His computer has a special alarm.
   d. His computer has important
      information on it.

3. What will happen if the robber uses the computer?
   a. The police will find the car.
   b. The police will find the computer.
   c. The police will call Arthur.
   d. The police will call the robber.

4. What happened at the bank?
   a. Someone left the bank.
   b. Someone closed the bank.
   c. Someone cleaned up the bank.
   d. Someone stole cash from the bank.

3 Complete the story.

break into   came over   got into   robber   stole   worried

Yesterday, I put my gloves on the kitchen table.
I came back a few minutes later, and they were
gone. I was _____worried_____. I thought,
                    1
"Did someone _____ the house?
                    2
Was there a _____ here?" Then
                    3
one of my neighbors _____. He
                    4
had my gloves in his hand. He said, "My cat

_____ your house through the
        5
window and _____ the gloves!
                    6
I don't know why, but he loves gloves. I'm so sorry."

4 Circle the correct words.

1. Two men **robbed** / **stole** a bank on Main Street.

2. The same night, three robbers **broke into** / **came over** a supermarket on Park Avenue.

3. The men made a big **crime** / **mess** in the store. Cans and bottles were all over the floor.

4. The robbers set off the alarm, so the police **came over** / **got into** right away.

5. The police said, "We were busy with two **crimes** / **robbers** on the same night."

5 What happened in the story? Listen. Then check (✓) the correct answer.

☐ The police caught the robbers when they were driving down Lombard Avenue.

☐ The robbers ran away because the car didn't have any gas in it.

☐ The robbers parked the car because the police were chasing them.

Study the chart and explanation on page 130.

1 **Complete the conversations. Use the past continuous.**

1. **A** What were you doing last night around 6:00 p.m.?

   B I _____was eating_____ dinner.
   (eat)

2. **A** What was Julie doing yesterday afternoon?

   B She _____ her cousin's children.
   (babysit)

3. **A** What were Phuong and Tim doing on Sunday morning?

   B They _____ a neighbor.
   (visit)

4. **A** What were Lisa and Alan doing on Monday night?

   B They _____ the kitchen.
   (clean)

5. **A** What was Kemal doing at 4:30 p.m.?

   B He was _____ a newspaper.
   (read)

2 **What were these people doing at 8:00 a.m. yesterday? Complete the sentences.**

drive   knit   sleep   study   talk   watch

1. Taline   Aram

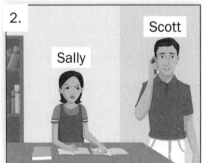
2. Sally   Scott

3. Leo   Ron

1. Taline _____was knitting_____ a sweater. Aram _____was watching_____ TV.

2. Sally _____. Scott _____ on the phone.

3. Leo _____. Ron _____ to work.

3 **Look at the chart. Answer the questions.**

	9:00 a.m.	2:00 p.m.	5:00 p.m.
Anna	eat breakfast	study English	clean the house
Pete	paint the bedroom	study English	watch a movie
Louise	drive to work	attend a meeting	clean the house
Fareed	drive to work	read a book	watch a movie

1. **A** Was Louise studying English at 2:00 p.m.?

   B _No, she wasn't. She was attending a meeting._

2. **A** Were Anna and Louise cleaning the house at 5:00 p.m.?

   B _____

3. **A** Were Louise and Fareed driving to work at 9:00 a.m.?

   B _____

4. **A** Was Pete studying English at 5:00 p.m.?

   B _____

4 **Write questions and answers. Use the present continuous and the chart in Exercise 3.**

1. Anna / 9:00 a.m.

   A What _was Anna doing at 9:00 a.m._?

   B _She was eating breakfast_.

2. Fareed / 2:00 p.m.

   A What _____?

   B _____.

3. Pete / 9:00 a.m.

   A What _____?

   B _____.

4. Anna and Pete / 2:00 p.m.

   A What _____?

   B _____.

Check your answers. See page 140.

Lesson C Past continuous and simple past

Study the explanation on page 130.

1 **Underline the past continuous in each sentence.**

1. We <u>were jogging</u> in the park when it started to rain.
2. I ran out of gas while I was driving to work.
3. Seema was having lunch with a friend when someone stole her car.
4. When the fire started, I was making cookies in the kitchen.
5. While the neighbors were attending a meeting, someone called the police.
6. Fatima was talking on the phone when her husband came home.

2 **Complete the paragraph. Use the past continuous or the simple past.**

While I _____*was working*_____ in the garden yesterday,
          1. work

I _____*heard*_____ a loud noise in the street. It sounded
     2. hear

like a car accident. When I looked in the street, two strangers

_____. One of them looked very upset.
     3. talk

The other driver _____ too fast when she
         4. drive

_____ a tree. The tree then _____
     5. hit   6. fall

on the other person's car. What a mess!

3 **Write sentences. Use the past continuous and the simple past.**

1. While we (eat lunch), the lights (go out).

   While we were eating lunch, the lights went out.

2. Ellen (sleep) when the fire alarm (go off) in her home.

   _____

3. When we (shop) at the mall, we (get) a parking ticket.

   _____

4. While Francisco (jog), it (start) to rain.

   _____

5. While I (cook) dinner, my husband (attend) a meeting.

   _____

6. Julio and Tia (work) in the garden when Julio (fall) off the ladder.

   _____

4 **Combine the sentences. Use the past continuous and the simple past.**

1. Chang watched TV. The fire alarm went off.

   While *Chang was watching TV, the fire alarm went off* .

2. The lights went out. We visited our neighbors.

   When _____ , _____ .

3. I baked a cake. An earthquake started.

   _____ when _____ .

4. We ate dinner. A thief stole my purse.

   _____ when _____ .

5. It began to rain. Fernando and Luis painted the house.

   _____ while _____ .

6. We drove in a bad storm. A tree fell on our car.

   _____ when _____ .

7. Maria took a grammar test. Yan did her homework.

   While _____ , _____ .

Lesson D Reading

1 **Read and circle the correct answers. Then listen.**

A Helping Hand

by Rodrigo and Elena Gonzalez

A year ago, a huge hurricane hit our state. It was the largest hurricane in 40 years, and it destroyed many of the homes in our neighborhood. Everyone had to evacuate. Some people lost everything – their home, their furniture, their car. Luckily, our home was OK, but we felt we had to help our neighbors.

The next day, we started to collect money, clothes, shoes, and food. Everyone was very generous and gave as much as they could. We used the money to buy food and water bottles. Two days later, we had three cars full of supplies. We took them over to the park and set up a shelter.

For the next three days, we stayed at the shelter. While people were looking for their families and gathering their things, we cooked food, served tea and coffee, and handed out clothes, food, and water. They were really glad to have our support. And we were very glad to have the chance to help them. One year later, we started a neighborhood organization to help everyone in our community in difficult times. It's important to know you can get help from your neighbors.

1. What is the main idea of this article?
   a. Hurricanes are dangerous.
   b. People should ask for help.
   c. Some people lost everything.
   d. Neighbors should help each other.

2. Which event happened first?
   a. The writers set up a shelter.
   b. The writers bought food and water.
   c. The writers collected food and money.
   d. The writers started a neighborhood organization.

3. What happened when the writers started to collect supplies?
   a. People didn't give any money.
   b. People gave clothes, food, and money.
   c. People gave tents and water bottles.
   d. People did not give very much.

4. Why did the writers feel good?
   a. They had to evacuate.
   b. They got to rebuild their home.
   c. They didn't need help.
   d. They were able to help their neighbors.

2 Underline the time phrases. Answer the questions.

1. We moved to this country <u>in 2015</u>. <u>A year later</u> we had a baby.

   A When did they have a baby?

   B *In 2016.*

2. A hurricane destroyed our home in August. Two months later, we rebuilt our home.

   A When did they rebuild their home?

   B _____

3. In July, there was a terrible fire in our town. For the next three months, we collected money and clothes.

   A When did they stop collecting money and clothes?

   B _____

4. At 6:00 p.m., we heard the fire alarm. Four minutes later, we evacuated the building.

   A At what time did they evacuate the building?

   B _____

3 Match the bold words with the correct meaning.

1. a. They were **gathering** apples in the backyard.
   b. A crowd was **gathering** in the street.

   _b_ meeting   _a_ collecting

2. a. Daniel needs a scholarship to **support** his college education.
   b. Thank you for your **support** after the hurricane.

   _____ help   _____ pay for

3. a. A thief **grabbed** my wallet on the bus.
   b. I **grabbed** as many photographs as I could during the fire.

   _____ stole   _____ took quickly

4. a. They gave us a **generous** amount of money.
   b. Our neighbors were very **generous** to us after the earthquake.

   _____ large   _____ helpful

5. a. We **lost** everything in the earthquake.
   b. We **lost** the game.

   _____ didn't win   _____ don't have it anymore

Lesson E Writing

1 **Read. Then answer the questions.**

One evening last week, I was driving home from work. I was driving slowly through my neighborhood when my cell phone rang. I pulled over to the curb and answered it. It was my wife. She asked me to pick up some food for dinner from the supermarket on the way home. I was turning off my cell phone and pulling back out when a cat ran across the street. I immediately turned the car to the right, and I hit a fire hydrant. Water went everywhere.

Luckily, I was OK. I didn't hit the cat, but the car was damaged. Firefighters came to fix the fire hydrant. The police arrived, and I had to fill out an accident report. While I was talking to the police, my wife called again. She wanted to know what happened to me. I said, "Well, I think I'll be a little late tonight."

1. What is the story about?

   The story is about a car accident.

2. When did the accident happen?

   _____

3. Where did the accident happen?

   _____

4. What was the writer doing when the story started?

   _____

5. Why did the accident happen?

   _____

6. How did the story end?

   _____

2 **Look at the pictures. Circle the correct answers.**

1. When did the story start?   a. at 5:55 a.m.   (b.) at 5:55 p.m.

2. Where did the story happen?   a. on a train   b. on a plane

3. What was Joe doing when the
   story started?   a. reading   b. talking

4. What was next to Joe?   a. a friend   b. a box

5. What happened while he was
   getting off the train?   a. He found his box.   b. He saw a friend.

6. What happened when the
   train doors closed?   a. He remembered his box.   b. He forgot his book.

7. How did the story end?   a. The doors opened,   b. The doors closed,
                                                           and he took his box.   and he lost his box.

3 **Write a narrative paragraph about what happened to Joe
in Exercise 2. Use the past continuous. Write at least one
sentence with *when* and one sentence with *while*.**

One evening at 5:55 p.m., Joe was sitting on a train.

Lesson F Another view

1 **Read the questions. Look at the chart. Then fill in the correct answers.**

Top ten cities in the U.S. in rank order by population size		
	2000	2017
New York, NY	1	1
Los Angeles, CA	2	2
Chicago, IL	3	3
Houston, TX	4	4
Philadelphia, PA	5	5
Phoenix, AZ	6	6
San Antonio, TX	9	7
San Diego, CA	7	8
Dallas, TX	8	9
San José, CA	11	10

Sources: U.S. Census Bureau.

1. Which state has the highest number of top ten cities by population size in 2000?

   ● Texas

   (B) Arizona

   (C) California

   (D) New York

2. Which states have the highest number of top ten cities by population size in 2017?

   (A) Texas and Arizona

   (B) Arizona and Illinois

   (C) California and Texas

   (D) New York and Pennsylvania

3. Which of the following cities had the same ranking in 2000 and in 2017?

   (A) Dallas

   (B) San José

   (C) San Antonio

   (D) Los Angeles

4. Which of the following cities had a different ranking?

   (A) New York

   (B) Houston

   (C) San Diego

   (D) Philadelphia

5. Which city was not on the top ten list in 2000?

   (A) Dallas

   (B) San José

   (C) San Diego

   (D) Phoenix

6. Which city had a smaller population in 2017 than it did in 2000?

   (A) Chicago

   (B) Dallas

   (C) San Antonio

   (D) Philadelphia

2 **How do these sentences use the present continuous? Mark them N (now), OE (ongoing event), or NF (near future).**

_N_ 1. It's snowing outside.

_____ 2. My husband is cleaning the snow off the sidewalk.

_____ 3. Later today, we're going shopping.

_____ 4. We're cooking dinner for some friends tonight.

_____ 5. We're both taking cooking classes at the Culinary Institute this month.

_____ 6. Next week, we're learning to prepare some Asian foods.

_____ 7. I'm volunteering to cook at the community center this year.

_____ 8. At the moment, I'm just watching the snow come down.

3 **Look at the chart. Complete the sentences.**

	Greg	Nicole	Hamoud
Now	work in garden	fill out a job application	call some friends to ask them to give food
Ongoing event	take a class at the garden center	try to find a job as a salesperson	collect food for a family that lost their home in a flood
Near future	take some vegetables to the county fair	go to a department store for an interview	take the food to the family

Greg:

1. This summer, _Greg is taking a class at the garden center_____.

2. Next Saturday, he _____.

3. At the moment, _____.

Nicole:

4. This month, _____.

5. Right now, _____.

6. On Friday, _____.

Hamoud:

7. This week, _____.

8. Next Saturday, _____.

9. At the moment, _____.

UNIT 10 FREE TIME

Lesson A Listening

1 Read and complete the paragraph. Then listen.

books   days off   discounts   reserve   round-trip   tax

Fabiola has three ___*days off*___ next week. She wants to go on vacation.
                        1
She went on the Internet and found some good _____ on flights
                                                      2
to Washington, D.C. She can get a _____ ticket for $95.00 if she
                                          3
_____ her flight five days ahead. The flight takes one hour. It leaves
        4
at 2:00 p.m. on Monday, and the return flight leaves Washington, D.C., at 11:00 a.m.

on Wednesday. The hotel costs $120 a night plus _____, which is
                                                          5
$14.50 per night.

If she takes the train, the trip will take three hours. The train leaves at 8:00 a.m. on

Monday, and the return train leaves Washington, D.C., at 6:00 p.m. on Tuesday. She does

not need to _____ a hotel room for two nights. The train costs $175.00,
                  6
but she can stay just one night and still have two full days of sightseeing.

2 Complete the chart. Use the information in Exercise 1.

	Cost of transportation	Cost of lodging	Total cost
By plane	$95.00		
By train			

Fabiola's trip is cheaper if she travels by _____.

3 Make sentences. Match the sentence parts.

1. You should reserve a room early __*d*__   a. come here during the summer.

2. You should book a flight in advance _____   b. doesn't usually include tax.

3. The advertised room rate _____   c. to get the best discounts.

4. Many tourists _____   d. because hotels are very busy at this time.

4 **Look at the bold words. Write sentences. Use words from the box with a similar meaning.**

days off   discount   high   reserve   tired

1. Room rates are **expensive** in the summer. *Room rates are high in the summer.*

2. You can get a **cheaper rate** if you book ahead. _____

3. You can **book** your hotel room online. _____

4. Sam has three **vacation days**. _____

5. Erin was **exhausted** after the long flight. _____

5 **Solve the problems.**

1. Sal and his wife Dana need a vacation. They want to take a weekend trip to Miami and stay two nights. They have never been there before. They can get a round-trip plane ticket for $150.00 each. The hotel costs $150.00 per night plus tax. The tax is $19.00 per night. How much will their transportation and lodging cost? _____

2. Joanna and her husband Andy have a few days off. They have $1,200.00 to spend. They want to go to Orlando for three nights. Round-trip plane tickets cost $250.00 for each person. The hotel costs $120.00 plus $13.00 for tax each night. How much money will they have after they have paid for transportation and lodging? _____

6 **Listen. Then mark the sentences as S (Sure) or NS (Not Sure).**

_NS_ 1. Arturo and Hana will stay at the Mount Green Ski Lodge.

_____ 2. Arturo and Hana will go skiing at Mount Green this weekend.

_____ 3. Arturo and Hana will borrow a cabin from Arturo's friend Mark.

_____ 4. Arturo's office will be closed on Friday.

Lesson B Conditionals

Study the explanation on page 133.

1 Circle the correct forms of the verbs.

1. If we **get** / **will get** a few days off, we **go** / **will go** to the beach.

2. Rosa **travels** / **will travel** by plane if the tickets **aren't** / **won't be** too expensive.

3. If the weather **is** / **will be** good, we **ride** / **will ride** our bicycles.

4. If Charlie **visits** / **will visit** San Diego, he **stays** / **will stay** with his sister.

5. If we **don't** / **won't** find a cheap hotel, we **don't** / **won't** go to New York.

2 Look at the pictures. Answer the questions.

1.

2.

3.

4.

1. What will Jack do if his friends come over this afternoon?

   If Jack's friends come over this afternoon, they'll play soccer.

2. What will the Perez family do if the weather is good?

   _____

3. What will Stacey do if she has the day off?

   _____

4. What will Robert do this weekend if it rains?

   _____

3 **Complete the conversation. Use the simple present or future form of the verbs.**

A What will you do this summer if you have a few days off?

B If I ___*have*___ enough money, I _____ my family in California.
1. have 2. visit

A That sounds fun! What _____ you _____ if you _____
3. do 4. not / have
enough money?

B I guess I'll stay home. What about you?

A If my brother _____ from Chicago, we _____ camping. But if he
5. come 6. go
_____ , I _____ my friends in Houston.
7. not / come 8. visit

4 **Write questions with *if*. Then answer the questions.**

1. Brian / do / have time off this summer

A What *will Brian do if he has time off this summer* ?

B He *will go swimming* .
(go swimming)

2. Tam and Chen / do / the weather is beautiful this weekend

A What _____ ?

B They _____ .
(work in the garden)

3. Sara / do / get some extra money for her birthday

A What _____ ?

B She _____ .
(go shopping)

4. you / do / have a three-day weekend

A What _____ ?

B I _____ .
(go hiking)

5. we / do / the weather is bad

A What _____ ?

B We _____ .
(clean the house)

Lesson C Future time clauses

Study the explanation on page 133.

1 **Read and complete the sentences. Use the correct form of the verb. Then listen.**

Sanjit is planning a trip to Colorado. He has

decided to make a list of things he needs to do

before he ___*leaves*___ . Before he _____
     1. leave   2. go

on his trip, he _____ some books about
                3. read

Colorado. After he _____ the books, he
                     4. read

_____ a map and choose the best route for
  5. find

his trip. He _____ some campsites and make
              6. choose

reservations before he _____ . On the day before he _____ ,
                         7. leave   8. leave

he _____ some food and first-aid supplies. He _____ some gas at the gas
   9. buy   10. get

station, too. After he does all that, he _____ his baggage into the car. Then he'll
                                          11. put

be ready for his trip!

2 **Complete the sentences. Use the simple present or future with *will*.**

1. Victor / book a flight to Dallas / talk to a travel agent

   Before *Victor books a flight to Dallas* , *he will talk to a travel agent* .

2. Victor / make a hotel reservation / fly to Dallas

   _____ before _____ .

3. Victor / clean up the house / leave for the airport

   After _____ , _____ .

4. Victor / go through security / check in

   _____ after _____ .

5. Victor / get on the plane / turn off his cell phone

   Before _____ , _____ .

3 **Look at Pedro's calendar. Write sentences about his plans. Use *before* and *after*.**

Monday, November 26		Tuesday, November 27	
9:30–5:30 p.m.	Work	9:30–5:30 p.m.	Work
6:00 p.m.	Buy concert tickets	6:15 p.m.	Meet Nick
7:00 p.m.	Invite Nick to the concert	6:30 p.m.	Eat dinner at a restaurant
7:30 p.m.	Make dinner reservations	8:30 p.m.	Concert

1. Pedro / buy the concert tickets / invite Nick to the concert

    a. *Pedro will buy concert tickets before he invites Nick to the concert.*

    b. *Pedro will invite Nick to the concert after he buys concert tickets.*

2. He / invite Nick to the concert / make dinner reservations

    a. *He will invite Nick to the concert before* _____

    b. *He will make dinner reservations after* _____

3. He / meet Nick / finish work

    a. _____

    b. _____

4. He / go to the concert / eat dinner at a restaurant

    a. _____

    b. _____

4 **Complete the conversations.**

1. **A** What *will you do before you go on your trip* _____? (before)
   B Before I go on my trip, I will learn a few words in French.

2. **A** What _____? (before)
   B Before Trina goes on vacation, she will get a passport.

3. **A** Where _____? (after)
   B They will go to Philadelphia after they leave New York.

4. **A** What _____? (before)
   B Suzanna will buy a cup of coffee before she reads the newspaper.

Lesson D Reading

1 **Read and circle *T* (True) or *F* (False). Then listen.**

The Statue of Liberty

The Statue of Liberty is one of the most popular tourist sights in New York City and a symbol of freedom for many Americans. The statue is on Liberty Island in the middle of New York Harbor. The people of France gave the statue to the people of the United States in 1886 as a gift of friendship.

Many people call the statue by its popular name, "Lady Liberty." The statue is a woman wearing a long robe and a crown with seven points. The points represent the seven continents and seven seas. She holds a flat piece of stone in her left hand and a burning torch high in her right hand. The stone has the date "JULY IV MDCCLXXVI" (July 4, 1776), the day of America's independence from Britain. There are 354 steps inside the statue and 25 windows in the crown. The 25 windows represent the 25 natural minerals of the earth.

It takes a lot of work to keep the Statue of Liberty in good condition. Sometimes the statue is closed for repairs. At these times, visitors are still able to visit the island and tour the park, but they aren't allowed to go into the statue. When the Statue of Liberty is open, visitors can learn about the statue at the museum in the base of the statue. A limited number of people can get a pass and climb up into the crown. From there, they can see a wonderful view of New York Harbor and the city's skyline.

To get to the Statue of Liberty, you must board a ferry. Private boats are not allowed to land on the island. It's a good idea to buy your tickets in advance, as the lines can be very long, and sometimes the tickets sell out.

1. The article gives information about the history of the statue. (T) F
2. The article describes the statue. T F
3. The article gives information about how to visit the statue. T F
4. The statue is over 300 years old. T F
5. The torch is in Lady Liberty's left hand. T F
6. France gave the statue as a gift in 1776. T F
7. Lady Liberty's crown has seven points. T F
8. You cannot buy tickets in advance to see the Statue of Liberty. T F

2 **Answer the questions. Use the information in Exercise 1.**

1. What is the main topic of the article?

   The Statue of Liberty is the main topic of this article.

2. Where is the statue located?

   _____

3. What happened in 1886?

   _____

4. Why did the people of France give the statue to the United States?

   _____

5. Why does "July 4, 1776" appear on the statue?

   _____

6. How many steps are inside the statue?

   _____

7. What can you see from inside the crown?

   _____

8. How do you get to the Statue of Liberty?

   _____

3 **Scan the article for the bold words. Underline them. Then circle the words with a similar meaning.**

1. **sights**
   a. attractions
   b. parks

2. **symbol**
   a. sign
   b. gift

3. **gift**
   a. promise
   b. present

4. **robe**
   a. dress
   b. jacket

5. **torch**
   a. pen
   b. fire

6. **independence**
   a. freedom
   b. friendship

7. **pass**
   a. entrance
   b. ticket

8. **board**
   a. get on
   b. get off

Lesson E Writing

1 **Read the paragraph. Then answer the questions.**

Central Park

Central Park, one of the most popular tourist attractions in New York City, is popular because it offers something for everyone. It is right in the heart of the city and is a perfect place to relax after a shopping trip or before you go to the theater. The zoo is open every day. If your children like animals, they will love the children's zoo, where children can touch animals such as goats and sheep. Older children can go to a beginner climbing course with special indoor and outdoor climbing walls. If the weather is nice, you can enjoy the beautiful weather and row boats on the lake. If you love culture and music, you'll enjoy one of the concerts or a theater performance of Shakespeare in the open-air theater. Finally, if you feel tired after a day of sightseeing and shopping, you can take a relaxing and romantic ride around the park in a horse-drawn carriage.

1. What is the main idea of the paragraph?

   Central Park is a popular attraction because it offers something for everyone.

2. What are four examples of things to do in Central Park?

   a. _____

   b. _____

   c. _____

   d. _____

3. What is the conclusion?

   _____

2 **Read the information. Then write a paragraph about Hollywood. Include a main idea, at least three examples of things to do in Hollywood, and a conclusion.**

Visit HOLLYWOOD
Birthplace of the Movies! Los Angeles, California

Visit movie studios

HOLLYWOOD

See the footprints of movie stars

Walk along the Hollywood Walk of Fame

Go to a concert at the Hollywood Bowl

One of the most popular tourist attractions in California is Hollywood.
Hollywood has something for everyone.

Lesson F Another view

1 **Read the questions. Look at the amusement park information. Then fill in the correct answers.**

	Family Fun Amusement Park	**Great Days Amusement Park**
Admission	One-day adult admission $39.95 Junior (3–8) $29.95 Senior (55+) $32.95 Children under 3 are free	One-day adult admission $29.95 Junior (5–12) $19.95 Senior (65+) $24.95 Children under 5 are free
Amenities	Water rides and family rides Indoor and outdoor swimming pools 4 movie theaters Restaurants / cafés	Mini-golf and go-kart racing Climbing courses for all ages Child play center Restaurants / cafés
Restaurants	Price Range • Appetizers: $5.00–$7.50 • Main courses: $8.99–$15.00 • Desserts: $4.75–$7.50	Price Range • Appetizers: $5.00–$15.00 • Main courses: $12.00–$24.00 • Desserts: $5.50–$8.00
Driving distance from destinations	San Francisco, CA (2 hours) Los Angeles, CA (6 hours)	Boston, MA (4 hours) Washington, D.C. (5 hours)

1. What is the admission for a person aged 66 at Family Fun Amusement Park?

   (A) $24.95

   (B) $29.95

   (●) $32.95

   (D) $39.95

2. Which is the cheapest?

   (A) one junior admission at Family Fun

   (B) one junior admission at Great Days

   (C) one senior admission at Family Fun

   (D) one senior admission at Great Days

3. Which statement is true?

   (A) Children under five are free at Family Fun.

   (B) Children over three are free at Family Fun.

   (C) Children over three are free at Great Days.

   (D) Children under five are free at Great Days.

4. How far is Great Days from Boston?

   (A) 1.5 hours

   (B) 4 hours

   (C) 4.5 hours

   (D) 6 hours

5. Which statement is true?

   (A) Great Days has a child play center.

   (B) Great Days has a movie theater.

   (C) Family Fun has a climbing course.

   (D) Family Fun has mini-golf.

6. How much is the most expensive main course at Family Fun?

   (A) $8.99

   (B) $12.00

   (C) $15.00

   (D) $24.00

2 How do these sentences use the present perfect? Mark them A, B, or C as follows:

A = events that begin in the past and continue until now

B = events that happened once in the past, time unclear

C = events that have been repeated in the past

1. She's been to the Louvre Museum in Paris and has seen the Mona Lisa. _B_

2. I've already visited Alcatraz. I don't want to go again. _____

3. The Bradleys have been in Hawaii for two weeks. They'll be back tomorrow. _____

4. We're at the county fair. We've been on the Ferris wheel, and we've seen the fireworks. _____

5. I've read *The Lord of the Rings* four times. I'll probably read it again some day. _____

6. We've been standing in line to buy tickets to Sea Adventure for an hour now. _____

7. Jim said that he and his wife have eaten several meals at that restaurant, and they've all been good. _____

8. I know I've stayed at this hotel before, but I can't remember when. _____

3 Circle the best answer to complete the conversation.

1. **A** I've been to New York three times.
   B _____ ?
   (a.) Do you think you'll go again some day?
   b. How long have you been there?

2. **A** We've been in Peru for two weeks, but we haven't gone to Cuzco.
   B _____ ?
   a. Are you still in Peru?
   b. Will you go to Cuzco before you leave?

3. **A** I've visited Loch Ness in Scotland, but I didn't see the monster.
   B _____ ?
   a. When did you go there?
   b. How long have you been there?

4. **A** We're in Tokyo now.
   B _____ ?
   a. How long did you stay there?
   b. How long have you been there?

5. **A** We haven't been to Nova Scotia yet.
   B _____ ?
   a. When did you go there?
   b. Do you want to go?

6. **A** I've visited the museum more than once, but I haven't seen everything.
   B _____ ?
   a. How many times have you been there?
   b. How long have you been there?

REFERENCE

Verbs + gerunds

A gerund is the base form of a verb + -ing.
Gerunds often follow verbs that talk about preferences. Use a gerund like a noun: *I love <u>dancing</u>*.

Spelling rules for gerunds

- Verbs ending in a vowel-consonant pair repeat the consonant before adding -ing:
  stop → stopping get → getting
- Verbs ending in silent -e drop the e before -ing:
  dance → dancing exercise → exercising

  but:

  be → being   see → seeing

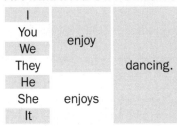

QUESTIONS

Do	I / you / we / they	enjoy dancing?
Does	he / she / it	

AFFIRMATIVE STATEMENTS

I / You / We / They	enjoy	dancing.
He / She / It	enjoys	

NEGATIVE STATEMENTS

I / You / We / They	don't enjoy	dancing.
He / She / It	doesn't enjoy	

Verbs gerunds often follow

avoid	feel like	love	quit
can't help	finish	mind	recommend
dislike	hate	miss	regret
enjoy	like	practice	suggest

Gerunds after prepositions

Prepositions are words like *in*, *of*, *about*, and *for*. Prepositions are often used in phrases with adjectives (*excited about*, *interested in*) and verbs (*think about*). Gerunds often follow these phrases.

WH- QUESTIONS: WHAT

What	am	I	tired of doing?
	are	you / we / they	
	is	he / she / it	

AFFIRMATIVE STATEMENTS

I	am	tired of working.
You / We / They	are	
He / She / It	is	

Phrases gerunds often follow

afraid of	famous for	nervous about	thank (someone) for
amazed by	good at	plan on	think about
angry at	happy about	pleased about	tired of
bad at	interested in	sad about	worried about
excited about	look forward to	talk about	

Verbs + infinitives

An infinitive is *to* + the base form of a verb.
Infinitives often follow verbs that talk about future ideas. See below for a list of verbs that infinitives often follow.

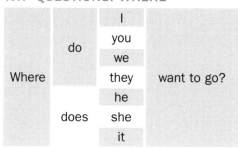

WH- QUESTIONS: *WHERE*

Where	do	I / you / we / they	want to go?
	does	he / she / it	

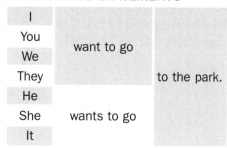

AFFIRMATIVE STATEMENTS

I / You / We / They	want to go	to the park.
He / She / It	wants to go	

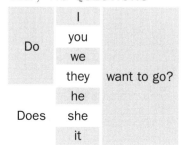

YES / NO QUESTIONS

Do	I / you / we / they	want to go?
Does	he / she / it	

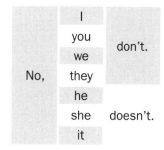

SHORT ANSWERS

Yes,	I / you / we / they	do.
	he / she / it	does.

No,	I / you / we / they	don't.
	he / she / it	doesn't.

Verbs infinitives often follow

agree	hope	need	promise
can / can't afford	intend	offer	refuse
decide	learn	plan	volunteer
expect	manage	prepare	want
help	mean	pretend	would like

don't = do not
doesn't = does not

Present perfect

The present perfect is *have* or *has* + past participle. Use the present perfect to talk about actions that started in the past and continue to now. See page 131 for a list of past participles with irregular verbs.
Use *how long* + present perfect to ask about length of time.
Use *for* with a period of time to answer questions with *how long*.
Use *since* with a point in time to answer questions with *how long*.

WH- QUESTIONS: *HOW LONG*

How long	have	I / you / we / they	been	here?
	has	he / she / it	been	

AFFIRMATIVE STATEMENTS: *FOR* AND *SINCE*

I / You / We / They	have been	here	for two hours. since 6:00 p.m.
He / She / It	has been		

Use *ever* with the present perfect to ask *Yes / No* questions about things that happened at any time before now.

haven't	=	have not
hasn't	=	has not

YES / NO QUESTIONS: *EVER*

Have	I / you / we / they	ever	been late?
Has	he / she / it	ever	been late?

SHORT ANSWERS

Yes,	I / you / we / they	have.
Yes,	he / she / it	has.

No,	I / you / we / they	haven't.
No,	he / she / it	hasn't.

Use *recently* and *lately* with the present perfect to talk about things that happened in the very recent past, not very long ago.

YES / NO QUESTIONS: RECENTLY AND LATELY

Have	I / you / we / they / he	been	early recently? early lately?
Has	she / it		

Use *already* and *yet* with the present perfect to talk about actions based on expectations.

AFFIRMATIVE STATEMENTS: *ALREADY*

I / You / We / They	have	already	eaten.
He / She / It	has		

NEGATIVE STATEMENTS: *YET*

I / You / We / They	haven't	eaten	yet.
He / She / It	hasn't		

Present perfect continuous

The present perfect continuous is *have* or *has* + *been* + present participle.
Use the present perfect continuous to talk about actions that started in the past, continue to now, and will probably continue in the future.

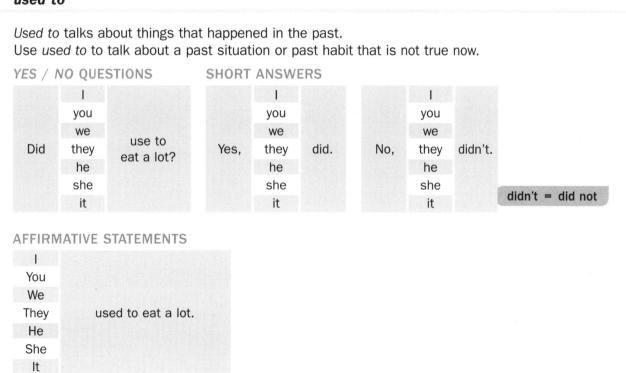

YES / NO QUESTIONS

| Have | I / you / we / they / he | been sitting here for a long time? |
| Has | she / it | |

SHORT ANSWERS

| Yes, | I / you / we / they | have. |
| | he / she / it | has. |

| No, | I / you / we / they | haven't. |
| | he / she / it | hasn't. |

WH- QUESTIONS: *HOW LONG*

| How long | have | I / you / we / they | been sitting here? |
| | has | he / she / it | |

AFFIRMATIVE STATEMENTS: *FOR* AND *SINCE*

| I / You / We / They | have been sitting here | for an hour. since 10 a.m. |
| He / She / It | has been sitting here | |

used to

Used to talks about things that happened in the past.
Use *used to* to talk about a past situation or past habit that is not true now.

YES / NO QUESTIONS

| Did | I / you / we / they / he / she / it | use to eat a lot? |

SHORT ANSWERS

| Yes, | I / you / we / they / he / she / it | did. |

| No, | I / you / we / they / he / she / it | didn't. |

didn't = did not

AFFIRMATIVE STATEMENTS

| I / You / We / They / He / She / It | used to eat a lot. |

Past continuous

Use the past continuous to talk about actions that were happening at a specific time in the past. The actions were not completed at that time.

WH- QUESTIONS: WHAT

What	was	I	doing last night?
	were	you	
		we	
		they	
	was	he	
		she	
		it	

AFFIRMATIVE STATEMENTS

I	was	working.
You	were	
We		
They		
He	was	
She		
It		

YES / NO QUESTIONS

Was	I	working?
Were	you	
	we	
	they	
	he	
Was	she	
	it	

SHORT ANSWERS

Yes,	I	was.
	you	were.
	we	
	they	
	he	was.
	she	
	it	

No,	I	wasn't.
	you	weren't.
	we	
	they	
	he	wasn't.
	she	
	it	

wasn't = was not
weren't = were not

could and should

Use *could* to give suggestions. Use *should* to give advice. *Should* gives stronger advice than *could*.

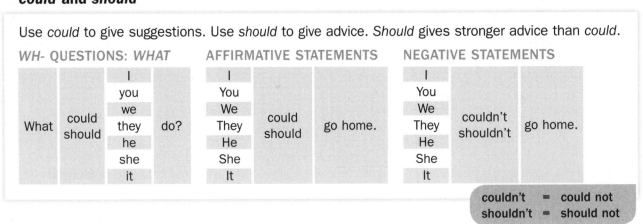

WH- QUESTIONS: WHAT

What	could	I	do?
	should	you	
		we	
		they	
		he	
		she	
		it	

AFFIRMATIVE STATEMENTS

I	could	go home.
You	should	
We		
They		
He		
She		
It		

NEGATIVE STATEMENTS

I	couldn't	go home.
You	shouldn't	
We		
They		
He		
She		
It		

couldn't = could not
shouldn't = should not

Irregular verbs

Base form	Simple past	Past participle	Base form	Simple past	Past participle
be	was / were	been	leave	left	left
become	became	become	lose	lost	lost
begin	began	begun	make	made	made
break	broke	broken	meet	met	met
bring	brought	brought	pay	paid	paid
build	built	built	put	put	put
buy	bought	bought	read	read	read
catch	caught	caught	ride	rode	ridden
choose	chose	chosen	run	ran	run
come	came	come	say	said	said
cost	cost	cost	see	saw	seen
cut	cut	cut	sell	sold	sold
do	did	done	send	sent	sent
drink	drank	drunk	set	set	set
drive	drove	driven	show	showed	shown
eat	ate	eaten	sing	sang	sung
fall	fell	fallen	sit	sat	sat
feel	felt	felt	sleep	slept	slept
fight	fought	fought	speak	spoke	spoken
find	found	found	spend	spent	spent
fly	flew	flown	stand	stood	stood
forget	forgot	forgotten	steal	stole	stolen
get	got	gotten / got	swim	swam	swum
give	gave	given	take	took	taken
go	went	gone	teach	taught	taught
have	had	had	tell	told	told
hear	heard	heard	think	thought	thought
hide	hid	hidden	throw	threw	thrown
hit	hit	hit	understand	understood	understood
hold	held	held	wake	woke	woken
hurt	hurt	hurt	wear	wore	worn
keep	kept	kept	win	won	won
know	knew	known	write	wrote	written

Spelling rules for regular past participles

- To form the past participle of regular verbs, add -ed to the base form:
  listen → listened
- For regular verbs ending in a consonant + -y, change y to i and add -ed:
  study → studied
- For regular verbs ending in a vowel + -y, add -ed:
  play → played
- For regular verbs ending in -e, add -d:
  live → lived

Grammar explanations

Separable phrasal verbs

A phrasal verb is a verb + preposition. The meaning of the phrasal verb is different from the meaning of the verb alone.

> He *handed out* the papers to the class. = He *gave* the papers to the class.

A separable phrasal verb can have a noun between the verb and the preposition.

> He *handed **the papers** out*.

A separable phrasal verb can have a pronoun between the verb and the preposition.

> He *handed **them** out*.

Common separable phrasal verbs

call back	cut off	find out	look up	throw away / out
call up	do over	give back	pick out	turn down
clean up	fill in	hand in	put away / back	turn off
cross out	fill out	hand out	shut off	turn up
cut down	fill up	leave on	tear up	

Comparisons

Use *more than*, *less than*, and *as much as* to compare nouns and gerunds. A gerund is the base form of a verb + *ing*. It is often used as a noun. You can compare activities by using gerunds and *more than*, *less than*, and *as much as*.

> I enjoy *walking more than driving*.
> She likes *cooking less than eating*.
> They enjoy *singing as much as dancing*.

Giving reasons and explanations with *because* and *because of*

Use a *because* clause or a *because of* phrase to give an explanation. A *because* clause is the part of the sentence that begins with *because* and has a subject and verb. A *because of* phrase is the part of the sentence that begins with *because of* and has a noun phrase. Use a comma (,) when the *because* clause or *because of* phrase begins the sentence.

> I came to Ohio *because of my children*.
> *Because of my children*, I came to Ohio.

> I came to Ohio *because my children are here*.
> *Because my children are here*, I came to Ohio.

Adjectives with *too* and *enough*

Use *too* + adjective to talk about more than the right amount.

> The ladder is *too tall*.

Use an adjective + *enough* to talk about the right amount of something.

> The ladder is *tall enough* to reach the ceiling.

Use *not* + adjective + *enough* to talk about less than the right amount.

> The ladder is *not tall enough*.

Capitalization rules

Capitalize the first, last, and other important words in titles.	**My** **S**trategies for **L**earning **E**nglish **S**alsa **S**tarz at **C**entury **P**ark **E**scape from **A**lcatraz
Capitalize letters in abbreviations.	**TV** (television) **DVD** (digital video disc or digital versatile disc) **ATM** (automated teller machine or automatic teller machine)
Capitalize titles when they follow a name.	Latisha Holmes, **P**resident, Rolling Hills Neighborhood Watch Janice Hill, **P**ersonnel **M**anager, Smart Shop

Adverb clauses

A clause is a part of a sentence that has a subject and a verb. A dependent clause often begins with time words such as *when*, *before*, and *after*. The dependent clause can come at the beginning or end of a sentence. Use a comma (,) after dependent clauses that come at the beginning of a sentence. Do not use a comma when a dependent clause comes at the end of a sentence.

when: Use *when* + present time verbs to talk about habits.

> *When I have a lot to do*, I make a to-do list.
> I make a to-do list *when I have a lot to do*.

before: Use *before* to order events in a sentence. *Before* introduces the second event.

Use *before* with the simple present to talk about habits.

> First, she reads the newspaper. Second, she eats breakfast. =
> She reads the newspaper *before she eats breakfast*.
> *Before she eats breakfast*, she reads the newspaper.

Use *before* with the simple present and future to talk about future plans.

> First, he'll finish school. Second, he'll take a vacation. =
> He'll finish school *before he takes a vacation*.
> *Before he takes a vacation*, he'll finish school.

after: Use *after* to order events in a sentence. *After* introduces the first event.

Use *after* with the simple present to talk about habits.

> First, I eat dinner. Second, I watch the news. =
> I watch the news *after I eat dinner*.
> *After I eat dinner*, I watch the news.

Use *after* with the simple present and future to talk about future plans.

> First, he'll finish school. Second, he'll take a vacation. =
> He'll take a vacation *after he finishes school*.
> *After he finishes school*, he'll take a vacation.

when and ***while***: Use *when* or *while* with the past continuous and simple past to show that one past action interrupted another past action.

Use *when* with the simple past for the action that interrupted.

> They were sleeping *when the fire started*.
> *When the fire started*, they were sleeping.

Use *while* with the past continuous to show the action that was happening before the interruption.

> The fire started *while they were sleeping*.
> *While they were sleeping*, the fire started.

if: Use *if* clauses to talk about future possibility. Use the simple present in the clause with *if*. Use the future in the other clause to talk about what could happen.

> She won't go *if the weather is bad*.
> *If the weather is bad*, she won't go.

ANSWER KEY

Welcome

Exercise 1 page 2
1. c   2. b   3. b   4. a   5. b   6. a

Exercise 2 page 3
1. wants to get
2. needs to improve
3. needs to take
4. needs to get
5. needs to apply
6. wants to work

Exercise 3 page 3
1. Emile wants to open a men's clothing store.
2. He needs to find a good location for the store.
3. Farah and Ali want to study engineering in college.
4. They need to take a lot of math classes.
5. Monica wants to pass the GED exam.
6. She needs to take some special classes.
7. Adrian wants to buy a new car.
8. He needs to save his money.

Exercise 4 page 4
1. is
2. is living
3. has
4. is working
5. puts, checks
6. wants
7. goes
8. is learning

Exercise 5 page 4
1. At the moment, Miguel is living with his brother Tony.
2. Tony has a job at a computer store.
3. Right now he is working as a salesperson.
4. He wants to become a computer technician.
5. Tony is taking English classes every Thursday evening.
6. Tony and Miguel are studying English together now.
7. Their teacher always gives a lot of homework.

Exercise 6 page 5
1. came
2. wanted
3. played
4. began
5. decided
6. will start
7. liked
8. will teach

Exercise 7 page 5
1. did you come to this country
2. did you come to this country
3. did you play for
4. did you play for them
5. did you decide to change your career plan
6. will you start your new job
7. will you teach
8. will you stay here

Unit 1: Personal information

Lesson A: Listening

Exercise 1 page 6
1. a   2. c   3. b   4. c   5. a   6. c

Exercise 2 page 7
1. outgoing
2. enjoys
3. going out
4. dislikes
5. shy
6. alone

Exercise 3 page 7
1. dislikes
2. enjoys
3. enjoys
4. dislikes
5. dislikes

Exercise 4 page 7
1. outgoing
2. quiet
3. stay home
4. dislike

Exercise 5 page 7
reading books, fixing old cars, listening to music, talking about movies

Lesson B: Verbs + gerunds

Exercise 1 page 8
1. getting up early
2. doing homework
3. doing homework
4. playing soccer
5. playing soccer
6. getting up early

Exercise 2 page 8
1. Yes, he does.
2. No, she doesn't.
3. No, he doesn't.
4. Yes, they do.
5. No, he doesn't.
6. No, he doesn't.

Exercise 3 page 9
1. going out
2. being
3. working
4. reading
5. listening
6. taking
7. doing
8. playing
9. using
10. cleaning

Exercise 4 page 9
1A. going out
1B. Yes, he does.
2A. being
2B. Yes, he does.
3A. reading
3B. No, he doesn't.
4A. doing
4B. No, he doesn't.

Exercise 5 page 9
1. Do you enjoy going to the beach?
2. Do you dislike standing in line?
3. Do you hate working out?
4. Do you like playing video games?
5. Do you mind taking out the garbage?
6. Do you avoid eating vegetables?

Lesson C: Comparisons

Exercise 1 page 10
1. playing sports
2. socializing with friends
3. dancing
4. cooking
5. watching movies
6. reading

Exercise 2 page 10
1. Angelina likes watching movies less than cooking.
2. Angelina likes watching movies more than reading.
3. Angelina likes cooking less than dancing.
4. Angelina likes socializing with friends more than dancing.
5. Angelina likes playing sports as much as socializing with friends.

Exercise 3 page 11
1. Ling likes painting more than playing an instrument.
2. Frank enjoys riding a bicycle more than driving a car.
3. Suzanna enjoys reading more than washing the dishes.
4. Annie and Steve like going to the movies more than shopping.

Exercise 4 page 11
1. Annie and Steve like shopping less <u>than</u> watching movies.
2. Ling likes playing an instrument <u>less</u> than painting.
3. Suzanna enjoys washing dishes less <u>than</u> reading.
4. Frank enjoys riding a bike <u>more</u> than driving a car.

Lesson D: Reading

Exercise 1 page 12
1. architect
2. computer programmer
3. teacher

Exercise 2 page 12
1. architect
2. computer programmer
3. teacher
4. computer programmer
5. teacher
6. architect

Exercise 3 page 13
Computer programmers: find answers to problems, like working alone
Teachers: help students, like learning about people
Architects: design new homes, imagine new ideas

Exercise 4 page 13
1. personality
2. intellectual
3. creative
4. artist
5. friendly
6. type
7. outgoing

Lesson E: Writing

Exercise 1 page 14
Jobs: architect, designer, scientist, social worker, teacher
Personality adjectives: creative, friendly, helpful, outgoing, reliable
Activities: drawing, finding answers, helping people, using social media, talking

Exercise 2 page 14
Name: Peter Jones
Job: social worker
Place of work: community center
Personality: friendly and outgoing
Likes: meeting and helping people

Exercise 3 page 15
1. computer programmer
2. intellectual
3. hardworking
4. finding answers

Exercise 4 page 15
Answer may vary.

Lesson F: Another view

Exercise 1 page 16

1. C   2. A   3. A   4. D   5. C   6. B

Exercise 2 page 17

1. c; Ruben must be a little shy.
2. a; Miguel must love music.
3. d; Adriana must be very intelligent.
4. a; Hana must like sports a lot.

Exercise 3 page 17

1. She must not be a very good cook.
2. He must be very creative.
3. He must not be a reliable employee.
4. She must not like working out.
5. She must know how to swim.

Unit 2: At school

Lesson A: Listening

Exercise 1 page 18

1. paper   4. index cards
2. list   5. concentrate
3. underline   6. discouraged

Exercise 2 page 18

1. b   2. c   3. b   4. a

Exercise 3 page 19

1. d   2. a   3. f   4. e   5. b   6. c

Exercise 4 page 19

1. list   5. vocabulary
2. paper   6. index cards
3. concentrate   7. boring
4. active   8. discouraged

Exercise 5 page 19

Bad study habits: doesn't study new words, is late for class, hands in homework late, forgets homework, doesn't study for tests
Good study habits: makes to-do lists, writes new words on index cards, underlines the main ideas

Exercise 6 page 19

Mr. Wilson has talked about learning strategies in class.

Lesson B: Present perfect

Exercise 1 page 20

1. for   3. since   5. since   7. for
2. since   4. for   6. since   8. since

Exercise 2 page 20

1. have   3. has   5. has
2. have   4. have   6. have

Exercise 3 page 20

1. has worked   4. has had
2. have lived   5. has taught
3. have studied   6. has been

Exercise 4 page 21

1A. has he been
1B. four hours, 3:00 p.m.
2A. has she known
2B. four months, August 1
3A. has he lived
3B. two years, June 25, 2013

Exercise 5 page 21

1. have they worked in this school
2. has she had a driver's license
3. has he lived in this apartment
4. have you been married

Lesson C: Present perfect

Exercise 1 page 22

1. lost   4. taken
2. forgotten   5. gotten
3. read

Exercise 2 page 22

1A. Has, studied
1B. Yes, she has.
2A. Have, talked
2B. No, they haven't.
3A. Has, made
3B. Yes, she has.
4A. Have, written
4B. Yes, they have.
5A. Has, done
5B. No, he hasn't.

Exercise 3 page 23

1. Have you ever used
2. Has your teacher ever talked
3. Have your friends ever studied
4. Have you ever written
5. Have you ever underlined
6. Have they ever gotten

Exercise 4 page 23

1. Melissa hasn't ever forgotten to study for a test. She has lost her textbook.
2. Franco has had trouble concentrating on his homework. He hasn't ever done the wrong homework.
3. Rose has read the newspaper in English. She hasn't ever tried to speak English with her neighbors.

Lesson D: Reading

Exercise 1 page 24

1. The article is about strategies for learning new words.
2. 1. Keep a vocabulary notebook.
   2. Make vocabulary cards.
   3. Use new words in conversations every day.
3. Make vocabulary cards.

Exercise 2 page 25

1. b   2. d   3. a   4. b

Exercise 3 page 25

1. c   2. d   3. e   4. a   5. b

Exercise 4 page 25

1. strategies
2. set
3. plan
4. practice
5. clues
6. gestures

Lesson E: Writing

Exercise 1 page 26

Listening strategies: Listen to the radio. Watch movies in English. Watch the news in English
Speaking strategies: Ask questions in class every day. Talk to people at work in English. Use new words in everyday conversation.
Reading strategies: Look up new words in a dictionary. Read newspapers in English. Underline new words with colored pens.

Exercise 2 page 26

1. Omar's first strategy is to read newspapers or magazines in English. He is going to read a newspaper article in English every day.

2. Omar's second strategy is to use colored pens to underline new words. He is going to use a yellow pen for new and difficult words. He is going to use a blue pen when he can guess the meaning of words.

3. Omar's third strategy is to use his dictionary more often. He is going to choose five words he doesn't know each day and check their meanings.

Exercise 3 page 27

1. 4   2. 2   3. 3   4. 1

Exercise 4 page 27

Answer may vary.

Lesson F: Another view

Exercise 1 page 28

1. Read   5. worry
2. Skim   6. Make
3. Answer   7. look
4. spend

Exercise 2 page 28

1. 4   2. 5   3. 6   4. 7   5. 2   6. 3   7. 1

Exercise 3 page 29

1. has been   6. started
2. has always gotten 7. has worked
3. have gone   8. talked
4. had   9. gave
5. needed   10. have improved

Exercise 4 page 29

1. Has Tran ever forgotten to put his name on a test?
   Yes. He forgot to put his name on a history test last week.
2. Has Naomi ever watched a TV show in English?
   Yes. She watched the news on the BBC last night.
3. Have Naomi and Tran ever studied geometry?
   Yes. They studied geometry in the first year of high school.

Unit 3: Friends and family

Lesson A: Listening

Exercise 1 page 30

1. came over   4. borrow
2. favor   5. noisy
3. broken   6. complain

Exercise 2 page 30

1. a   2. b   3. d   4. a

Exercise 3 page 31

1. borrow   5. complained
2. battery   6. noise
3. appreciates   7. favor
4. owe   8. come over

Exercise 4 page 31

1. lent   3. borrowed
2. borrowed   4. lent

Exercise 5 page 31

1. lend   3. borrow
2. lend   4. borrow

Exercise 6 page 31

He's going to borrow a key from the building manager.

Lesson B: Clauses and phrases with *because*

Exercise 1 page 32
1. c   2. a   3. e   4. b   5. d

Exercise 2 page 32
1. because
2. because
3. because of
4. because of
5. because of
6. because

Exercise 3 page 32
1. We couldn't sleep because of the noise.
2. We couldn't play soccer because of the rain.
3. They were late for the appointment because of the traffic.
4. Reyna stayed at home because of the flu.
5. Sam stayed up late because of the basketball game.
6. Beatriz moved to this country because of her children.

Exercise 4 page 33
1. because
2. because
3. because of
4. because of
5. because

Exercise 5 page 33
1. because it was closed
2. because of the rain
3. because it was her son's birthday
4. because of the smoke
5. because he was sick
6. because there were so many people

Lesson C: Adverbs of degree

Exercise 1 page 34
1. hot
2. tall
3. small
4. strong
5. close
6. young

Exercise 2 page 34
1. hot
2. tall
3. strong
4. small
5. young
6. close

Exercise 3 page 34
1. too young
2. old enough
3. too weak
4. strong enough
5. too small
6. big enough

Exercise 4 page 35
1A. too noisy
1B. not quiet enough
2A. too expensive
2B. not cheap enough
3A. too small
3B. not big enough
4A. too difficult
4B. not easy enough
5A. too boring
5B. not interesting enough
6A. too young
6B. not old enough

Exercise 5 page 35
1. big enough
2. tall enough
3. old enough
4. too high
5. strong enough
6. too young
7. experienced enough
8. too weak

Lesson D: Reading

Exercise 1 page 36
1. The writer gets together with her neighbors once a month.
2. Some teenagers painted the graffiti.
3. The writer's neighbors shouted at the teenagers, and they ran away.
4. The writer's neighborhood is safe.

Exercise 2 page 37
1. c   2. a   3. b   4. d

Exercise 3 page 37
1. get into
2. get together
3. look after
4. goes off
5. run away
6. break into

Exercise 4 page 37
1. run away
2. look after
3. get together
4. goes off
5. get into
6. break into

Lesson E: Writing

Exercise 1 page 38
1. today's date
2. problem
3. request
4. writer

Exercise 2 page 38
1. F
2. F
3. F
4. T
5. T
6. T
7. F
8. T

Exercise 3 page 39
1. soon
2. because
3. very
4. advance
5. because of

Exercise 4 page 39
Answer may vary.

Lesson F: Another view

Exercise 1 page 40
1. A   2. C   3. C   4. B   5. B   6. B

Exercise 2 page 41
1. aren't / are not able to do
2. are able to
3. aren't / are not able to have
4. 's / is able to open
5. isn't / is not able to fix
6. isn't / is not able to be
7. 're / are able to rent
8. 'm / am not able to leave

Exercise 3 page 41
1. I'm (not) able to run a mile in 10 minutes.
2. I'm (not) able to lift 50 pounds with one hand.
3. I'm (not) able to speak Japanese.
4. I'm (not) able to play the piano for my classmates.
5. I'm (not) able to fix a computer.
6. I'm (not) able to change a flat tire.

Unit 4: Health

Lesson A: Listening

Exercise 1 page 42
1. diet
2. exercise
3. pressure
4. weight
5. tired
6. advice

Exercise 2 page 42
1. a   2. b   3. b   4. b

Exercise 3 page 43
Healthy activities: check your weight, eat breakfast, eat fish, ride a bicycle,

Unhealthy activities: drink a lot of soda, eat a lot of hamburgers, gain 20 pounds, go to bed late

Exercise 4 page 43
1. diet
2. medication
3. weight
4. exercise
5. healthy

Exercise 5 page 43
Past: eat fast food for lunch; take the elevator; work 12 hours a day;
Now: have soup for lunch; walk up the stairs; eat breakfast; go to the gym; leave work at 5:30

Lesson B: Present perfect

Exercise 1 page 44
1. have gained
2. have given
3. have not eaten
4. have started
5. have exercised
6. has gone
7. have not been

Exercise 2 page 44
1. You haven't exercised this week.
2. Paul has gained weight recently.
3. Ray and Louisa have lost weight recently.
4. Alicia has been unhappy lately.
5. My blood pressure has gone up recently.
6. Greg hasn't visited a dentist recently.
7. Sarah has given up desserts lately.

Exercise 3 page 45
1. Annette hasn't checked her blood pressure recently.
2. Annette has gone to the gym recently.
3. Annette has eaten more fruits and vegetables recently.
4. Annette has slept eight hours a day recently.
5. Annette hasn't taken vitamins recently.

Exercise 4 page 45
1A. Has Bill lost weight recently?
1B. he hasn't.
2A. Have Tina and Mario given up desserts recently?
2B. they have.
3A. Have you checked your blood pressure lately?
3B. I haven't.
4A. Has Barbara slept much lately?
4B. she has.
5A. Has Lisa started taking vitamins recently?
5B. she hasn't.

Lesson C: *Used to*

Exercise 1 page 46
1. use
2. used
3. used
4. use
5. used
6. use

Exercise 2 page 46
1. used to
2. use to
3. used to
4. used to
5. use to
6. used to

Exercise 3 page 46
1. used to eat
2. eats
3. takes
4. used to exercise
5. goes
6. used to drive
7. rides
8. used to drink
9. drinks
10. used to feel
11. has

Exercise 4 page 47
1. Emilia used to stay up until 2:00 a.m., but now she goes to bed at 10:00 p.m.
2. Emilia used to eat meat every day, but now she eats fish twice a week.
3. Emilia used to go straight home after work, but now she goes to the gym three times a week.
4. Emilia used to eat a lot of fatty foods, but now she eats salad and vegetables.
5. Emilia used to skip breakfast, but now she eats fruit and yogurt for breakfast.

Exercise 5 page 47
1A. Did Emilia use to stay up until 2:00 a.m.?
1B. Yes, she did.
2A. Did Emilia use to eat meat every day?
2B. Yes, she did.
3A. Did Emilia use to go to the gym three times a week?
3B. No, she didn't.

Lesson D: Reading

Exercise 1 page 48
1. Mint is good for treating indigestion.
2. Lavender is good for treating headaches.
3. Mint is good for treating stomachaches.
4. Thyme tea can help treat a cough or a sore throat.

Exercise 2 page 49
Thyme: Use it to make tea. Use it to cook chicken and fish. Use it to treat a cough and sore throat.
Lavender: Use it to make tea. Use it to cook meat. Use it to treat headaches and high blood pressure.
Mint: Use it to make tea. Use it to cook meat and fish. Use it to treat indigestion and upset stomachs.

Exercise 3 page 49
1. digestion   4. herbal
2. treatment   5. digest
3. prevent   6. treat

Exercise 4 page 49
1. adjective   5. verb
2. noun   6. verb
3. verb or noun   7. noun
4. noun

Lesson E: Writing

Exercise 1 page 50
1. cooking and medicine
2. green-gray leaves and purple flowers
3. sore throats and breathing problems
4. to add flavor to meat and vegetables
5. as a mouthwash

Exercise 2 page 50
1. Rosemary
2. garden or in your home
3. sharp, narrow leaves
4. headaches
5. add flavor to meat or oil

Exercise 3 page 51
1. in hot, dry places
2. long, spiky leaves with juice inside
3. burns, insect bites, and dry skin
4. skin creams and lotions, shampoos, and soaps

Exercise 4 page 51
Answer may vary.

Lesson F: Another view

Exercise 1 page 52
1. B   2. D   3. D   4. C

Exercise 2 page 53
1. Dr. Chang told Harry Johnson not to eat sweets between meals.
2. He also told him to try to get more exercise.
3. Alec's mother told him to take his vitamins.
4. His father told him not to stay out late every night.
5. Ms. Bailey told the class not to stay up late studying for the test.
6. She also told them to eat a good breakfast in the morning.
7. Magda told Helen to use mint leaves to make iced tea.
8. Then she told her not to put too much sugar in it.

Unit 5: Around town

Lesson A: Listening

Exercise 1 page 54
1. B   2. D   3. C   4. A

Exercise 2 page 54
1. events   4. admission
2. concerts   5. storytelling
3. afford   6. exhibits

Exercise 3 page 55
1. d   3. d   5. b
2. c   4. b   6. c

Exercise 4 page 55
go to a museum, go out for coffee

Lesson B: Verbs + infinitives

Exercise 1 page 56
1. to go   4. to eat
2. to see   5. to take
3. to meet   6. to come home

Exercise 2 page 56
1. want to ride
2. plans to eat
3. intends to meet
4. need to take
5. she expects to be
6. would like to buy
7. hopes to find

Exercise 3 page 57
1. Tony promises to visit his family every year.
2. Lee expects to finish work early tonight.
3. I plan to go to Florida this winter.
4. Shin intends to buy some concert tickets tomorrow.
5. We hope to visit our daughter in California next month.
6. Paul refuses to go to the beach this weekend.
7. I want to meet my friends on my birthday.
8. I would like to take a trip with my family next year.

Exercise 4 page 57
1. Chris plans to watch less TV.
2. Chris intends to go to an art museum.
3. Chris wants to visit relatives more often.
4. Chris plans to walk to work every day.
5. Chris would like to give up desserts.
6. Chris hopes to buy organic vegetables.

Lesson C: Present perfect

Exercise 1 page 58
1. seen   3. read   5. bought
2. made   4. paid   6. done

Exercise 2 page 58
1. hasn't started yet   3. has already ended
2. has already closed   4. hasn't opened yet

Exercise 3 page 59
1. Has, brought / Yes, he has.
2. Has, invited / Yes, she has.
3. Has, gotten / No, he hasn't.
4. Has, baked / No, she hasn't
5. Has, bought / Yes, he has.
6. Have, put up / Yes, they have.
7. Have, set up / No, they haven't.

Exercise 4 page 59
1. We haven't gone to the park <u>yet</u>.
2. Our favorite TV show hasn't <u>started</u> yet.
3. Have <u>you</u> bought tickets for the fund-raiser yet?
4. They <u>haven't</u> eaten lunch yet.
5. Ivan and Alex <u>have</u> already been to that restaurant.
6. <u>Has</u> Julie visited the art exhibit yet?

Lesson D: Reading

Exercise 1 page 60
1. F 2. F 3. F 4. T 5. T 6. F 7. T

Exercise 2 page 61
1. d   2. d   3. b   4. d   5. b

Exercise 3 page 61
1. We missed the concert.
2. The concert was superb.
3. There was a crowd.
4. The waiting time was excessive.
5. There were five musicians.
6. The stage was unremarkable.

Lesson E: Writing

Exercise 1 page 62
Positive: amazing, fabulous, incredible, superb
Negative: excessive, irritating, ominous, unremarkable

Exercise 2 page 62
Positive adjectives: fabulous, incredible, amazing
Negative adjectives: terrible, irritating, unremarkable

Exercise 3 page 63
1. b, N   3. e, N   5. d, N
2. a, N   4. c, P

Exercise 4 page 63
Answer may vary.

Lesson F: Another view

Exercise 1 page 64
1. A 2. C 3. D 4. C 5. B 6. D

Exercise 2 page 65
1. reading   5. listening
2. to go   6. to see
3. to buy   7. walking
4. being   8. to study

Exercise 3 page 65
1. Betty prefers going to crafts fairs, not to the mall.
2. x

3. The lights went out, but the musicians continued to play.
4. x
5. I started to read the book last night, and I've already finished it.
6. x
7. x
8. Raul hates driving in the city during rush hour.

Unit 6: Time
Lesson A: Listening
Exercise 1 page 66
1. chores
2. deadline
3. due
4. tasks
5. procrastinating
6. prioritize
7. impatient

Exercise 2 page 66
1. to-do list
2. procrastinating
3. chores
4. due
5. prioritize
6. impatient

Exercise 3 page 67
1. a
2. b
3. b
4. c
5. b
6. a

Exercise 4 page 67
1. b
2. f
3. e
4. c
5. a
6. d

Exercise 5 page 67
2. Alicia has learned to manage her time.
3. Thomas often procrastinates.

Lesson B: Adverb clauses
Exercise 1 page 68
1. b
2. e
3. a
4. f
5. c
6. d

Exercise 2 page 68
1. When Parvana has a lot of homework, she makes a to-do list of her tasks.
2. When she wants to concentrate, she goes to the library.
3. She looks at the clock when she starts her work.
4. When she finishes a task, she checks it off her to-do list.
5. She takes a short break when she feels tired.
6. When she doesn't hand in her homework on time, her teacher is upset.
7. She eats a snack when she feels hungry.
8. When she needs to focus, she doesn't answer the phone.
9. She does the difficult tasks first when she has a lot of work to do.
10. When she has a deadline, she doesn't procrastinate.

Exercise 3 page 69
1. When I finish my homework, I take a break.
2. no comma
3. no comma
4. When we don't hand in our homework, our teacher is very upset.
5. When I have a deadline, I stay up late.
6. no comma

Exercise 4 page 69
1A. What do you do when you finish a difficult task?
1B. I take a break.
2A. What do you do when you need to concentrate?
2B. I go to the library.
3A. What do you do when you don't understand the homework?
3B. I ask my teacher.
4A. What do you do when you have a quiz or a test?
4B. I study my notes.
5A. What do you do when you feel tired?
5B. I rest.
6A. What do you do when you don't want to work?
6B. I procrastinate.

Lesson C: Adverb clauses
Exercise 1 page 70
1. after he wakes up
2. after he gets dressed
3. after he eats breakfast
4. after he works out
5. after he takes a shower

Exercise 2 page 70
1. Janet gets home before she eats dinner.
2. Janet eats dinner before she walks the dog.
3. Janet walks the dog before she watches TV.
4. Janet watches TV before she reads a book.

Exercise 3 page 71
1A. What does Mannie do before he eats breakfast?
1B. He gets dressed.
2A. What does Mannie do before he works out?
2B. He eats breakfast.
3A. What does Mannie do before he goes to work?
3B. He takes a shower.
4A. What does Janet do after she gets home?
4B. She eats dinner.
5A. What does Janet do after she watches TV?
5B. She reads a book.
6A. What does Janet do after she reads a book?
6B. She goes to bed.

Exercise 4 page 71
1. I watch TV after I have dinner.
2. Before Sandy goes to work, she buys a newspaper.
3. Ivana goes to school after she finishes work.
4. After Simon finishes his homework, he takes a break.
5. They usually go swimming after they go to the park.
6. Before you go out, you need to take out the trash.
7. Melanie puts on makeup after she takes a shower.
8. Alan washes the dishes before he goes to bed.

Lesson D: Reading
Exercise 1 page 72
1. c
2. a
3. b
4. d

Exercise 2 page 73
1. impolite
2. impatient
3. unspoken
4. irresponsible
5. uncommon

Exercise 3 page 73
1. It is uncommon to miss a plane.
2. It is impolite to be late.
3. It is unusual to be early for a party.
4. He is impatient.
5. They are irresponsible.
6. She is disorganized.

Exercise 4 page 73
1. lucky
2. possible
3. honest
4. friendly
5. kind
6. rational

Lesson E: Writing
Exercise 1 page 74
1. Nita is a very organized person.
2. She keeps all of her class notes in one binder with different sections.
3. She writes all of her homework assignments and due dates in a special notebook.
4. In summary

Exercise 2 page 74
1. She writes all her homework assignments and due dates in a special notebook.
2. She keeps all her notes in one binder with different sections.
3. She checks her bag carefully and makes sure she has all the books she needs.
4. She plans how much time she will need for each assignment.
5. She takes a short break.

Exercise 3 page 75
My boss Frida is a very impatient person. For example, she often gets angry when you are three minutes late. She is also not a good listener, and she often interrupts. Finally, she is always in a hurry and never has enough time. In conclusion, Frida is a very impatient person, and it is difficult to work for her.

Exercise 4 page 75
Answer may vary.

Lesson F: Another view
Exercise 1 page 76
1. C
2. D
3. C
4. B
5. A

Exercise 2 page 77
1. Before
2. when
3. When
4. after
5. When
6. before

Exercise 3 page 77
1. Before she took out the trash, Mary ate dinner.
2. After the Walters finished their hike, the rain began. OR The rain began after the Walters finished their hike.
3. I brushed my teeth before I went to bed OR Before I went to bed, I brushed my teeth.
4. After Deidre fed the cat, she watched the news. OR Deidre watched the news after she fed the cat.
5. Before he arrived at work, Eduardo made a to-do list. OR Eduardo made a to-do list before he arrived at work.

Exercise 4 page 77

1. Sometimes I read the newspaper when I eat breakfast.
2. Jane usually checks her email before she goes to bed. OR Before she goes to bed, Jane usually checks her email.
3. Did you buy tickets for the concert after they went on sale? OR After they went on sale, did you buy tickets for the concert?
4. Before I make dinner, I go to the supermarket to buy food. OR I go to the supermarket to buy food before I make dinner.

Unit 7: Shopping
Lesson A: Listening
Exercise 1 page 78

1. d   2. d   3. c   4. b

Exercise 2 page 79

1. afford   3. cash   5. pay off
2. credit   4. interest   6. balance

Exercise 3 page 79

1. $2,500.00
2. $250.00
3. $500.00

Exercise 4 page 79

1. $2,500   3. $100
2. 24   4. $550

Lesson B: Modals
Exercise 1 page 80

1. b 2. e 3. d 4. f 5. c 6. a

Exercise 2 page 80

1. buy   3. use   5. apply
2. taking   4. talk   6. looking

Exercise 3 page 80

1. should   3. should   5. could
2. could   4. should   6. should

Exercise 4 page 81

1. using your credit card
2. buy a used one
3. buy a new one
4. walking more often
5. looking for a cheaper plan
6. open a savings account

Exercise 5 page 81

1. should we do   4. should I make
2. should I tell   5. should I wear
3. should I buy

Lesson C: Gerunds after prepositions
Exercise 1 page 82

1. applying   6. lending   11. paying
2. being   7. losing   12. spending
3. buying   8. making   13. studying
4. finding   9. moving   14. waiting
5. getting   10. opening

Exercise 2 page 82

1. waiting   4. opening
2. buying   5. studying
3. applying   6. getting

Exercise 3 page 83

1. about   4. about
2. about   5. for
3. of

Exercise 4 page 83

1. about finding a job
2. for driving me to work
3. about getting a scholarship
4. of getting up early
5. of losing their jobs
6. in learning about computers

Exercise 5 page 83

1. Ron is excited about going to college.
2. Miguel is afraid of losing his job.
3. Vincent and Anna are happy about paying off their loan.
4. Tim and Betsy are worried about getting into debt.
5. Steve is interested in buying a new car.

Lesson D: Reading
Exercise 1 page 84

1. They can't afford the minimum payments.
2. They offer a 10–15 percent discount.
3. You won't have to pay any interest.
4. They say you should have at least two cards.

Exercise 2 page 85

1. Choose credit cards with low interest rates.
2. Keep the account balance low.
3. Always try to pay more than just the minimum payment.
4. Have no more than six cards.

Exercise 3 page 85

1. e   2. a   3. d   4. c   5. b

Exercise 4 page 85

1. credit   4. minimum
2. interest   5. counselor
3. budget

Exercise 5 page 85

1. interest rate   4. debt counselor
2. family budget   5. minimum payment
3. credit card

Lesson E: Writing
Exercise 1 page 86

1. c   2. d   3. b   4. a

Exercise 2 page 86

1. Gas is very expensive. His car uses a lot of gas. He needs to see an auto mechanic for repairs. He is worried about having his car break down.
2. Ask a co-worker to give you a ride to work and share the cost of gas. Drive to work three times a week and take the bus twice a week. Take the bus for a couple of months and save money.

Exercise 4 page 87

Answer may vary.

Lesson F: Another view
Exercise 1 page 88

1. a 2. c 3. b 4. b 5. a 6. d

Exercise 2 page 89

1. took   4. takes   7. get
2. gets   5. take   8. getting
3. got   6. take

Exercise 3 page 89

1. You should always take notes during class.
2. Milos and Judy were married, but last month they got divorced.
3. I'm tired. I'm going to take a nap.

4. Harriet used to work for the phone company, but she got fired last week.
5. It takes Lucy an hour to get dressed.
6. I'm going to take a trip next month.

Unit 8: Work
Lesson A: Listening
Exercise 1 page 90

1. employed   5. degree
2. strengths   6. personnel
3. reliable   7. shift
4. gets along

Exercise 2 page 90

1. reservations clerk
2. Senegal
3. cashier
4. computer, copy machine, and fax machine
5. responsible and friendly

Exercise 3 page 91

1. I'm from Senegal.
2. I'm a cashier in a pharmacy.
3. I can use a computer, a copy machine, and a fax machine.
4. I speak French fluently and English very well.
5. Yes, I am going to college to get a degree in hotel management.
6. I am reliable and friendly.

Exercise 4 page 91

1. get along   4. interview
2. employed   5. shift
3. strengths   6. background

Exercise 5 page 91

1. building manager   3. custodian
2. Argentina   4. hard-working

Lesson B: Present perfect continuous
Exercise 1 page 92

for: a long time, one hour, three months, two weeks
since: September, Tuesday, 2:00 p.m., 2010
all: day, morning, week, year

Exercise 2 page 92

1. Kendra has been working in the library since October.
2. Frank and Marta have been studying computers for two years.
3. Carla has been looking for a job since January.
4. I have been waiting for an interview since 1:30 p.m.
5. You have been talking on the phone for two hours.
6. We have been using the library computers all morning.
7. Kemal has been driving a cab for 20 years.
8. Gloria has been cooking food all day.

Exercise 3 page 93

1A. How long have Alicia and Claire been painting the house?
1B. Since 11:00 a.m.
    For 30 minutes.
2A. How long has Inez been cooking?
2B. Since 4:00 p.m.
    For two hours.
3A. How long have Tony and Leon been studying computers?
3B. Since June 1st.
    For one month.

4A. How long has Yoshi been working in the restaurant?
4B. Since Tuesday.
For five days.
5A. How long have you been using a computer?
5B. Since August.
For three months.
6A. How long has Lenka been driving?
6B. Since 10:00 a.m.
For three hours.
7A. How long has Juan been attending this school?
7B. Since January.
For three weeks.

Lesson C: Phrasal verbs
Exercise 1 page 94
1. back
2. out
3. down
4. up
5. away

Exercise 2 page 94
1. needs to turn it down
2. is cleaning it up
3. is throwing them away
4. are putting them away
5. need to call him back

Exercise 3 page 94
1. them away
2. it up
3. him back
4. it up
5. it out

Exercise 4 page 95
1. I don't have time to call him back.
2. Please throw it out.
3. Please put them away.
4. Let's turn it on.
5. Please turn it off.

Exercise 5 page 95
1. She's putting away her clothes.
She's putting her clothes away.
She's putting them away.
2. He's handing out the tests.
He's handing the tests out.
He's handing them out.
3. She's cleaning up her kitchen
She's cleaning her kitchen up.
She's cleaning it up.
4. He's calling back Doctor Kim.
He's calling Doctor Kim back.
He's calling him back.

Lesson D: Reading
Exercise 1 page 96
1. Ivan wrote the blog.
2. The blog is about Ivan's new job.
3. Ivan has been writing the blog for five days.
4. He asks readers to share tips with him about starting a new job.

Exercise 2 page 97
5, 2, 4, 1, 6, 3

Exercise 3 page 97
1. d   2. a   3. e   4. b   5. c

Exercise 4 page 97
1. a   2. b   3. a   4. b   5. b   6. b

Exercise 5 page 97
1. confidence
2. depression
3. excitement
4. patience
5. seriousness

Lesson E: Writing
Exercise 1 page 98
To: arobinson@cityofficeservices.com
From: sarah.bonarelli3@netmail.com
Subject: Interview
Date: August 18, 2018

Dear Ms. Robinson:
I would like to thank you for the job interview I had with you on August 17th. I appreciate the time you spent with me. I enjoyed seeing the office and learning more about the company. Thank you again for your time. I hope to hear from you soon.
Sincerely,
Sarah Bonarelli

Exercise 2 page 99
Answer may vary.

Lesson F: Another view
Exercise 1 page 100
1. B   2. B   3. D   4. D   5. D   6. B

Exercise 2 page 101
1. Eliza's reading a mystery story
She's been reading
2. The Jensens are living in Miami
They've been living
3. I'm studying Russian
I've been studying
4. Esteban is looking for a job
He's been looking for a job
5. Jun is organizing his papers
He's been organizing
6. Julie is writing her blog
She's been writing

Exercise 3 page 101
1. has been working
2. 's / has been feeling
3. 's / has been looking
4. 's / is planning
5. 's / is writing
6. 's / reading
7. 've / have been going
8. 'm / am making

Unit 9: Daily living
Lesson A: Listening
Exercise 1 page 102
1. broke into
2. stole
3. robber
4. robbed
5. crime

Exercise 2 page 102
1. b   2. d   3. b   4. d

Exercise 3 page 103
1. worried
2. break into
3. robber
4. came over
5. got into
6. stole

Exercise 4 page 103
1. robbed
2. broke into
3. mess
4. came over
5. crimes

Exercise 5 page 103
The robbers ran away because the car didn't have any gas in it.

Lesson B: Past continuous
Exercise 1 page 104
1. was eating
2. was babysitting
3. were visiting
4. were cleaning
5. was reading

Exercise 2 page 104
1. was knitting, was watching
2. was studying, was talking
3. was sleeping, was driving

Exercise 3 page 105
1. No, she wasn't. She was attending a meeting.
2. Yes, they were. They were cleaning the house.
3. Yes, they were. They were driving to work.
4. No, he wasn't. He was watching a movie.

Exercise 4 page 105
1A. What was Anna doing at 9:00 a.m.?
1B. She was eating breakfast.
2A. What was Fareed doing at 2:00 p.m.?
2B. He was reading a book.
3A. What was Pete doing at 9:00 a.m.?
3B. He was painting the bedroom.
4A. What were Anna and Pete doing at 2:00 p.m.?
4B. They were studying English.

Lesson C: Past continuous and simple past
Exercise 1 page 106
1. We were jogging in the park when it started to rain.
2. I ran out of gas while I was driving to work.
3. Seema was having lunch with a friend when someone stole her car.
4. When the fire started, I was making cookies in the kitchen.
5. While the neighbors were attending a meeting, someone called the police.
6. Fatima was talking on the phone when her husband came home.

Exercise 2 page 106
1. was working
2. heard
3. were talking
4. was driving
5. hit
6. fell

Exercise 3 page 107
1. While we were eating lunch, the lights went out.
2. Ellen was sleeping when the fire alarm went off in her home.
3. When we got a parking ticket, we were shopping at the mall.
4. While Francisco was jogging, it started to rain.
5. While I was cooking dinner, my husband attended a meeting.
6. Julio and Tia were working in the garden when Julio fell off the ladder.

Exercise 4 page 107
1. While Chang was watching TV, the fire alarm went off.
2. When the lights went out, we were visiting our neighbors.
3. I was baking a cake when the earthquake started.
4. We were eating dinner when a thief stole my purse.
5. It began to rain while Fernando and Luis were painting the house.

6. We were driving in a bad storm when a tree fell on our car.
7. While Maria was taking a grammar test, Yan did her homework.

Lesson D: Reading

Exercise 1 page 108
1. d 2. c 3. b 4. d

Exercise 2 page 109
1. in 2015; A year later
   1B. In 2016.
2. in August; Two months later
   2B. In October.
3. In July; For the next three months
   3B. In October.
4. At 6:00 p.m.; Four minutes later
   4B. At 6:04 p.m.

Exercise 3 page 109
1. b, a 2. b, a 3. a, b 4. a, b 5. b, a

Lesson E: Writing

Exercise 1 page 110
1. The story is about a car accident.
2. The accident happened one evening last week.
3. The accident happened in the writer's neighborhood.
4. He was driving home from work.
5. A cat ran across the street, the writer turned the car, and then he hit a fire hydrant.
6. The writer told his wife he was going to be late.

Exercise 2 page 111
1. b 4. b 6. a
2. a 5. b 7. b
3. a

Exercise 3 page 111
Answer may vary.

Lesson F: Another view

Exercise 1 page 112
1. A 2. C 3. D 4. C 5. B 6. B

Exercise 2 page 113
1. N 3. NF 5. OE 7. OE
2. N 4. NF 6. NF 8. N

Exercise 3 page 113
1. Greg is taking a class at the garden center
2. 's / is taking some vegetables to the county fair
3. he is working in his garden
4. Nicole is trying to find a job as a salesperson
5. she's / is filling out a job application
6. she's / is going to a department store for an interview
7. Hamoud is collecting food for a family that lost their home in a flood.
8. he's / is taking the food to the family
9. he's / is calling some friends to ask them to give food

Unit 10: Free time

Lesson A: Listening

Exercise 1 page 114
1. days off 4. books
2. discounts 5. tax
3. round-trip 6. reserve

Exercise 2 page 114
By plane: $95.00, $269.00, $364.00
By train: $175.00, $134.50, $309.50
It is cheaper for Fabiola to travel by train.

Exercise 3 page 114
1. d 2. c 3. b 4. a

Exercise 4 page 115
1. Room rates are high in the summer.
2. You can get a discount if you book ahead.
3. You can reserve your hotel room online.
4. Sam has three days off.
5. Erin was tired after the long flight.

Exercise 5 page 115
1. $638.00
2. $301.00

Exercise 6 page 115
1. NS 2. S 3. NS 4. S

Lesson B: Conditionals

Exercise 1 page 116
1. get, will go 4. visits, will stay
2. will travel, aren't 5. don't, won't
3. is, will ride

Exercise 2 page 116
1. If Jack's friends come over this afternoon, they'll play soccer.
2. If the weather is good, the Perez family will go hiking.
3. If Stacey has the day off, she will go shopping.
4. If it rains this weekend, Robert will read a book.

Exercise 3 page 117
1. have 5. comes
2. will visit 6. will go
3. will, do 7. doesn't come
4. don't have 8. will visit

Exercise 4 page 117
1A. What will Brian do if he has time off this summer?
1B. He will go swimming.
2A. What will Tam and Chen do if the weather is beautiful this weekend?
2B. They will work in the garden.
3A. What will Sara do if she gets some extra money for her birthday?
3B. She will go shopping.
4A. What will you do if you have a three-day weekend?
4B. I will go hiking.
5A. What will we do if the weather is bad?
5B. We will clean the house.

Lesson C: Future time clauses

Exercise 1 page 118
1. leaves 5. will find 9. will buy
2. goes 6. will choose 10. will get
3. will read 7. leaves 11. will put
4. reads 8. leaves

Exercise 2 page 118
1. Before Victor books a flight to Dallas, he will talk to a travel agent.
2. Victor will make a hotel reservation before he flies to Dallas.
3. After Victor cleans up the house, he will leave for the airport.
4. Victor will go through security after he checks in.
5. Before Victor gets on the plane, he will turn off his cell phone.

Exercise 3 page 119
1. a. Pedro will buy concert tickets before he invites Nick to the concert.
   b. Pedro will invite Nick to the concert after he buys concert tickets.
2. a. He will invite Nick to the concert before he makes dinner reservations.
   b. He will make dinner reservations after he invites Nick to the concert.
3. a. He will meet Nick after he finishes work.
   b. He will finish work before he meets Nick.
4. a. He will go to the concert after he eats dinner at a restaurant.
   b. He will eat dinner at a restaurant before he goes to the concert.

Exercise 4 page 119
1. What will you do before you go on your trip?
2. What will Trina do before she goes on vacation?
3. Where will they go after they leave New York?
4. What will Suzanna buy before she reads the newspaper?

Lesson D: Reading

Exercise 1 page 120
1. T 4. F 7. T
2. T 5. F 8. F
3. T 6. F

Exercise 2 page 121
1. The Statue of Liberty is the main topic of this article.
2. It's located in the middle of New York Harbor.
3. France gave the Statue of Liberty to the United States.
4. They gave it as a gift of friendship.
5. It's the day of America's independence from Britain.
6. There are 354 steps inside the statue.
7. You can see New York Harbor and the city's skyline from the crown.
8. You must take a ferry.

Exercise 3 page 121
1. a 4. a 7. b
2. a 5. b 8. a
3. b 6. a

Lesson E: Writing

Exercise 1 page 122
Answers may vary.

Exercise 2 page 123
Answer may vary.

Lesson F: Another view

Exercise 1 page 124
1. C 3. D 5. A
2. B 4. B 6. C

Exercise 2 page 125
1. B 4. A 7. C
2. B 5. C 8. B
3. A 6. A

Exercise 3 page 125
1. a 2. b 3. a 4. b 5. b 6. a

ACKNOWLEDGMENTS

The authors and publishers acknowledge the following sources of copyright material and are grateful for the permissions granted. While every effort has been made, it has not always been possible to identify the sources of all the material used, or to trace all copyright holders. If any omissions are brought to our notice, we will be happy to include the appropriate acknowledgements on reprinting and in the next update to the digital edition, as applicable.

Key: TR = Top Right, BR = Below Right, T = Top, C = Center, B = Below, Ex = Exercise.

Photos

All photos are sourced from Getty Images

p. 3: Alison Wright/Corbis Documentary; p. 4, p. 54 (Ex 1.B): Tetra Images; p. 12 (T): Monty Rakusen/Cultura, p. 12 (C): Caiaimage/Chris Cross/Caiaimage, p. 12 (B): PeopleImages/DigitalVision; p. 14: Ezra Bailey/Iconica; p. 15: Jacqueline Veissid/Blend Images; p. 22 (Janice): Ulrike Hammerich/EyeEm/EyeEm, p. 22 (Hiroshi): Yasuhide Fumoto/DigitalVision; p. 42: suedhang/Cultura; p. 54 (Ex 1.A): vojce/iStock/Getty Images Plus; p. 54 (Ex 1.C): monkeybusinessimages/iStock/Getty Images Plus, p. 54 (Ex 1.D): Matt Champlin/Moment; p. 55: qingwa/iStock/ Getty Images Plus; p. 56: pkline; p. 64 (fair): 77DZIGN/DigitalVision Vectors, p. 64 (animal): Stefan Huwiler/ imageBROKER, p. 64 (tour): kali9/iStock/Getty Images Plus, p. 64 (barbecue): LauriPatterson/E+; p. 70 (T): Rob Lewine, p. 70 (B): Tim Robberts/The Image Bank; p. 84: scanrail/iStock/Getty Images Plus; p. 96: Dmitrii Rusev/EyeEm; p. 120: AndreaAstes/iStock/Getty Images Plus; p. 122: federicogarcia guschmer/RooM; p. 123 (walk of fame): Meinzahn/iStock Editorial/Getty Images Plus, p. 123 (studio): Axelle/Bauer-Griffin/Contributor/GC Images, p. 123 (footprints): csfotoimages/iStock Editorial/Getty Images Plus, p. 123 (concert): Joe Sohm/Visions of America/Universal Images Group.

Illustrations

p. 2, p. 11, p. 27, p. 29, p. 33, p. 34, p. 47, p. 51, p. 53, p. 65, p. 80, p. 101, p. 103, p. 104 (1–2), p. 106: Q2A Media Services; p. 6: Nina Edwards; p. 8 (1–3): Cyrille Berger; p. 21 (1), p. 82 (1–6), p. 108: Monika Roe, p. 21 (2–3): Monike Roe; p. 36, p. 78, p. 110, p. 118: Kim Johnson; p. 95 (1–4): Brad Hamann; p. 116 (1–4): Cindy Luu.

Back cover photography by pressureUA/iStock/Getty Images Plus; Adidet Chaiwattanakul/EyeEm; pixelfit/E+/GettyImages.

Front cover photography by Peathegee Inc/Blend Images/GettyImages.

Audio produced by CityVox.

3rd Edition
Ventures 3
WORKBOOK

Gretchen Bitterlin ▪ **Dennis Johnson** ▪ **Donna Price** ▪ **Sylvia Ramirez**
K. Lynn Savage (Series Editor)

CAMBRIDGE
UNIVERSITY PRESS

CAMBRIDGE
UNIVERSITY PRESS

University Printing House, Cambridge CB2 8BS, United Kingdom

One Liberty Plaza, 20th Floor, New York, NY 10006, USA

477 Williamstown Road, Port Melbourne, VIC 3207, Australia

314–321, 3rd Floor, Plot 3, Splendor Forum, Jasola District Centre, New Delhi – 110025, India

79 Anson Road, #06–04/06, Singapore 079906

Cambridge University Press is part of the University of Cambridge.

It furthers the University's mission by disseminating knowledge in the pursuit of education, learning and research at the highest international levels of excellence.

www.cambridge.org
Information on this title: www.cambridge.org/9781108450560

© Cambridge University Press 2018

This publication is in copyright. Subject to statutory exception and to the provisions of relevant collective licensing agreements, no reproduction of any part may take place without the written permission of Cambridge University Press.

First published 2008
Second edition 2014

20 19 18 17 16 15 14 13 12 11 10

Printed in Mexico by Editorial Impresora Apolo, S.A. de C.V.

A catalogue record for this publication is available from the British Library

ISBN 978-1-108-44957-1 Student's Book
ISBN 978-1-108-44942-7 Online Workbook
ISBN 978-1-108-63615-5 Teacher's Edition
ISBN 978-1-108-44922-9 Class Audio CDs
ISBN 978-1-108-45035-5 Presentation Plus

Additional resources for this publication at www.cambridge.org/ventures

Cambridge University Press has no responsibility for the persistence or accuracy of URLs for external or third-party internet websites referred to in this publication, and does not guarantee that any content on such websites is, or will remain, accurate or appropriate. Information regarding prices, travel timetables, and other factual information given in this work is correct at the time of first printing but Cambridge University Press does not guarantee the accuracy of such information thereafter.